Asian American Actors

Asian American Actors

Oral Histories from Stage, Screen, and Television

by

Joann Faung Jean Lee

McFarland & Company, Inc., Publishers
Jefferson, North Carolina, and London

On the cover: Nancy Kwan, Lia Chang, Lane Nishikawa, Raymond Moy, Cherylene Lee, Billy Chang and Karen Tsen Lee

To David Chow,
With Love...

Library of Congress Cataloguing-in-Publication Data

Lee, Joann Faung Jean, 1950–
    Asian American actors : oral histories from stage, screen, and television / by Joann Faung Jean Lee
        p.   cm.
    Includes bibliographical references and index.

    ISBN-13: 978-0-7864-0730-9
    (softcover : 50# alkaline paper) ∞

    1. Asian-American actors—Biography.   I. Title.
PN2286.2.L44   2000
792'.028'08995073—dc21   00-42108
[B]

British Library cataloguing data are available

Manufactured in the United States of America

*McFarland & Company, Inc., Publishers
Box 611, Jefferson, North Carolina 28640
www.mcfarlandpub.com*

Contents

Preface

As an Asian American I am struck constantly by two phenomena within media: the invisibility of Asians in general, and the limited, stereotypical roles granted Asian actors on screen. An Asian male is often portrayed as a villain, gangster, dope peddler, or a weakling in distress. An Asian woman is often seen as available and easy, or as the lotus blossom (à la Madame Butterfly): an accessible and willing mistress to the white man. These are images that are played out often in television, film and theater. I often wondered why Asians are portrayed in such a negative fashion. Furthermore, I also wondered why Asian actors would stoop to playing these marginal roles when there seems very limited opportunity to attain superstar status in mainstream media. For these reasons I became interested in Asian American actors as a realm of research.

On one level I have a generalized understanding that mainstream media are reflective of majority audience interests. However as an Asian American I also feel the absence of strong Asian American images in film, television and theater amounts to an invisibility in cultural arenas that is ultimately problematic to Asian Americans. Very little has been written about Asian Americans in media, and this study would, it is hoped, add to the small but growing body of literature in this area.

This book attempts to explore the modern image of Asian Americans in film, theater and television, as seen through the eyes of actors who are called upon to play those roles.

Over a four month period I attended rehearsals, auditions, readings and performances to learn more about the actors in New York. Interviews with West Coast actors were conducted in San Francisco and Los Angeles.

Discussions were reconstructed as personal narratives. In so doing the intent was to grammatically shape the material so that the text would not be disjointed or confusing. Answers were grouped together to provide a continuity of thought and logic. I strove to retain the original tone and content of the answers, to stay as close to the overall responses as possible, and to provide the information I deemed relevant to the research focus of this project. The interviews are in the speakers' own words. I eliminated repetitive phrasing and rearranged text primarily for grammatical purposes and continuity of thought.

How I came to interview these particular actors is partly a matter of interconnection. Karen Tsen Lee was one of the first actors contacted. Through her I was able to make connections with others. To all those interviewed who shared their lives and dreams with me, I am indebted to their generous spirit and donation of time.

Introduction

Asian faces and more significantly whites playing Asians in major roles have been a part of Hollywood films for close to a century. The earliest documented instance of Americans seeking out Asians as thematic subjects for films dates back to 1896 (Wong, 1978, p. 2). Historically Hollywood used white actors made up to look "Asian" for roles featuring Asian characters. One classic example is D. W. Griffith's 1919 film *Broken Blossoms*, where the leading role—a Chinese male—was played by Richard Barthelmess.[1] Ironically the most well-known of Asian characters featured in Hollywood films have traditionally been played by white actors costumed to look Asian: Charlie Chan, Fu Manchu, and Mr. Moto.[2] The practice of using well-known white faces to play major Asian roles persisted throughout the 1950s to 1980: Marlon Brando in *Tea House of the August Moon* (1956); Shirley MacLaine in *My Geisha* (1962); Peter Sellers in *The Fiendish Plot of Dr. Fu Manchu* (1980)[3] to name a few.

Today, the casting of non–Asians in Asian roles persists on Broadway. *The King and I* returned to Broadway in March 1996, with the lead role of King of Siam played by Lou Diamond Phillips, who is part Hispanic.[4] In 1990 the casting of a British actor in one of the leading roles in the Broadway production of *Miss Saigon* prompted protests from outraged Asian American actors.[5]

Because the theater, film, and television industries are such powerful forms of mass communication, the images they generate have a tremendous impact on cultural and social perceptions. No one since Wong (1978) has compiled as comprehensive a historical documentation and content analysis of Asians and American films. He argues that historically American motion pictures have systematically treated Asians as racial inferiors, whereby the Asians presented to the American film audience have been largely a patchwork of traditionally inaccurate images and clichés, totally the products of white society (p. 15), that consequently the impact of this practice is yet to be assessed in a directed way. Moy (1993) traces the role of the Chinese in Hollywood films as constructed stereotypes fostered by a need to demean or dehumanize "othered" people to maintain an advantage for the dominant culture. Conversely, many of the roles Asian American actors play on the big screen today continue to be minor ones, derived from images of "otherness," exotica, or that of a foreign collective with accents. Yet despite continuing dissatisfaction with such parts, Asian Americans compete in ever increasing numbers for such roles.

Asian American actors have experienced a series of constraints driven by what Wong (1978) describes as institutionalized racism within the movie industry. Within those constraints is the relationship between profit making priorities (therefore the need to draw mass audiences) and concepts of white American social ideals as epitomized by the big stars of Hollywood. It is not so much individual racism, as Wong (1978) suggests, as it is the institutional barriers which bar Asian actors from major roles, relegating them for the most part to extras. As a racial minority, Asian Americans do not fit the profile of most big Hollywood stars. Asians are often cast as adjuncts to main characters to fulfill various functions—often ethnic parts—as dictated by particular genres. Although this is not discriminatory, what is of import is the lack of opportunity to play major roles—roles that are not linked solely to race specific characterization, roles that are essentially all–American.

Despite these limitations, a handful of Asian American acting companies have sprung up over the past decade in New York. These include the Pan Asian Repertory, National Asian American Theater Company, Pin Chong and Company, Silk Road Playhouse, and Four Seas Players, to name a few.[6] On the West Coast, the Asian American Theater Company, and East West Players have become major forces in staging Asian American productions. Such companies provide Asian Americans opportunities to act in local companies and fulfill the cultural needs of the Asian American community. Yet while Asians have become more visible in Asian repertory companies, television, and films, the roles they play remain essentially race specific and culture-conscious.

American films represent 85 percent of all films distributed worldwide, with foreign distribution accounting for a steadily increasing portion of a movie's profit potential (Donahue, 1987, p. 68). As media companies look toward a global marketplace for profits, Asian Americans are very gradually emerging from their media invisibility. Films in recent years have opened up somewhat to Asian faces, owing to the emergence of more Asian American playwrights. But beyond the works of such ethnic directors as Wayne Wang and Frank Chin, what sort of roles are Asians being cast in today, and in the eyes of Asian actors how much does race play in the quest for ultimate big star status? Why are these concerns important? Images from Hollywood films as well as television are a dominant part of our culture, often mirroring and even shaping our perceptions of society. We are at a crossroads of multiculturalism, where the myth of a white dominated Anglo America is undergoing redefinition from a multitude of ethnic voices. Looking at how a particular racial group fares in this evolution would be a starting point from which to explore how films—as a form of mass communication—have been touched by the multicultural debate.

Jowett and Linton (1980) wrote:

> The motion picture industry was more than just a successful business institution, for unlike steel mills or breakfast cereals the movies became an important factor in the actual shaping of the way in which Americans (and those in other parts of the world) thought and how they perceived the world around them. Perhaps more than any other social and cultural institution since the Catholic Church in the middle ages, the movies caught and held the imagination of hundreds of millions of people. The movies in many ways epitomized and paralleled the development of a "consumer society" in the twentieth century, and an eager public readily and enthusiastically embraced the 'movie star' as a symbol of both fantasy and success [p. 69].

Within this context, Asians as the "movie star" symbol is fantasy. Why, then, do Asians aspire to a career in acting when the fantasy is even more elusive given their racial difference, and how do they go about striving to overcome their "otherness" in competing for stardom? Furthermore, what does this inform us about theater, film, and television as mass culture?

One could argue that in a media culture rooted in predominantly a Western/European/white matrix, the opportunities for Asians, or any minority, to play the leading roles are limited just because that is the way things are. But it is hoped this work can raise and therefore help to better understand the issues inherent in conditions of exclusion. As our society moves toward a more pluralistic mosaic, the effects of discrimination—especially when they are culturally bound—need to be recognized beyond the context of minority problems within a majority culture.

Hollywood, Culture and Business

A great deal of research has been done to examine films as mass communication, the effect of film on culture, and the roles Asians have historically had in Hollywood films. But no book-length scholarly study exists in English that is written from the perspective of Asian American actors exploring how the industry—as it is currently structured—shapes and influences their professional self-image and goals. There are essentially two areas of literature researched for this book: the area of film and culture as related to ethnicity and race, and the film industry as a business.

Within the scope of film and culture, writers such as Dissanayake (1994), Marchetti (1993), Oehling (1980), Toplin (1993) and Wong (1978) have researched ethnic or Asian stereotypes by examining a range of Hollywood films. In particular Marchetti (1993) and Wong (1978) have provided comprehensive overviews. Wong (1978) investigated motion pictures and visual media racism of Asians by studying Hollywood films produced between 1930 and 1975. He studied hundreds of films in which Asians or Asian themes were present, and he wrote about the subject matter in the context of the larger social, political, and military climate of the United States. He ties Hollywood's interest in Asians in war films to the fact that the last three major wars in which the United States was involved were all with Asian countries: Japan, Korea, and Vietnam. But Wong's book was completed close to twenty years ago, and since then the push toward multiculturalism and changes in social and cultural perceptions regarding Asian Americans have led to changes in the way Asians are portrayed in media, as well as opportunities for Asian American actors and actresses. This work, it is hoped, will add to this research from a more current perspective. Moreover, the advent of postmodernism has opened up new approaches in filmmaking (Gitlin, 1989; Kaplan, 1988).

Marchetti (1993) focuses on narratives featuring Asian-Caucasian sexual liaisons through a study of 17 mainstream fictional Hollywood films and television movies between 1915 and 1986. In her work she details the characterization of Asian men in films as less than positive, often as villainous, sexually depraved, or eunuch-like characters. Conversely, Asian women were cast in roles of the Madame Butterfly genre (sacrificing the self for the white male), as submissive flowers, or as sexually available.

Leong (1991) attempts through an anthology of fifty media and cultural works to convey a sense of how Asian and Pacific Americans view themselves and have created film, video and radio alternatives to Hollywood portrayals and mass media images.

Indeed, numerous other researchers, among them Corrigan (1991), Higashi (1991), Masavisut, Simson and Smith (1994), and Summerfield (1993), have grappled with the effects of film on culture. Cowen (1991) even constructs a taxonomy of films in which ethnicity plays a role, and Landy (1993) suggests a taxonomy of roles based on theatrical characterization of types.

Asian presence in recent films tends to be linked with certain social issues—issues that have a connection to changes in the immigration laws in 1965 which enabled a large influx of Asians to enter the United States. A look at films of the 1980s and 1990s shows a repetition of five genres: immigration as a source of conflict (*Armed Response*, 1986); criminalized immigrant groups (*Year of the Dragon*, 1985); economic competition with mainstream Americans (*Alamo Bay*, 1985); war (*Platoon* 1986); and violence between ethnic groups (*China Girl*, 1987). But even these tend to be stories where centrality is tied to some aspect of Americaness—either in values, clash of culture, or confrontation. In essence, Asian presence in Hollywood film remains a prop.

As for motion pictures, researchers and industry critics Armes (1987), Donahue (1987), Gomery (1992), Izod (1988), and Prindle (1993) have written extensively on the film industry as a three-tier process involving producers, distributors, and exhibitors. Of the three, many argue that distributors are by far the most powerful of the triad. "Distribution is the means by which a film becomes available to the public, and is therefore, a crucial factor in the ultimate success or failure of a film.... Because of high cost of distribution, studios find it unprofitable to distribute a film with a gross rental potential of less than $10 million" (Donahue, 1987, p. 1).

Increasingly, studios are going for blockbusters, films that will draw the mass market audience. Distribution strategy is crucial as demonstrated, for example, by *Batman Forever* (1995). It opened in 3,600 theaters nationwide, grossing $53 million in its first weekend, topping the previous record set by *Jurassic Park* in 1993. Clearly, producers make films with an audience in mind (Prindle, 1993). But what audiences want and how they will respond to films are often unpredictable variables.

Conversely, Jowett and Linton (1980) argue that "individuals can learn from movies and that the psychology of moviegoing is subject to a variety of factors such as the social context, the type of movie theater, and even the type of content.... The movie industry makes use of the psychology of the moviegoer both to measure the effectiveness of certain movies and to create appeals for new product. Movies do play an important part in the collective consciousness (or unconsciousness) of our society" (p. 87).

Additionally, Hollywood movies superimpose Americanness as a self-ascribing category, according to Friedman (1991). "At the same time that Hollywood has as most of its big stars, people who are white, English speaking and Christian, it also participates in the process of assimilating Americans of diverse origin, not by enforcing Norman Rockwell lifestyles at home, but rather by projecting and promoting a picture of American culture and society more homogenized than true" (p. 96).

The motion picture, wrote Jowett and Linton (1980), "was much more than merely entertainment.... There were other factors which helped to give the movies their prominent place in the American social structure. First, movies were the culmination of the development of a mass society in the United States, a process which brought together the dynamic forces of urbanization, industrialization, and the national forms of mass communication. When combined, these three forces created a form of social interaction which encouraged a greater degree of homogeneity in society than had previously been the case. Despite the diverse character of the American population, the increasing similarity of their socializing experiences meant that from a cultural perspective Americans were becoming more alike in their tastes. The mass media in general and the movies in particular were major contributors to this increased cultural homogeneity" (p. 69).

Schiller writes that a community's economic life cannot be separated from its symbolic content. Together, they represent the totality of a culture (1989, p. 31). Film, television, and theater are all part of the culture industry, and as such they are produced for the purpose of selling them to those who can pay for them.

In light of this, this study provides a body of information from which to begin a closer examination of the impact of multiculturalism on myths of cultural homogeneity within images generated by both Hollywood films, television and theater.

What does it say about film, television and theater as mass media industries when race is still a key factor in the chance for success? This is especially significant when the cultural and educational direction of the United States in the past decade has been driven by a call to equalize opportunity and to include diversity in the workplace. For Asians in media, whatever the justification the color line clearly remains a wall along which sinews of racism continue to cling. The intent of this study is to shed light on how this issue is navigated in relation to Asian American actors' experiences.

Mass Communication Structures and Society

In recent years increasing attention has been given to mass media and the relationship of media ownership and cultural power by such media ecologists and scholars as Bagdikian (1992), Ewen (1976), Gitlin (1983), Postman (1985), and Schiller (1989). Those who own the industry have a tremendous power over what is produced and exhibited in mass media films (Donahue, 1987; Schiller, 1989). Within that context producers and casting directors in particular greatly influence the development of roles and casting practices. How do artists of color see themselves within a culture that has traditionally favored white actors of European descent? With industry-wide takeovers of major motion picture studios in the 1980s (Bagdikian, 1992) and the restructuring of media companies to encompass a range of products from television, films, and video tapes to publishing, the commercial reach of such companies now blankets the American landscape and dominates the global media markets (Schiller, 1989).

The main realm of research with which media ecologists have been concerned is the relationship between mass media and society. Through researching the experiences of Asian American actors, the hope is to render a stronger understanding of mass communication structures such as Hollywood films, television, and theater, as they relate to societal values in a cultural context. Even though television and films are two separate mediums, they are essentially two sides of the same coin in that the images from both have the same "media-specific production elements, although the projection modes are different" (Hilton, 1982, p. iii).

The principal goal of this study is to shed light on how aspiring Asian actors deal with constraints within film, television and theater, given their racial minority status. I have studied the professional lives of Asian American actors as they go about the business of trying for roles in films and in television. Additionally, I have interviewed veteran actors to determine from their individual perspectives how past industry barriers to media stardom have changed relative to conditions in the profession today.

This study is undertaken as a piece of a larger inquiry within the general domain of prejudice and cultural domination in mass media. The problem of exclusion in film, television and theater as related to the African American experience has been extensively documented by numerous scholars (Brown, 1972; Cripps, 1990; Dates and Barlow, 1990; Fredrickson, 1971; and Kellner, 1987). This has not been the case however for the Asian American experience. In *Racism and Anti-Racism in American Popular Culture*, Silk (1990) wrote:

> The portrayal of Blacks in the early cinema was highly demeaning. Black people were shown as crude stereotypes, either as objects of derision or as poor passive creatures. Sometimes they were given major roles but only as apologia for slavery and segregation. Many of these parts were in fact acted by Whites in Black face…. The economic power of the major studios and the enormous size of the White audience ensured that portrayals of Blacks on film seen by most people to the end of the silent era were those that Hollywood chose to depict. This is a pattern that, with rare exception, has continued to the present day. Anxious to avoid controversy that might reduce box-office takings, the studios expressed racism either by ignoring Blacks completely or assigning them peripheral and demeaning roles…. Those who got parts were thankful for the work, while many others were dismayed by the results [p. 131].

"Television creates two worlds—one white, the other non–White," according to Palmer, Smith and Strawser (1993, p. 149). "White children learn from television that it is a White world. White characters comprise a large majority of TV roles. Furthermore, Whites, especially men, are depicted in highly professional, powerful settings whereas blacks and other non–Whites are pigeonholed into less desirable, stereotypical roles. Black men especially bear the brunt of the burden. When a black couple is shown, they usually appear in the pattern of the weak man and strong woman" (p. 149). Dates and Barlow (1990) suggest that

> the dominant trend in African American portraiture has been created and nurtured by succeeding generations of White image makers, beginning as far back as the colonial era. Its opposite has been created and maintained by Black image makers in response to the omissions and distortions of the former. This war of images casts light on the historical trajectory of the race issue in American society from both sides of the controversy. Thus the definition and control of Black images in the mass media have been contested from the outset along racial lines, with White cultural domination provoking African American cultural resistance [p. 3].

Like African Americans, Asian American actors have encountered racism in media, though cultural resistance has not been as extensively documented. One reason for this lack is that the concept of the Asian American as a unifying political and cultural construct encompassing all Americans of Asian and Pacific Island ancestry is relatively new (Chan and Hune 1995). "In the late 1960's Asian Americans articulated a new racialist collectivity. The end of the exclusionary and discriminatory immigration policies in 1965, and the conclusion of the Vietnam War in 1975, reconstructed the ethnic, social and political character of 'Asian America' in less than one generation" (pp. 216–17).

Also within this generation the power of mass media companies transformed the cultural and informational space of America. Schiller (1989) maintains that culture industries, such as film and television, dominate cultural creations for the purpose of profit: "Speech, dance, drama (ritual), music, and the visual and plastic arts have been vital, indeed necessary, features of human experience from earliest times. What distinguishes their situation in the industrial-capitalist era, and especially in its most recent development, are the relentless and successful efforts to separate these elemental expressions of human creativity from their group and community origins for the purpose of *selling them* to those who can pay for them" (1989, p. 31). "The determining factor in the large majority of decisions about what products and services are made," Schiller asserts, "*must be* commercial profitability" (1989 p. 43). Indeed, commercial profitability as the primary motivation for what is produced in motion pictures and aired on television has been extensively documented by such writers as Gitlin (1983) and Huston (1992).

With culture industries such as theater, film and television increasingly concentrated in fewer and fewer hands (Bagdikian, 1992), and profit as the locus of their existence, privatized media companies are enveloping the informational and cultural landscape in the quest for corporate earnings. The fallout is culture as product, fashioned for a mass market audience.

Schiller (1984) maintains that in advanced market economies it is a freewheeling private sector that dominates communications activities outside the official sector. Within this he writes that

> a prescribed set of rules and codes are generally absent. There is rather what might be called institutionalized communications domination—much as the expression has been used with respect to race and sex. Institutional racism, for instance, argues that people are subject not to specific legislative acts of discrimination, though these may be present too, but that social existence is so structured that racism is inevitable. If Blacks for example, have been excluded in the past from adequate education, the dynamics of the system operate to perpetuate the existing imbalance in income and opportunity [p. 81].

Daniels and Kitano (1970) suggest "there can be discrimination without prejudice, and prejudice without discrimination.... The power of discriminatory behavior lies in its effectiveness in validating and maintaining the 'inferiority' of a group. Once discrimination is institutionalized it pervades the entire system so that those with racial prejudices find validation for their biased prejudgments, while those without initial racial prejudice eventually adhere to what has been known in the past as the 'earned reputation' theory.... Such phrases as 'If they'd only shape up,' or 'It's really their own fault that they remain where they are,' are still common" (pp. 22–23).

The point is not whether media power brokers as individuals are prejudiced, but that a system of institutionalized domination discriminates. In this context, how do minority actors navigate the barriers inherent in culture industries which cater for the most part to white audiences? According to Postman (1985), "Our media are our metaphors. Our metaphors create the content of our culture" (p. 15).

Data Collection, Methodology, and Delimitations

How do aspiring Asian American actors navigate the color line in theater, film, or television in their quest for stardom? To answer this question, a series of subordinate questions had to be formed: How do aspiring Asian American actors cope with the issue and barrier of race in an industry where physical appearance is a key factor to success? What is it like to be an Asian face aspiring to succeed in an industry where stars have traditionally been white, of European descent, Christian, and American-born?

How are the barriers to stardom for an Asian American actor today different from those of the past? How do the brokers of stardom—agents, casting directors and producers—see Asian American actors in relation to their potential to achieve stardom in the media?

Terminology: Asian American actors are both men and women of Asian descent with acting careers in the United States. In preliminary discussions with several women, all indicated they referred to themselves as actors rather than actresses.

The term "color line," used metaphorically, is a racial barrier within theater, film, television, and media, centered on the notion that America is about white culture. Accordingly, various forms of media entertainment are generated primarily for a white audience. Nonwhites have on occasions crossed that line. But for all intents and purposes mainstream media remain a white domain, in which Asian American actors have little opportunity to enter.

Mainstream media, used in a broad context, is primarily that segment of the industry owned and controlled by American media giants, such as the broadcast networks and the Hollywood studios which employ actors.

As a case study, findings are not intended to serve as definitive generalizations on or about all Asian American actors. Rather, the purpose of the researcher is to build a detailed picture of the lives and thoughts of various aspiring Asian American actors to suggest directions for future research and also to provide background for future researchers.

The experience of white and other nonwhite actors are not included in this study. The purpose of this study is not to compare experiences of whites and other nonwhite actors with that of Asian American actors. Rather, it is to look at the perceptions of Asian American actors and their responses to their professional lives.

Neither does this book include a study of the images of other racial minorities as portrayed in films or on television. The primary focus is on deriving a portrait of how various aspiring Asian American actors cope with the challenges of being a racial minority in a profession where physical appearance is deemed a factor to success.

Furthermore, it is not the intent of this study to undertake the task of providing content analysis or a historical survey of films in which Asians characters or actors have appeared. A review of related literature reflects the existence of an established though limited amount of scholarship in this realm.

The method of inquiry selected for this research is ethnographic case studies. Using a qualitative approach, field observations were incorporated with a series of open-ended interviews and oral histories. The goal was to negotiate a deep understanding for the experience of Asian American actors struggling to attain mainstream stardom.

In contacting aspiring Asian American actors geography was a determining factor. Part One of the book includes research gathered in New York City. Part Two consists of interviews with Asian American actors in San Francisco and Los Angeles. The three cities of New York, San Francisco, and Los Angeles were selected because they have the largest Asian American populations. Los Angeles and New York are also known as cities where acting opportunities tend to be more abundant.

Nancy Kwan is probably the most nationally well-known Asian American actor interviewed for this book. The participants included are at varying stages in their careers. Repeated attempts to interview other well-known actors were unsuccessful.

Part One focuses on the work and thoughts of six aspiring Asian American actors. These actors (three men, and three women) are at various stages in their careers; their experience levels range from three to ten years or more in the business. None of the six are superstars, as the key purpose of this study is to examine the efforts of aspiring actors struggling to achieve celebrity status.

To contrast their experiences the perspectives of four veteran actors are also included. In order to gauge and give context to the shifts that have occurred over the years, it is important to find actors who tried to enter the profession at least during the 1970s. The choice of two or more decades as a parameter of time is somewhat arbitrary. It is based on the informed assumption that an Asian American collective and political consciousness emerged in the mid–1960s, and subsequent to that, pan-ethnic groups have organized to oppose media misrepresentations and to seek more opportunities for Asian Americans in theater, film, and television (Chan and Hune, 1995, p. 216).

While their oral histories aren't definitive reflections of the kinds of past conditions all Asian American actors have worked under, they do provide a historical perspective from which to further understand Asian American actors' experiences.

The decision to cast actors generally falls in the hands of producers and casting directors, while the roles of managers and agents are to represent actors. For further context, two interviews with talent brokers—one casting director and one agent—are included. How talent brokers see Asians is significant. While their views of Asian American actors and the acting experience are not definitive, they do shed light on perspectives of the entertainment industry.

Part Two consists of interviews conducted in San Francisco and Los Angeles. Here the purpose was to examine and contrast the experiences of the actors with the experiences of their East Coast counterparts. All of those interviewed said they had worked with the Asian American Theater Company (AATC) at some point in their careers, and AATC served as a great source of support and personal development for them.

Notes

1. Data provided by *Blockbuster Video Guide to Movies and Video* CD, 1995.

2. Warner Oland played Charlie Chan in 12 films, from 1931 to 1938. Sidney Toler took over the role as Chan in 9 films from 1938 to 1944. Peter Lorre played Mr. Moto in 8 films from 1937 to 1939. Warner Oland played Dr. Fu Manchu in 1929. Data provided by *Blockbuster Video Guide to Movies and Video* CD, 1995.

3. Data provided by *Blockbuster Video Guide to Movies and Video* CD, 1995.

4. *The New Yorker*, "Goings on about town", March 18, 1996, p 14.

5. Jonathan Pryce played the role of the Engineer, a sleazy Eurasian brothel operator, in the initial London production of *Miss Saigon* for two years When he was cast for the role in the United States, Asian American actors protested, charging that the show producers did not consider casting an Asian for the role. Pryce had used prosthetics on his eyes in the London production, a practice he said he would drop if it offended Asian Americans. *Backstage*, vol. 31; no. 33; p. 1; August 17, 1990.

6. Asian American Arts Organizations in New York and New Jersey, Asian American Arts Alliance, New York NY 1993.

—PART I—

Asian American Actors in New York City

1

Aspiring Actors

Karen Tsen Lee said she had no idea from day to day what her schedule would look like. Oftentimes she would get calls as late as 9 P.M. for auditions or work for the next day. There was no such thing as planning her life in advance. Every day was left flexible. We had talked over the phone several times, and the first time I got to meet her face to face she agreed to allow me to catch up with her at an audition. The location was 440 Lafayette Street. The audition was for a film, *Final Act*. She was auditioning for the role of a reporter.

I was supposed to meet her at 3:50. I was early. I walked into this very bare looking room which was an alcove to a series of hallways. The receptionist said the audition was in room M, but I walked down the hall and there was no room marked M. I asked again, and she said it would be the room that was unmarked.

The lighting was bare incandescent. The hallway was lined with a row of seats on each side. They were the sort of seats one sees in a theater. Plush, with arm rests. Red. The floor was red, the wall was painted a puke white with a red stripe running along all the way around. The place looked anonymous in that there were really no pictures, and no hint of what this place was for. There were about six different red doors along the hallway, all closed. Loud talk, some music and even singing filtered out from inside.

There was an air of hopefulness among the people milling about. They seemed oblivious to the drabness of the surroundings. Behind one door marked for women there was a changing room. It had mirrors along the wall and benches against the wall. Then there was a bathroom.

The people there were mostly in their twenties or thirties. I didn't see anyone who appeared to be 50 or older, but there were some children. Most were women sitting along the bench outside the various studio or audition rooms, looking at what looked like some scripts, and mouthing to themselves.

There was a feeling of anticipation in the air.

Karen wasn't quite sure who was producing the film; her agent called her the night before to tell her about the "go see" as it is called in the business.

She arrived wearing a short, purple silk dress with a tan blazer. Her shoulder length hair was curled at the ends. It was summer and she had on beige pumps. She said she had just come from a "print" shoot. She said she did quite a bit of print modeling—it was sort of her bread and butter between acting roles. She had on a black digital wristwatch with an alarm. She said she wore it to keep herself on track with her schedule which was set for her next appointment across town. She had been on the run since 8 A.M. she said. Her makeup was from her previous assignment. She took out some water from her knapsack, drank briefly from it, brushed her hair, then settled down to read the part handed to her. Within 15 minutes she was called in to read.

By 5:30 P.M. she was finished. She tied her hair back into a ponytail and changed from pumps to sneakers. She was on her way to a kung fu class, and then to meet with some friends. She said there was no such thing as a typical day. She showed me her daily planner. It was little squares of her schedule filled in, pen marks highlighted in pink, yellow, lime green. She explained she used the different colors to track her various appointments—professional, social, and personal.

When I next saw Karen she said she didn't hear from the casting director, which meant she didn't get the part. But she was doing a reading that evening sponsored by the Women's Project and Productions Playwrights' Lab. Readings, she explained, were ways for the writer to hear his or her work in progress. It was also a means to showcase the work of emerging writers to a select audience. Actors are not paid to do readings. They donate their time, and receive maybe $10 for transportation. The actors hold their scripts in their hands and there is little costuming or staging involved.

This evening the reading was at Marymount Manhattan College Theater. Karen read from *Rowing to America*, a play by Kitty Chen about two Chinese sisters exchanging their hopes and pains about coming to the United States. This was the first opportunity I had to see Karen perform. Her role was that of the older sister who had apparently seen the darker side of life. She played the part with a presence and conviction that to me was very professional. I was quite moved by her performance.

It was here I met another female aspiring actor included in this study. Fay Ann Lee played the role of the younger sister. Her character did much of the rowing in a make-believe boat on stage, dreaming of opportunities of an America paved in gold. When Fay sang I was struck with how strong and beautiful her voice was. It turns out Fay got her start playing a hooker in the *Miss Saigon* chorus in 1992. She left the company after two years because she said she needed to grow professionally. She said she did not feel good about playing a hooker and as time went by she developed a great dislike for playing a role where Asian women are portrayed in such a demeaning light.

Lia Chang, a photojournalist, actor, and writer, was also part of a group doing a reading that evening for a play involving three women who meet as strangers, but who end up exploring commonalities in their lives.

Mel Gionson, one of the aspiring actors interviewed, has appeared in numerous regional productions. He had one of the leading roles in the off Broadway play *The Innocence of Ghosts*, produced by Pan Asian Repertory during autumn 1996.

The world of Asian American actors in New York City appears also to be a community where actors know about other actors and it is not unusual for them to audition against each other for the same parts. That is especially common in race specific roles such as a Chinese gang member or an Asian with kung fu abilities. As such some actors have found it professionally important to list as part of their training Chinese martial arts skills.

In the world of kung fu training Raymond Moy has been a t'ai chi ch'uan instructor and knows kung fu and sword fighting. He also lists on his résumé tennis and baseball as skills.

Raymond grew up in Queens and married a woman I knew who grew up in Chinatown. Raymond had appeared as a gang leader in *China Girl*, a 1988 motion picture version of *Romeo and Juliet* involving Italians and Chinese. Raymond said he has become disillusioned with the possibilities of "making it" as an actor because of the limited roles available for Asian men in films. After I interviewed him he referred me to his former agent Michael Amato. Billy Chang, one of the male aspiring actors included in this study, is Michael's client. Billy in contrast to Raymond has a very upbeat perspective about being an Asian American actor.

Raymond also directed me to his manager Jadin Wong. It turned out that Jadin had an acting and entertainment career of her own. She started out in San Francisco in the 1930s. I include her in this study as one of the veteran actors.

Another veteran actor interviewed is Peter Kwong, who started in the business 22 years ago. Getting to speak with an Asian American male who has been in the business for at least two decades was difficult, as many live in California as opposed to New York. I was fortunate enough to meet Peter Kwong when he visited New York to attend a board meeting with the American Federation of Television and Radio Artists.

Pat Suzuki, who starred on Broadway's *Flower Drum Song*, was doing a staged reading of *Knock Off Balance*, a play by Cherylene Lee (interviewed in Part Two of this book) when I saw her. I interviewed her as a veteran actor.

Tisa Chang, founder and artistic director of Pan Asian Repertory Theater, is the fourth veteran actor included in this section. Pan Asian Rep is the largest and most well known Asian American theater company in New York.

Raymond Moy

He was born in New York City and raised in Queens. His film credits include China Girl, Working Girls, *and* Party Girls; *he has appeared twice as a villainous gang member in the television series* The Equalizer; *played a Korean grocer in* Strapped *(HBO movie); in cabaret theater he's played a warrior and ninja. He was cast as a Vietnamese guard in an off Broadway production,* A Place Called Heartbreak. *He said most of the roles he has played has been as villains or grocery clerks, and said he has become very bitter over the years about this. He still auditions for films but said he has given up on doing a lot of the auditions for gangsters and villains. He said he will not play those roles anymore because that is not how he sees Asians.*

He started in the acting business in 1982 and was cast in his first major motion film in 1988. Currently he is acting on a part-time basis. He supports his family by selling dental equipment. He said he is in his 40s. He is married, has a daughter in preschool, and lives in a suburban New Jersey home.

HOW IT STARTED

Somewhere about 15–16 years ago I started questioning what I wanted to do with the rest of my life and I guess I always wanted to be an actor but didn't know how to begin or who to speak to, where to start.

A friend at work had done some modeling and we were talking one night and we decided that we were going to take acting lessons. To make the story short, she ended up not doing it and I did it. I started studying theater down in the Village. I guess that was about '80 or '82, I don't really remember exactly, but that's how I started. Just to get my feet wet. After a year or two of studying I felt confident enough that I could hold my own with the professional actors in the class and I got pictures and résumés made up. I started sending and handing them out to whomever would take one. And that's how it started.

Raymond Moy

I would say six months after I handed everything out, I hadn't gotten one reply. Then about six months later somebody called and sent me out to do some audition or a "go see" for print, which is like magazine or newspaper work and I didn't get it. But it was exciting, going for a first audition. And then one day, I think it was 1984, they were filming this big movie in Central Park—it was *Ghostbusters*, and they needed a bunch of actors who were not in the union, and I got picked. That was really my first taste of working as an actor. It was kind of neat. I didn't have any lines, but I was an FBI agent and there's a segment in there, where if you know where to look, I'm standing there with a trench coat. So that was really exciting, sort of encouraged me to keep going. Kept studying, kept getting sent out. I think it was around 1986 I got my first break in the sense of a real role in a movie with lines; a real part in a movie. They were searching and searching for the right person and they finally came back to me. They had seen me and then wasn't interested and then came back and then I got a part in a movie and I was real happy and I guess that kept me going for a little longer.

It was a Chinese gangster movie. It was called *China Girl*. I played this character, Tommy Chan, who was, I guess, the enforcer. He was second in command. So it was kind of, to me, a glamorous role too because I got to play a tough guy. What happened then was nice but it was kind of bad in a way. I got other parts, but it was always the gangster. I had done a couple episodes of *The Equalizer*, playing gangsters and various tough guy roles, and that became tiresome after a while.

But what I found was once I got sort of in the business there was really nowhere else to go for me. Other than playing either a gangster or a crooked business man, a grocer, some kind of restaurant guy, I found that my real life was more glamorous than the roles I was chosen to play. So I decided my real life was better in a lot of ways because I don't see myself as a gangster whatsoever, and I see myself as a regular person and I never get a chance to play a regular person. Disheartening.

I have a happy family life, I don't love what I do for a living, but I like it enough. I don't hate it. I'm good at what I do. I'm a good person, well liked in my community. I have my hobbies that most people don't do. I do my tai chi. I do my acting whenever I can. I read books. I have an interesting philosophy on life. That's much bigger than any role that I've ever gotten. So my real life is much bigger in life than the movie roles that I've been given so far.

It should be the other way around. Usually in the movies you get to play a bigger role than you are in life, get to play a king, get to play a cop, a super cop, get to play a hero. I don't get to play any of those things so my real life is much larger than any of the roles I've been offered.

Think about that: that's pretty heavy. People can't understand. Well, yeah, but Sean Connery goes to work and he's James Bond or he's the King of England and Bruce Willis gets to blow up New York and hang around with Cybil Sheppard. I go there, I get to stab somebody; I get to give someone a piece of salami; I get to stand there and look mean as a business man and that's not interesting. That's so one dimensional; that's so horrible.

On Roles

My most recent roles? One was for HBO where I played a Korean grocer. It was a small part but it played a pivotal role in the movie. I got a lot of recognition for it. No work, but a lot of recognition. And a small budget film that got very good reviews at Cannes and at the Sundance Festival. Again, I played not a Korean grocer this time, but a Chinese grocer. I was thankful to get away from the gangster roles but then I was stuck playing grocers, I think. It kind of pissed me off.

The other route I suppose I could have taken was to get into the kung fu roles, because I do have a martial arts background. But I decided, well, I've sold out in one aspect of my life, I don't want to sell out in every aspect. So I decided that's for my own—my martial arts is for my own enjoyment, for my own satisfaction.

I mean this is every actor's dream when they start out—I'm not talking so much about being a star, but being someone who can portray someone bigger than life, on the screen or on the stage. I feel like as an Asian actor, we're never, never given that opportunity. Maybe some people are, but even then it's once or twice in their life and that's it. Whereas with American actors that's not the case. They get one or two big roles and then they're onto being a big, big star.

As far as selling out, what I mean is roles that are left over are playing a criminal, playing someone who is subservient, playing someone who's a minority but doesn't have any dimension to their character, like playing a grocer. There's nothing to it; it's just a stereotype. So not giving in to the stereotypes would not be selling out, but if you don't give in to the stereotypes then you don't work at all, which is fine with me at this point.

How did I reconcile playing a stereotypical gangster when I know that most Asians aren't like that in real life? It's very easy. I worked so infrequently even in those days, that I was happy to get a part where I would play Charlie Manson if they asked me. That's how I used to feel.

When I think about the part I played in *China Girl* it was really horrible. The whole script was horrible; it was hell. The Chinese and the Italians are fighting it out and I grew up in Chinatown and other than a couple of bloody noses, Chinese got along fabulously with the Italians, adults and the kids. They coexisted for a hundred years. That never got in the script. I was so happy I got a part that I just forgot about it to tell you the truth. I think about it now. I thought about it afterwards but while I was doing it, it didn't cross my mind whatsoever. It's like someone who has all these principles, and you starve that person to death and then you hand them a piece of bread. He'll grab that piece of bread and then worry about his principles afterwards. I think that's how I felt. Maybe not how I feel, but that's how I felt. I've hopefully gone beyond that.

My uncle is an actor. He's a lot older than I am. He played the title role of the cabby in Wayne Wang's first film about the taxi driver, *Chan Is Missing*.

I was so excited when the movie came out. I flew out to California to talk to him. Basically in so many words he said to me, "Well, I can think of a few good businesses I could recommend that you should do," and this and that. And I said, no. What about being an actor? And he said, "Well, you know, if you want to play Chinese gangsters."

I said, "Chinese gangsters?"

He said, "Well yeah, if you want to play Chinese gangsters there are some roles, but there haven't been any other roles offered to me since then."

Even though he was in a nice film that got critical acclaim and Wayne Wang's a real talented director, he never really worked a heck of a lot after that. So he was trying to be kind to me and I was angered by it because I said, well, what if I can make a difference?

We all think that, what if we can make a difference? I suppose making a difference means not selling out. But that's like a double-edged sword. Either you sell out and play the roles that are offered to you, which are, to me in my way of seeing things, reinforcing stereotypes, which we don't need, or not working at all. Because there aren't really too many other roles.

Has it changed any in the past ten years? Not at all. I feel that it's gotten worse. I suppose emotionally I got very upset about being in the business over this particular incident: I had a friend that produced films and writes, a screenwriter. He was actually one of my students from when I used to teach tai chi; we decided to write. And I thought it was a fantastic screenplay. It was about my brother-in-law's father, who was the first Chinese Treasury agent. It was in the 1940s, it was very exciting. He had a very exciting life, to be the first Chinese T-Man and I wanted to write a script about his life with me doing the title role. And he said, "Great." And after we sketched out the script, he rewrote it and said, "Ray, I think it'd be best if we put an American actor in the title role, and you play second fiddle."

My heart sank about three thousand feet because I said, well, he is my friend. I know he's not doing this because he's belittling me, he's doing it because of what he knows about Hollywood. And I said to myself, I have an in, and even then I can't do what I really think is right.

This was maybe five years ago. I started thinking, well gee, what chances are there really for an Asian American actor?

We never did the script because I decided I didn't want to do it. I said, I've seen that a hundred times already. I don't want to be Tonto. I want to be the Lone Ranger. For once. And he said he understood and basically we tore up the script and that was it.

I'm not involved with any projects with him anymore. He's on his own. He still writes, but he does a lot of producing. He understands how I feel, he respects it, but he doesn't think he could change it and he's afraid. As a producer he's afraid of the money thing. So they're not really going to take a shot with an Asian American actor. I've done enough gangsters and grocers. I don't have to make a living doing that. If I never work again it's not going to bother me because I've dealt with those devils in my head. I've been doing it long enough that I could intelligently make that decision, I think.

I don't have that anger in me strong enough to play the gangsters anymore. The reason I got that gangster role [in *China Girl*] was because I was very angry about getting any role at all and I used that for the audition and it carried for a while. I just don't have that energy for that anymore.

Maybe I'm blind, but I don't see one Asian American male on any TV show that's on any of the 97 channels on TV. I'm not talking about repeats, I'm talking about recent shows. I don't see any. I don't see that improving. It's gotten worse. I could remember there were at least a certain minority years ago when I used to watch TV even if it was a small role. But I don't see any roles. So there are less calls, too, than there were a few years ago, I think. I'm not sure, but I think.

"JUST A GUY," PASSION, AND PLAYING SECOND FIDDLE

I suppose that the one most discouraging thing was that there was never a title role for me, ever, that I can recall, other than a Hong Kong–made movie, one that could be offered to me that I could even qualify for. That's pretty scary when you think about it.

See, it's not quite the same when you look at an American or a non–Asian or a non-minority actor because when they're lumped in a category they basically all look a certain way. They don't look like a matinee idol, they don't look like the star type. Everyone knows what that is; that image comes to mind.

Asians are mostly put into a character type, a character category. Being an Asian and not looking like a particular character type is a big disadvantage. For me the turning point was several years ago when they started to cast certain roles that weren't stereotypes of an Asian American character type but say more of the lead type roles; there were a couple available. I felt that I had no shot whatsoever to get them because I was up against these extremely, extremely good looking Asian men and I feel like I'm somewhere in between.

Don't take this the wrong way, but what discouraged me was going out for a couple of roles, I'm not going to mention my friend's name, but not getting it simply because my friend was just so much better looking than I was that I think he dazzled them. And he got the role and I realized that no matter how much I learn how to act, I'm never going to be as good looking as him. So if you ask me what the most discouraging blow was, it was that. It was like I was stunned.

It changed my whole perspective. I quit taking acting lessons the very next week.

That had nothing to do with being Asian, and it had nothing to do with acting either, but there was an Asian role to be cast. He showed up and I showed up and they picked him because he was just marvelous and I realized that that was a big fact, too: how pretty you are. I felt that my chances as an Asian actor was already slim because I was an Asian actor; but to be not pretty enough and then not get the part, that was just too much to take. I'm not a character type, I'm not a leading guy; I'm just a guy. And there were no roles for just a guy. That's what I want to be: just a guy. I don't want to be, you know, Paul Newman and I don't want to be Ralph Kramden, I just want to be a guy. And that's where I see myself; just a guy. Bruce Willis is just a guy. Really, without his muscles Arnold Schwartzenegger is just a guy. I can go on and on. Chuck Norris is just a guy. Steven Segal is just a guy, yeah he knows a little bit of Aikido, but there are many. There are many who are stars. Stars. Even Kevin Costner is really just a guy. Harrison Ford is just really a guy. He's cute but he's just a guy. I mean, you could probably say I'm cute, you know what I'm saying? You probably could say that, but I'm just a guy. That's what I mean. That's the way I see myself. That's why I don't see any hope for me in the way they cast because when they do cast they're either going to take a really good looking guy or some guy like the butcher who's really good with the two Chinese knives, butcher knives. Unless they decide to go against type.

It's partially racism. I'm not going to be naive as to think that it isn't. It's partially that they're oblivious that we exist and it's partially because they don't give a shit. Who cares? So what? What are you going to do? With black people, politically, and population-wise they have a voice. We don't have any voice. Asian Americans, we have no voice. Like if they make some movie that some segment of the Asian American political population decides is not politically correct they get like 300 actors to carry banners. That's not a voice that gets on the 5 o'clock news. The movie goes on anyway and those actors who are in the movie are happy to be a part of the movie. And if I had a part in that movie I'd be happy to be in the movie, too. You know, to be honest.

Let's talk in terms of the big picture. You take a person like John

Lone who was in a film that got like eight Academy Awards [*The Last Emperor* (1987)] and [he] doesn't even get nominated. If he was white, even if he didn't get any Academy Awards and he was in a big picture he would have gotten like three, four film offers back to back. Because I know this. I know other actors that aren't Asian and once they have a little bit of a track record they already have back to back movies. But that's not the case with Lone. He's not a household name. Asian actors know who he is. Asian people, some of them know who he is. But this guy is a fine actor.

You take someone like Russell Wong, he's a good looking guy, I mean a really good looking guy and if he was an American actor he'd be Brad Pitt. He would be an incredible star. So it's not just me, it's even the best looking guys who are talented, like John, who really are not stars. I mean they're like nothing compared to even the crummiest American actor. You know, like a second fiddle actor to an American actor. And I think that's real sad. We're playing in a vacuum. That is the reality that we've got to face. Take Brad Pitt and you ship him off to the People's Republic of China or Japan, he's not going to be a star. They'll say, "Yeah, he's a nice looking, fine looking young man, a very good actor but we're not going to make him the star of a movie. We've got Bruce Lee, you know." That's the sad reality.

This was told to me in the very, very beginning when I wanted to be an actor and I understood it. I still understand it but I thought well, you know, there's always that chance. Look at Bruce Lee and look at Eddie Murphy. He's black and this is a white country and people will recognize him for his talent or charisma, whatever it is.

But that happens once in a lifetime. It doesn't happen for the majority of us. Ever. The sad thing is that it is a question of black and white but it's not all about being black and white. The question about being black and white is casting what appears in movies.

But what's not a question of black and white is what's inside; what talent a person has, feelings a person has that he can portray on the screen, portray in a play, portray on a TV show, goes beyond color. Look at James Earl Jones. It's real sad that as Asians we never get a chance to do that. I mean in a ten minute role where my job is to carve somebody up or carve a sandwich up for someone to eat, I'll never be able to give that piece of me that's inside my heart to the audience so they can experience and say, "Wow." And I think that's real sad. I'm not just talking for myself. There are a lot of fine Asian American actors out there.

I was given a role by Forest Whitaker—a small part, like I said, I played a Korean grocer, but I got a chance to do a small piece of me and because of that, it's an amazing thing, that small, small, part, a couple of years ago, two years ago. I will be recognized by black people everywhere.

I'm not saying I'm Robert De Niro, I'm just saying that I have a piece of me that needs to be expressed and maybe seen by people and they'll get some entertainment out of it and also maybe they'll feel something from it.

If I was playing a romantic role the way I could express my love for that other person in the script or in the movie, the play, whatever, would be special. In other words every person that does it has his own soul that he puts in—his own part of his soul that's different. I've already played the angry guy. I'd like to be able to play someone who can love someone.

There's a time frame, because I'm not getting any younger. Pretty soon the only love story I can do will be like Clint Eastwood and Meryl Streep [*The Bridges of Madison County*]. And in terms of being an action star, the only thing I will be able to do will be like Pat Morita, teach somebody else how to fight. So there it is. It's not too convincing anymore when Sean Connery beats somebody up. I've got a few good years left still and they're fading fast. It's all right. No, it's not all right.

How do I deal with that? I tell myself it's okay and that it wasn't meant to be. I'm out of shape anyway, so if I ever got a part I'd have to go on a diet, get one of those machines they have on TV to reduce my stomach. So, it's okay. But it's tough to deal with, all kidding aside. You have to move on, you have to realize that our generation of baby boomers have to step aside. We can't be the young "in" generation forever. We have to do other things. It's a hard thing to accept but you have to accept it.

It's age driven. I love Clint Eastwood but if you look at his last two, three roles, he's not convincing anymore as the male lead that the young woman falls in love with. It just doesn't really happen in real life. And how many guys can he really beat up? When he was in his prime being Dirty Harry, he was very convincing. So, it is age driven. It's an age-driven industry.

What role would I like to play? Maybe a Chinese philosopher like Confucius. If I had to pick.

Why do I choose a Chinese? Because I am. Problem is that because of what I look like, in people's eyes I've always been Chinese first and then someone else next.

It's sort of like I got a double whammy: first of all I get lumped as Asians play those parts, and second of all when I show up I don't look like the stereotype they have in their minds either.

There aren't any roles and when there are they aren't really suited for me anyhow. It's horrible.

SUCCESS VERSUS STARDOM

Success as an actor means being able to work as an actor and make a living as an actor; doing roles that go beyond what I am as an Asian. Success as a human being—I still haven't completely mastered that yet. That will probably take a lifetime or two. That's probably harder.

Is there a difference between being successful and being a star? Yeah, there is. Being a star, I suppose, I picture them in *People Magazine* every other week. I'll be walking around with Lady Di. I'll go to the Oscars and whatever, Emmy Awards that are going on. That, to me, is being a star. I probably don't have to be a star, that's not something that I think I have to be. I would be satisfied with doing one or two movies a year and having a substantial role in those movies. That would be nice. You know, playing a part. Playing a part that, not necessarily is the lead, but some sort of supporting role. If it is the lead then that's fine, but playing a supporting role is fine.

I used to believe that I might have that opportunity some day to play a leading role in a major film. But I don't know that I could memorize an entire script. That would probably be like an obstacle. Can it still happen? Who knows. It could always happen, I suppose as long as I'm alive. It could happen. Would I like it to happen? Yeah, sure, I'd love for it to happen.

ON CASTING AND OPPORTUNITIES

I go out for commercials because they don't bother me. I go out for commercials and I go out for commercial print because I stand there and smile and if they like my face I get picked. The parts are mostly as businessmen. I'm confining myself more or less to commercials so it's some crazy guy in a suit. It's specifically Asian. Sometimes they'll want Chinese, sometimes they'll want Japanese. I never, ever, get a call for a businessman and then you show up and you're an Asian and everybody else is not. That will never, ever happen 'cause then the casting director will call up your agent and probably yell at him and say, "Why did you send me a Chinese guy for a business man?" You know what I mean? Not an Asian businessman, a businessman. They're very specific. They're exclusive of each other.

The casting director's job has been to reinforce stereotypes. God forbid they should take a chance and say, "Hey! This guy is two inches shorter than what we want. He's got black hair instead of blonde hair. He kind of looks like Chiang Kai-shek and not Jimmy Carter. Let's pick him."

They would never, ever do that. I don't know where the order comes down from, maybe from the producers, maybe from the sponsors, I don't know. But I've never seen them ever take a chance. And when they have, I've never gotten the role. Never. Will that change? I hope to God it does change. Not just for me but for everybody else.

On off Broadway they're kind of avant-garde and they have something called nontraditional casting in which they'll give a minority actor a shot at playing a role. They're much more I guess, into the arts in theater.

In film, TV, commercials, print, you can forget it. If you pick up any magazine you're going to see ten people romping around in bathing suits, and maybe one black guy, maybe one Asian girl, that's it. God forbid three Asian guys and a Filipino girl, or two black girls. That would never happen. It's just mind-boggling. But it will not happen.

I think people are afraid to take a chance, stick their necks out and be different. My point being that someone's got to stick his neck out, someone's got to take a chance sometime and see if people will accept an Asian face in lead roles. My gut feeling is that they will. Change has got to come from producers. Word has got to come down from them to the casting people.

With writers, I don't think they really care what color the person is, it's what's inside them. But we're so far out of the loop that someone writing a screenplay or a play won't even think about us because, let's face it, they have to get what they write produced as well. So they're looking at what they see that's out there. We're so far away from it that they don't even give us a second thought.

As for films like *The Joy Luck Club* that's fine, but that's like a Spike Lee thing where once in a while you get a black movie out there that's good. And people say, "Oh, wow. That's great." And they turn around and they go back to writing stuff about the detective guy who has three girlfriends and he's like a James Bond guy and that's what they write. But it's white. It's so white that it's scary.

But certainly the producers and directors, it's up to them to make a difference. They see Asians the way our society sees Asians: as a marginal people that are invisible. What is the solution? The solution is that some Asian with some big money that wants to produce films will produce films with Asians in it. That's my belief.

ANGER, THE PROFESSION AND BEING A MINORITY

The anger? It's something that is not directed at acting, or at the movie business, or at show business. It's something that I think is there being a minority, growing up in a country that's a majority. That's always there. It's there because from childhood you realize that you're not like everybody else. You'll never be treated like everybody else for the most part. People judge you by your cover, a book by its cover. Some people once they get to know you, see what's inside you, grow to love that hopefully. But there's a certain segment that never will.

I find that people in show business in particular are afraid to rock the boat. I'm talking about the Establishment, they are afraid to ever take a stand where they're going to do something that's in the forefront. They'd rather reinforce stereotypes that are there. It's sad but it's a money business. They're worried about making money and they're worried about losing money. So why should they take a risk?

So that anger has to do with, I guess, opportunities and people's perceptions about minorities. Culturally.

But it spills over to the business because it's worse in the acting business. In the dental business I'm a Chinese man basically going out in a world that's, at best two, three percent Asian. And I write a lot of business with most people who aren't Asian. So obviously, barriers are not really that strong in real life, but on the screen they are. On the screen they're magnified. So it pisses me off. It pisses me off even more because I see this is bullshit. Why can't I play a dentist?

You know, I once had this argument with a director. I said, why can't I play Debbie's husband?

"Because you're Asian, because you're Chinese," he said.

I said, "So?"

He said, "Well, then people watching the show will say how come they cast—how come he isn't white?"

And I said, "Who gives a shit? You know, that happens in real life, you know."

That's why I like this one sitcom on TV now—it's with Jonathan Silverman and one of his friends is an Asian American woman and she just happens to be married to one of his other friends and, yeah, they allude to it occasionally, but that's the real world, you see? That's a very, very small part of what's being portrayed out there. It's mind-boggling. But that's the reality. It's sad. I think that if someone would take the chance, I don't think they would lose. Putting in a minority actor in a role that doesn't call for it but just is.

I've come to understand not just in the movie business but in all business whatsoever it's the money people that control everything. So I think there have got to be producers who could tell the writers and directors to do anything. So it's got to come through the producers.

If there were more Asian Americans with money who were producing projects that's how things would get done. Otherwise you're going to get a Wayne Wang film or a Spike Lee film where once in a while a minority script comes out that's fabulous and people say, Yeah. *The Last Emperor* was great and *Waiting to Exhale* was great and *The Joy Luck Club* was fabulous but they've come and gone. *Flower Drum Song* was great but that was forty years ago. I'm talking about mainstream stuff where the guy answers the door and there's a Chinese guy there, reading a paper and he says "Hey, what's going on?" and blah blah blah. I'm talking about that. That's what we need. And you know, as I look around at society I see more and more Asians all around and I can't understand why it isn't happening on the screen.

Art should be a reflection of life and if this is life maybe it should be reflected more. Have a Chinese guy mowing his lawn, or going down the block. What's wrong with that? Why does he have to be in a restaurant or sweat shop. That's the other thing; the sweat shop thing. Pretty scary.

It's harder for Asian actors than it is for black actors. On TV like 10 percent of the shows are black. I hope to God things will change. My daughter—six years old; by default, she's in the business. Hopefully it will change for her. I think my father hoped that it would change for me but it didn't.

I didn't realize this until long after he was gone. He died when I was very young. He always wanted to be an actor but he had seven kids to raise and he never got the chance to do it. I think he hoped it would change for me. I don't think I'll see it in my lifetime. It makes me sad to think that way, but I don't see it in my lifetime. Maybe it will change in my daughter's lifetime.

DRAWING THE LINE

Where is that line? The line is I will not play a role that reinforces the Chinese or the Asian stereotype. I won't play a role that portrays Asians as bad, as evil, because I don't think that's the case. Basically those are the two things that I kind of feel strongly about that I wouldn't play.

When I give that up what am I left with? Nothing. That's why I'm sitting here talking to you now. I suppose I could do theater, but I don't really have a lot of time to do theater. I have a family and a job and it's just difficult. Sad. Really. Sad.

I'll never get over it. I'll never get over it because enough people either that I know or don't know have seen me somewhere in some film or TV show and they always ask me what am I doing next and I don't have the heart to tell them I'm not doing anything next. But they're going to keep asking me that for a long time to come, probably. They're not going to forget it and I could not ask for them to possibly understand what it is to be an Asian actor in a country that's not Asian. I don't think that they could ever understand what that feels like. So I usually tell them, Oh, they're not picking me for anything so that's why I'm not doing anything. And then they feel bad for me and then that's the end of the story. But basically that's what happens because there really isn't a heck of a lot much else out there.

I think a lot of people feel the way I do but not quite as deeply. I think most Asian actors just scramble to get the work because you're committed to being an actor and they'll take whatever jobs they feel, and they're afraid to speak out really because it may jeopardize their chances of getting work. I don't really give two shits. I know that if there's a role for me they're going to give it to me anyway. 'Cause I can do the role better than anybody else so they'll give it to me. If that's the role. I'm not saying every role, but the role. And they probably agree with me anyhow. But I don't think they feel as deeply; they can't feel as deeply because then they wouldn't be able to work. I still could work. I feel this way but I could still do it. If something comes along that looks halfway interesting and I don't think is too much of a stereotype, I'd do it. If it's the manager of a restaurant I'll play it. There are plenty of Chinese guys who are managers of restaurants. And I don't think that's reinforcing stereotypes. I'll do it.

But what I really would like to do is the Bruce Willis roles or the Kevin Costner roles where I'm just a guy. There was one role in particular that I wished I could do but I never got the part. But I never heard of the movie, so it doesn't really matter. But it was part of an interracial romance between a Chinese actor, a Chinese man and a frontierswoman. I guess this was set over a hundred years ago. I though it was fabulous, I wanted to do it so badly. But I'd like to do a romantic role is what I'm saying. It was the only one that ever came up in all the years that I'm an actor that had that type of script. But it went over like a lead balloon.

IMAGE OF ASIAN MALE AND AUDITIONS

For a while I was auditioning for Chinese gangsters; the Chinese Mafia; Asian business men that are corrupt; Asian business men that are not corrupt; restaurant guys; store owners. That's about it. Pretty much those are the stereotypes. You don't ever see a Chinese dental salesman. Or a Chinese woman that writes novels and teaches college. So those are basically the roles that are offered which aren't too exciting.

It's kind of nice but not to do it every time you have a part to do. It gets stale. They could think, Oh, yeah, that guy. He always plays the bad guy. He always plays it the same way. There aren't really any working Asian American male veteran actors; I could name them really on my hand: there's James Hong, he's a fine actor, he's in everything; and Pat Morita does the karate things and once in a while something else, and that's it. Really. And these guys have been around for like close to fifty years. So there really isn't much for us to do.

How is it different for Asian women? God bless them but they're able to work more than we are able to. We see them in the media more. People find them less threatening. It goes back to that whole thing with Madame Butterfly. It's the big male white man and the female, you know what I mean? They don't see the female as threatening, they see the male. The Asian male is the one you got to watch out for. The Yellow Peril.

Look at Margaret Cho. She had her own show for a while. There are a lot of funny Chinese men, and Japanese and Korean men. I mean a lot of funny guys and God forbid they should have their own show. Probably would have made it because they're funnier than she is. She's great but there are some funny guys that I know. Yeah, it's the threatening thing. I don't know why they find us threatening, but we're threatening.

How do I encounter that? There will never be a Pacino role for an Asian guy because they don't want to show that we're intense. They'll show that he's a nice guy and he's Barney Miller's sidekick and very funny and he's not a threatening guy. But he's not carrying the Dirty Harry gun with the big pistol.

Do I think that's because producers don't envision that or the audiences won't buy that? Probably both. It's that they're afraid audiences won't buy it and they have to have a little bit of prejudice, I think, otherwise they would do it. It's like a double thing.

As for Denzel Washington, his popularity doesn't mean things have changed. You know why? Because Sidney Poitier did it thirty years ago. He's getting old, he can't do those roles anymore so they get some other black guy that does it. If I sound cynical it's because I am. Yeah, Denzel Washington is nothing but 1990's Sidney Poitier guy. It's not going to change nothing. The day I see a Chinese guy walking around with a big gun in a detective movie and he gets to kiss a girl that isn't Asian I'll be a happy guy. I'll break out a bottle of Dom Perignon.

What it says about the culture is that this is a white society and it's going to stay that way. And we have to keep fighting but it doesn't seem like there's much hope.

Do I think I would be much further ahead in my career if I were white? If I were white I would be married to Melanie Griffith or something and I would be living in Hollywood. And I would be commanding whatever script I want. Yeah, definitely, if I were white and I had the similar looks that I have and similar talent, even half the talent that I have, I think, I'd be a big star.

See it's very bizarre because I'm an American. I'm an Asian, but I'm an American. I could never live in Hong Kong and be happy. I'm happy here because I'm an American. Yet sometimes I forget that I'm Chinese when I look in the mirror. I still don't think I'm Chinese but I'm reminded sometimes that I am. So, therefore, I have to be Chinese. 'Cause I don't think my philosophy and the way that I think is so Chinese. I believe in some Asian philosophy and I believe in some Asian principles but basically the core of what's inside of me is American.

So as an Asian American actor I feel like that *Twilight Zone* movie where the guy is actually white and he runs through this white neighborhood in a racist South and they think he's black and they try to kill him and he's a WASP, but he goes to Germany and they think he's a Jew and they try to kill him. I mean, not as severe as that but basically that's how I feel because inside of me this is who I am, but from the outside I'm judged all these different ways. If I could sum up the experience of being an Asian American actor that would be it. That's it.

What does it mean to ratchet up a stereotype character? There are two perspectives. There's the perspective of the director, what he or she wants out of this. And you and what you think you can do to get the part. What happens most of the time is that I get wrapped up in thinking about what they want me to be and that's when I generally lose. They'll say, "All right, what we need here is you're the super in the building, and you're a Chinese guy and you just came over from the other side. You don't know the rules around here so you bring the garbage out on Tuesday, but you're supposed to bring it out on Wednesday. Can you do that Ray?" And I do it. And if I do it thinking, trying to put myself in their shoes, what they think, which is here's this guy fresh off the boat and he's an idiot and he's doing this and that, I usually don't get the part. And if I do it figuring I don't care what the director thinks I'm going to do what I think, and if I get the part or not at least I did what I think, sometimes I get the part. Sometimes they'll change the script. This has happened. The director will say, "Ray, you're no longer a guy from Hong Kong. You're a regular New Yorker and you're just going to do," and that makes everybody change. All of a sudden the other actor gets to change how he deals with it too.

What usually works best is I just push the stereotype aside and sometimes it works. But I try, because usually you don't get the part any-way. You can go on like a hundred auditions and maybe get one part any-way. That's the nature of the business.

But just about everybody has to audition. That's an actor's life. I should say to be fair about the whole thing that it is difficult for the Asian actor but it's just as difficult for non–Asian actors because there are that many more actors so their numbers are higher. You have fewer parts for Asian American actors, granted, but even though there are more parts for regular American actors, there are a lot more non–Asians competing for the same roles. There are like ten times or twenty times more actors. So competition is that much harder for any actor.

They have in their favor however the chance that someday they will be discovered. We really don't have that. We don't really have a shot.

Would I stay in the profession knowing the way it is? Yeah, I just have a different perspective. I feel like something inside has gotten dull. I feel the same way about acting as I do about dental supplies: that if I get work I'm going to go do it because it's a paycheck.

Think about it: If you pretty much know that all you're ever going to be is the restaurant guy or the plumber, it's just a job. You're going to do it and someone will see you and say, "Oh I remember you. You were the guy in the store and—" and that's about as far as it ever gets and it kind of kills something inside of you. So you lose that starry-eyedness, I guess. I feel that probably if I were a writer I would have a better chance because then people wouldn't have to see my face, they could just see the words. Or if I was a director. Look at the guy who did *Sense and Sensibility* [Ang Lee]. So what I'm saying is that people aren't outwardly racist and prejudiced, they're cautious and it's generally because of money. The underlying thing, they're afraid of risking their bucks. That's how I see it. It kind of saddens me because we all want to be before the camera. If we have to we'll do other things but what we wanted to do was be in front of the camera and now we do get to it but we have to play a tree or a rock and not the prince.

Billy Chang

He is 28 years old, raised in Atlantic City. He had a role as recurring character Clarence (a bad guy) in the TV series Kung Fu. *He attended Beaver College for two years, then Rutgers University where he took some acting classes. He starred in his first film role in 1990 and believes he has a natural ability to act. He*

Billy Chang

said he wants only to do film because this is the mass media where he says he can reach the most people.

Chang believes he has a chance to make it big because film is about the average guy, he says, and people want to see others that are like themselves. He says he is American in many ways even though he is Chinese and he thinks if someone like Wesley Snipes, a black man who is not exceptionally good looking, can make it, he has a chance too.

He has done mostly gangster, kung fu, and villain roles, but he says this does not bother him, as long as he can make the role into something special.

He supports himself selling real estate in Atlantic City. His manager is in New York and Chang commutes into the city for film auditions.

How It Started

My dad took me to see a Bruce Lee movie in 1973, right after Bruce Lee died. The theater was packed. All of a sudden you see somebody that's like—it's your own face up there. You see the whole crowd cheering every time he would hit somebody; they would jump up and clap and it was almost like a sporting event. In my entire life to this day it was one of my proudest moments. Even though it had nothing to do with me. It wasn't me up there. It wasn't my family. But I walked out of that theater ten feet tall. Basically that's where it started. Bruce Lee was very unique. I don't know if he was a great actor in the classical sense but he had a gift of self-expression in anything he did: in the way he fought, in the way he moved, in the way he picked up a glass of water. He had the gift of self-expression. And the reaction I had was, I would like to do that. Not do martial arts, but to be able to show people what's inside me. Not as a Chinese person, just as a person. Because my whole childhood I just watched others, I didn't speak my thoughts.

I had planned to be an actor since childhood. When you're young and filled with these dreams you think you can do anything. Then you reach a period when you lose that and you basically feel like—Well, I have to be a little more grounded in reality. Because it's taught to you. It's taught to you by the people that worry about you. But then I think I reached another level after that period where I started believing in myself again. And during that time an opportunity came up.

I started out acting to earn extra money. But the real break came in 1990. My mom called me and said, "You know, I just saw an ad in the Chinese paper in New York. They're looking for some extras for this Hong Kong film they're shooting in New York."

I had just finished final exams in college at the time and I said, all right, I'll give it a try. Maybe I can get some work for the summer. So I went and auditioned. And they called me back. I thought I had the part because I figured you don't audition extras again. There was another call back. I started auditioning and they kept calling me back over and over again. I started wondering to myself, what's going on? It turned out Russell Wong [another actor] was originally scheduled to play the part but there was a conflict so I got the leading role. The movie was about a Hong Kong cop sent to New York to investigate Asian organized crime, and the film was called *Taking Manhattan*. I've been acting ever since.

The way it was explained to me was that in Hong Kong the current crop of stars were aging, and they wanted to come to America to actually find a young face to bring back. But this was where my biggest frustration lay: I didn't want to go back to Hong Kong. If I was going to get into acting, if I was going to dedicate my life to it, I didn't want to do it because it was easy money. I did it for money when it was something on the side. But if I was going to dedicate my life to it I wanted to make it in America. I didn't want to be a Hong Kong star. I don't know the culture. I don't speak Cantonese. And it was a personal goal. I just wanted to make it in America because I didn't see any Asian actors making it big here.

Growing up, even though he had already died, I had Bruce Lee to look up to because at that time he was so big. It was the early seventies. I grew up in a section of Atlantic City; they idolized him basically. And even though he was dead I had his memory to live on and I was proud.

WHAT HOLLYWOOD WANTS

I have a deep feeling that, yes, it is possible to speak out. Only because if it weren't, I think I would lose hope in everything else. Because you have Hispanic stars, you have black stars. That wasn't possible twenty years ago. Back then nobody thought that someone like Wesley Snipes could star in his own movies and bring in ten million dollars a weekend. It would have been unheard of. It's done today and the market's growing for Hispanics now. I don't see why it shouldn't happen for Asians unless Asians are below everybody else, which I know they're not. I don't see why it shouldn't happen, it's just going to take somebody that has the drive who's not willing to concede to what Hollywood wants right now.

I think they want people to play—and don't get me wrong I think it's getting better, if you look at it now compared with ten years ago—I think they want filler, what I term "filler" roles. The Asian American population is growing very rapidly. They can't ignore this. They can't show an area or a scene where there are no Asians in it but at the same time I don't think they want to make them the center of attention. They don't want to make Asians the focus. Just look around, look at the films we see these days. You'll have an Asian here, an Asian there but to actually be focused upon? And if they're focused upon it's because they're Asian. It's because like—Oh, this is the Asian businessman from Japan. It's always something that has to deal with culture. You never see an Asian and say—that's just a person that's expressing himself, interacting with other people. If it's a weighty role it always has to do with culture. In other words, I can't just be me there.

I can't be just the guy next door.

ROLES, OPPORTUNITIES AND TRAINING

At least I had Bruce Lee when I was growing up. I told myself—the kids today what do they have? They have nothing and it's got to bother them, self-esteem wise. In the eighties I didn't see any Asian hero figures on screen.

There are many, many successful Asians, I'm not saying that there aren't. There are success stories everywhere about Asian Americans but you need them in the media. You need it because kids don't follow other things; they follow television, they follow movies. And that's what I wanted to do. So I turned down that offer to go to Hong Kong. I ended up doing a couple more Hong Kong films, but I never wanted to go there and market myself. I wanted to do it here.

I've done a few American films since then, one is called *Guns of the Dragon*. I also worked on several television series: *Law & Order*, *True Blue*, and a couple of stints on *America's Most Wanted*.

Then came the *Kung Fu* series which I locked into for a while. I was in the very first episode and I did the very last episode of this season. So, it's been about four years now with that show. I played a character named Clarence—he's basically the young, I don't want to say "Don" because that's more Italian, but he was the young leader that actually took the place of the Godfather when he died in Chinatown. So, it's an interesting character.

What types of characters have I played most in American productions? Mostly gangsters. You know what? I don't have a problem with that. You know, a lot of people, even Italian Americans, any ethnic group that gets locked into a certain role, and that role is negative, they tend to speak out against it. And it's true: There should be other roles besides gangsters and things like that for Asian Americans. But as an actor I don't mind playing gangsters. What I detest is when they show a gangster, an Asian gangster or any ethnic gangster who is pure evil, and they don't portray him as a person.

The *Godfather* movies romanticized the gangster era and showed that gangsters were people as well. They did these terrible things but they were people; they had family, they cared for them, they had feelings. And the only complaint that I have is when they paint a certain picture for Asian

American actors, Asian American gangsters, they don't show that. They don't show the human side of them. So what I do with *Kung Fu* actually— I work a lot with the writer/producer and said I wanted to inject certain human traits into my character and he was very, very generous about it. That's why this guy Clarence is always trying to go good in every single episode that he returns in. And out of the works that I've done I'm very happy with that character. I mean, you can actually see the human side of him. As long as they keep the gangster human it doesn't bother me.

My ideal role would be the sort of roles Al Pacino plays. I think he is a wonderful actor and I love his choice in roles. He's always playing the person who's going against the system, the person on the outside, and a person who's trying to speak out in a world that's gone wrong. It parallels a lot of what my own life is about so I would love to play such a role, something with no action, 'cause I'm tired of action. I'm tired of doing stunts ('cause I do my own stunts, as well), and something where you can actually look deeper into the soul for conflict.

I haven't had much of an opportunity to play such a role.

Although I think things are getting better, I haven't really seen the results of that progress yet. So what I'm doing now is working on my own script because independent films are basically the way to go now. I have to write my own roles because Hollywood's not creating them. I have to actually go and create these characters myself and hopefully one of these days they will get picked up.

I was working on rewriting the Green Hornet for a while, but I found out recently that it was picked up by Hollywood. Hollywood's doing it now.

Developing a script isn't too hard. It's following it through that is tough. The marketing is hard. I'm not an experienced writer, but I do have writing abilities. I studied acting at Rutgers and at HB Studios in the Village.

My formal training I got at these places but the heart of my strength I believe lies in the fact that my whole life I've been working on somehow communicating the turmoil that I felt growing up. My whole life I tried to hone those skills, and it was just constant practice. I love the craft of acting.

The turmoil I confronted growing up is the same turmoil that I'm confronting right now in the business. I sympathize with the Asian American dilemma in the business. There's a part of me that wants to show the world that I'm an Asian American and I'm going to make it. But there's another side of me that wants to be able to go into a casting of a movie and say, I want you to look at my character. I want you to look at my performance. Not as an Asian American actor just as a person. I want you to see what I feel.

This is from Billy Chang's perspective—that's all I want. Not, that's from an Asian American perspective.

That's how it was growing up. Everything I did was like—oh, is that how the Chinese people do things? Maybe a lot of it is a result of my upbringing but there are differences between me and other Asians. We're not one and the same.

CASTING ATTITUDES

I remember when I first read for Clarence in *Kung Fu*. It was a part where I was making a threat to a store owner. I had discussed it with my manager about whether to do it with an accent. I knew that other actors were going to do it and I said to myself, most of the Chinese gangsters that I know or have seen, or the ones that I've met in New York, they've been here a long time. They don't speak with that Fu Manchu 1930's sinister accent. They speak like Americans. So I went in and I did the role actually with a New York accent, a real gangster, south side type—and I was in and out of there in twenty seconds. I told myself, well, okay, I just blew it. Because everybody—people in before me were in for like twenty minutes, thirty minutes. I walked out a little bit angry with myself. I thought maybe I should have just conceded and just did it the way they expected. But they called me back and said, "You got the part. Your performance was so electrifying and so unique."

I was really happy about it but when it came time to shoot they wanted me to go back to the accent. And I fought with them. I said no, I don't want to do it with the accent. This is what makes the role. He's different, he's unique.

I didn't end up doing it with an accent. But that's what I'm talking about. They actually have an image of what it's supposed to be like and 90 percent of the time they're wrong. That's not how it is. Because they didn't grow up with the culture. They don't know.

How hard is it to change those preconceptions among people who are actually in the position of casting and producing or writing? I think it's next to impossible until they get to really know you. Like the writer-producer whom I worked with in *Kung Fu*, he has 100 percent confidence in me now. I won over his confidence from working with him.

But in general going into a casting? Or going into meet an agent? Or going into meet casting people? No. They have their ideas and they say, "Who is this young guy who thinks he's going to change the industry?

He's nobody." So to me it's near impossible until you get and actually make some strong ties, then you can push your ideas.

One thing that I am proud of and sometimes my pocket hurts because of it, I don't make a lot of concessions. I mean I basically go in with an actor's attitude and say, this is the way I feel the role should be played. And I know I've lost a lot of roles because of it. I know there were roles where if I read the way they wanted it to be read, that I could have gotten them. But I won't. I won't do it. Sometimes if it's a going series and you're talking about big money, that's where the conflict comes in. But I would rather walk out of there and just feel like I put my head high. And even if I were to get the role, if I were to play it the way they wanted me to, and it's recorded on film for all of posterity, I think that that would hurt me more than not getting a role. So, you can't. You can't really go in and try to please, even though that's the main objective; you want to actually get the role.

I'm hoping that the same things that are costing me work right now will make me unique one day and actually set me aside from the rest of the actors out there.

What do they want me to be that I find so objectionable? If you're auditioning for a gangster role for instance, as an Asian American, they want you to be sinister. They want you to be emotionless; they want you to be cold. All through history I don't think I've seen even 1 percent of anyone, no matter how bad, who didn't have a human side to him. They don't want you to show any human emotions. They want you to show how cold you can be—basically a calculating killer. And then when you go for other roles, like students, or doctors, or professors or things like that it's the total opposite. They don't want you to have any—how can I put this? They want you to be submissive. I remember auditioning a few years ago, as a doctor. It was an independent film, and they wanted him to be very submissive, you know, it was very demeaning actually, the dialogue in it. It was an Asian doctor. Those are some of the expectations. It's almost like opposite ends of the spectrum. It's never just a person that has strengths and weaknesses at the same time. It's either he's just no emotions or he's weak. It's never something in the middle which is where most of us fall. So it's really frustrating. That's one of the reasons I've actually gone into my own works, as far as writing and everything like that. I don't have the faintest idea whether these things will ever go into production, but I think writing is a therapy because even though I haven't played it, when I see the roles it's almost like encouragement to me: Well, wow, this is a great role for me, 'cause I'm not getting them anywhere else.

Outlook and Expectations

No matter who you are, Asian or Hispanic or whatever, one thing that always has to be kept in mind is that individuals are different. I could tell you that this is holding me back, that's holding me back, and certain factors obviously do, in any walk of life, but there are other things that hold you back that have nothing to do with your culture, that have nothing to do with your nationality, your race. I could tell you, yeah, this is all so difficult because of the Asian American situation in the industry. But at the same time even if the doors were completely open I might not have what it takes inside to make it.

I think one thing that has to be always kept in mind in the forefront is that individuals are different. Woody Harrelson and Bruce Willis made it as average looking guys but the industry held them back in a way, too, in the beginning because they were average looking. They were able to tap into something in the audience and I think that's really, really important.

What I think the American audience wants right now are individuals who don't have any pretensions; heroes who are very down to earth, who maybe aren't the best looking guys in the world or the smoothest, James Bond-ish types of characters but people who can connect with the common man, or the street people. That's why hip hop right now is such a phase. You know, rich kids from $200,000 neighborhoods are trying to be these little street kids. Why? Because they want that down-to-earth kind of quality—which might be good or bad for society, but I think that's what they're connecting with. So as long as you can connect with that, I think the possibility of making it is there. Wesley Snipes: there are much better looking black men than him but he made it because he reached the average guys of the audience who want to see themselves on the screen. They know they can never reach the dimensions of the impeccably-dressed, beautiful person, so they'd rather see the average Joe make it. That's the quality that needs to be tapped right now.

Being that I'm 28 years old, I feel that the good roles aren't going to come until I'm 30 years old. The roles I would like to play I don't think are going to start coming until now. In your mid-twenties you can't play teenagers anymore and you can't play older men. So you're kind of just stuck in this little void. I think that it's going to start opening up once I get into my late twenties, early thirties. I don't give myself a time frame to make it at all.

The stereotype right now is that Asian American men are not romantic. It's not a moral judgment here—good or bad—but they're just not very passionate. That's what the impression is. I could say until I'm blue in the face, it's Hollywood. It's Hollywood. It's Hollywood. But Hollywood has an image and that image wasn't developed in Hollywood. That image was developed in society. I can't sit here and say, let's talk about how unfair it is, all I can do as an individual is push myself. This is who I am. I can't change the world's impression about Asians or blacks or anybody else. I can change the world's impression about me. So what I try to do is market myself. I don't market myself as an Asian American actor. I just market myself. And I'm hoping to God that somebody will say, "Okay, this is a special young man here. I want to see if he can do something."

It's true there aren't those romantic roles that I'm sure a lot of Asian men would like to play. But it's up to me—and other Asian men to try to change that.

I watch Jackie Chan whose martial arts films are big box office smashes and I'm very happy that an Asian American is making it in America. But at the same time I also know that martial arts films—I can't do them. Because it would be like cashing in on another person's success. It's been done so many times by Asian Americans here. You think martial arts and you think Asians. You think Asians, you think martial arts. It kind of takes away from what I'm trying to do.

The thing I am stressing is you have to care about the character you are playing. It can be an action film, that's fine. If it's a film about two guys sitting in a closet for the whole day it doesn't matter as long as you can care about the character that I'm playing. Give him qualities; give him emotions.

It sounds so ridiculous because how can you write a character who basically has no feelings? Emotions are what acting is supposed to be about. The funny thing is that with Asian American roles you get parts that basically have no emotional content whatsoever. They're just filler roles. That's the thing that's the most frustrating. It's not the fact that there's little work out there or anything, it's just the fact that the roles that I do see, there's nothing to them.

The main thing I want to get across is that I don't know if I'll ever get to play the guy next door. But even if it's not the guy next door, just give a little window to the character's soul, that's all.

Have I thought of doing things other than film and television, such as theater? The artist side of me would love to do it. But the other side of me is more interested in reaching a mass audience to express myself.

There's a vanity side too. Maybe there is a little of that in all of us to different degrees. I've gotten to the point in my life where I was the one on the outside listening for so long that now I want to be in the center talking. And it's the same way if we go into a room now, a party, a club or anywhere. I want to be the one doing the talking. I love to listen too, I feel there is always something I can learn from other people. But I think my time is here and now, and I want to be the one expressing. In a local theater you can do that but it's going to be seen by a much smaller number. I want to be recognized.

If you're in the industry to get work, professional work, to make money you obviously want a mass audience, you obviously want a following.

You have actors who basically never do interviews and say they hate the stardom. How much can you really hate it if you're actually out there trying to get in films seen by millions of people. So reaching a mass audience is important to me. That's why I'm concentrating on the television aspects.

I feel I have a very strong passion for my craft. But I've met people who take it to another level. They love acting so much that they'll toil in small theaters and will be seen like by twelve people for the next six months just because they love it so much. You've got to be a little bit in your own world to be like that and I'm not that distanced from the population.

Recognition and stardom basically is—we all have our demons that we grew up with; my demons were that no one would listen. Recognition means I have the control to say what I want, express what I want. I have so much I kept inside of me and now I want everyone to see it. I listened to all of you for ten years now I want your attention. So that's what recognition is; it's not going down and signing autographs. It's the power, the creative control to express what you want to express. When I work with *Kung Fu* it's the ultimate high for me because people listen to me. If I say shouldn't the character be this—they'd say okay, you're right, you're right. They'd change it. And that's not vanity. It's just that as an artist, as a creative person in any field you want that kind of control. And I know that on stage you don't become the kind of star that basically says I want this changed or that changed. You can't do that because it's all about big money, because that's where the power comes from.

If your films are grossing ten million dollars a weekend like Jackie Chan's you can do whatever you want. It all boils down to being able to express myself eventually. That's what this all boils down to.

People say this is a one in a million chance, you gotta do what you gotta do. I don't see this as a one in a million chance. I see the odds a little bit better. Two in a million maybe, but that two is better than one. I do think it's possible to make it big, and stranger things have happened in the industry. We're talking about an entire ethnic group—Asians— that's growing faster than any other ethnic group. Why wouldn't one person, it shouldn't be one, it should be ten, it should be twenty, but why wouldn't one person be able after all these years to break through? Stranger things have happened. Whoever thought Joe Pesci, five feet tall, heavy set, with a funny accent would be a major star? That to me is stranger than one Asian American being able to make it in America. I don't see the odds as that great.

You have people at the top who basically don't know what they're doing when it comes to Asian characterization. They say "I think it should be played like this, and I think this would work, or that would work." And you say, well, an Asian American isn't played that way. They'll say "How come you don't have an accent? How come you're walking this way? Why do you think your shirt should be opened? Why do you think you should be carrying a briefcase?" They have certain stereotypes. And I'm thinking to myself, you don't know Asian American culture, you don't know me as an individual, or what I'm trying to bring to this role. You know what you see on the street. You know what you see on CNN. You know what you see on Channel Five News.

Even if I coat that with honey and sugar they'll think I'm attacking their perception of Asian Americans and so they wonder who is this Asian American to tell me I don't know about Asian Americans. It's frustrating and what's more I have a little bit of a volatile personality; not to the point where I would start trouble and argue with people but I will speak my mind.

But if I were not to express myself wouldn't that defeat my own purpose? My ultimate goal is expression. How can I go about it and not express myself along the way. I would never forgive myself for that.

I don't believe that Asians or any minority or anybody in general, should have to walk through society or an industry with their head down and basically say—whatever you want, whatever you want, it's not my territory it's your territory. This country was built on ideals.

I want to quote something. I wish I knew who said it because it would make it seem more intellectual if I knew where it came from. It goes: "A reasonable man adapts himself to the world around him. An unreasonable man expects the world to adapt to him. Therefore all progress depends on the unreasonable man." I love that quote. I live by that quote. So I'm trying to be as unreasonable as I can, hoping to change things.

Mel Gionson

Mel said he is in his early 40s. He has short, salt and pepper hair, and a chin mustache, about two inches long. He was raised in

Waipahu—a small rural town 15 miles from Honolulu. He came to New York City in 1980. In college he was an arts major, interested in pop culture. He took a drama class, and said he was attracted to the poetry of theater. He appeared in the off Broadway production of The Innocence of Ghosts *in October 1996.*

IN HAWAII

I was going to major in fine arts in college, but the lines to register were too long, so I ended up taking a drama course. In my first role I auditioned for a play called the *Basic Training of Pavlo Hummel*, a nontraditional production. The play is about the Vietnam protest. The original people who starred in the original Joseph Papp production was Tisa Chang and Al Pacino. Ironically I was cast as the Ivy League guy. In Hawaii we don't have the psycho-social pressures that people in the mainland have. I majored in drama from there.

In Hawaii we didn't talk in terms of races. We would just say, that girl looked like an ingenue, or that person looked like he could play a certain part.

I'm Hawaiian—that is I am a mix of Filipino, Chinese, Irish, Spanish. It's mixed in there. But culturally, I am basically Hawaiian. In Hawaii you could say this person is ethnically Chinese, or ethnically Japanese. But I'm a "local" boy. In Hawaii we share each other's foods, and you learn about each other's culture. In Hawaii they feel comfortable with everyone fitting into the larger community.

I acted a lot in Hawaii. I worked in the Kennedy Theater and worked for Hawaii Performing Arts. They do productions exploring the human condition, and what it means to grow up in the Hawaiian experience. After college I worked for the Honolulu Ballet company. I worked as an administrator then as a performer. Then I ended up in New York.

COMING TO NEW YORK

New York was where I wanted to be. I was attracted to the Warholian romance of New York. Los Angeles had no draw for me at all. I wanted to do theater, because I liked the literary bent. There is something about theater that is very transforming. Theater engages the audience and the imagination. It's not as passive as film. You feel the audience more.

The first thing I auditioned for in New York was a production of *Richard II*. It was done in a church. I was cast in a minor role as a replacement. It was a nontraditional show, a mixture of white and black. Joe Papp had already broken ground with nontraditional casting.

What attracted me to the theater and New York was seeing Shakespeare on public television. I saw people who looked like me participating in the classics. People like Raul Julia and James Earl Jones mixed in Shakespeare. I thought it was neat. It was something I was striving for.

I answer all kinds of calls. Any actor, regardless of race. My ethnicity is nondeniable. Even in nontraditional calls. They like to mix it up. Everything is based on race. Everything in the business is based on looks. And race is part of looks. Everything is based on imagery. The problem of stereotypes is the imagery—the perception of certain groups and how they fit into that imagery.

Say there are good guys and bad guys—how society sees what is a good guy versus a bad guy. Good is clear skin, blond hair, blue eyes, a certain look. Openness will denote goodness. Pockmarked face and bad hair will be bad. A lot of times the bad, or the other, is perceived in terms of race.

I've had calls for both good and bad guy types. Generally I don't get a lot of villain roles. Right now, I'm being called for roles of doctors, or white collar professionals—journalists. Depends on what the societal icon is. Like Kaity Tong. It's breaking barriers. So an Asian woman might play a reporter. Stereotypes are based on certain realities, but seen only from a certain point of view.

ROLES

I played a white physicist in a small local theater production. I didn't play a white person, only the role was written for a white physicist. I also did some things for the National Asian American Theater company—two George Bernard Shaw one act plays: *Village Wooing* and *How He Lied to Her Husband*. In the winter of '95-'96, I read for a part in *King Lear* in public theater. I was one of the people in the ensemble, a guy named Ken.

My agent submits pictures. Then the producers decide that this person looks like he might be good for this, or that role. So you go in and read those roles. So going in, the producers know what you look like. Sometimes those choices of casting are based on race, or your résumé. It depends on how well you do in the audition.

Sometimes they look at qualities on your face, which are not necessarily race specific. Do you look like a good person, the character they want? It depends on the producer.

I've also done regional theaters in various towns up and down the East

Coast, also Berkeley. I've worked in the play *Woman Warrior.* I played a Chinese diplomat on stage in Philadelphia. I played Bob Krachet in the *Christmas Carol* in Syracuse. The production lasted two months. It surprised a lot of people in the audience. A woman stopped me in a supermarket up there, and said she really liked the performance, but said she was taken aback by my playing the role, but after a while it didn't matter, because I had the qualities. It was heartwarming, because in a lot of the smaller communities they are all white, and they see blacks or Asians in a certain way.

I wasn't too surprised when I landed the role, because I was called to read for the part. There was a clue there. If they were willing to see me in the role in the audition, then it would have to do with how I auditioned as opposed to what I looked like.

I don't audition much for film, because most of the films are done in Los Angeles. When they do come to New York to shoot, most of the casting has already been done. In TV it's expanding. Television and everything in the commercial end are market place driven. In commercial productions they look at the bottom line. They want to see how much commercial time they can sell. In soap operas the hero is blond, blue eyed. The brunette is considered exotic. That's why they cast stars in TV and film. It's a sold package. A certain kind of icon. When you have film or TV, it's who will buy the ticket. Stars, like Cruise or Denzel, are a certain kind of icon who will draw in the dollars. There is no Asian American actor who is a star in that sense.

I've seen changes in the 16 years I've been here. A lot more Asian American actors are surfacing, to give it a try. How high can I go in this business? There's always hope. I'm a character actor. I don't see myself as a star. It's a limitation of talent and looks. The business is so weird. It's not just one thing. It's hard to mix in race with the business. Business has to do with talent, beauty. It's all very serendipitous. I don't see myself as a box office draw.

I'm proud that I'm an Asian American Pacific Islander working actor. I don't have to support myself by waiting tables. I'm not a waiter. I think it's an accomplishment to be proud of. I had this blond hair, blue eyed roommate when I first came to New York. She was freaking out that I was going on calls, and she wasn't. She looked like Goldie Hawn, and there are lots of people that look like that type. But the calls I was going on, the producers had fewer to choose from.

The roles I've done are challenging enough, so I don't get dispirited. It keeps me going. What do I see as the pinnacle? It's want everyone wants— to be a star, to have a place in the Hamptons, a home in California, a lot of people want that. Be a star. Make tons of money. Have a freedom that can be purchased with the dollars. It's like winning the lottery. Acting is a lottery. These are the numbers I want to play. Maybe I'll score.

Opportunities on Broadway? They're very limited. I'm not a song and dance man. Broadway is an addendum. Many of the shows are musicals, and they are produced for tourists. There are many revivals of musicals going on now. So it's the off Broadway gig that can be satisfying and lucrative. Broadway is commercial. Opportunities for me are in nonprofit theater. I've done an AT&T commercial, some industrials—films for teaching techniques.

Where do I want to be for the next ten years? A part of the New York market. Doing theater, working in the entertainment field, then I'll go back to Hawaii. I want to do more classics, though I haven't done any leading roles in the classics, I would like to. What are my chances? I don't know.

Right now it is very satisfying for me to be a card carrying union member. I take great pride in that. At any given time, according to Actors Equity, 98 percent of the actors are unemployed. So I am proud that I can support myself, working as an actor.

The millions you hear actors making actually only happens to a very small part of the population. The struggling actor makes an average of maybe $15,000 a year. If there is any accomplishment, it's in making a living at what you do. The rest is gravy. If you can make $10,000 extra on a role, that's lovely gravy.

Do I see myself as leading role material? You have to see yourself as leading role material. Perception is an odd thing. You can't put an impediment on what you can do. Anyone who enters into this, his heart will be at the wayside if he gets discouraged easily. When you enter acting it's a lifestyle. When you're a CEO, you have to dress like a CEO. As an actor, you have to dress like you're an actor. In theater, its not a job you go to, it's a job that's in you. In acting one day you might play the leading role, and the next day, a supporting character.

ASIAN MALE ROLES

It used to be that the roles for Asian males in films were very subservient. That's because most of the productions are produced by whites. So if a Chinese waiter is the only contact whites have with Asian males, then they are cast as waiters. That's their only sense of what Asians do. I think white Americans feel they own the country, and then there are these minorities around them. That's their point of view. If Asian Americans take a hand in the production then things might change.

I haven't seen an "ordinariness," which has to be reflected in film. Asian Americans as dads, or as sons. A villain is an extraordinary person. Asians are asked to play such parts. But how about your neighbor being Asian? That's an ordinary role. Yet we are not at the point where Asians can play ordinary roles. The point of view is still that Asians, when they appear, are either a point of the plot, or extraordinary as characters. The thing is, Asians as a driving force only has been around 20-30 years. White America didn't know of a black America, let alone an Asian American America.

Do I feel I would be further along in my career if I were white? Yes. I feel I would be. Face is an impediment. There is no question about it.

Karen Tsen Lee

She started out studying modern dance and later became interested in acting. She decided that dancing was limited because it was something that one could do only while young. So she took a few classes in acting, including a continuing ed class at NYU.

In television she has appeared in bit parts in the Cosby Mysteries, *on* New York Undercover, All My Children, The Equalizer, *and* Saturday Night Live. *She has played a number of roles on television: an attorney, a call girl, a Filipino bride, a student.*

In theater she has appeared off Broadway in the role of Nora, in A Doll House *(Pan Asian Repertory Theater). On off-off-Broadway she has appeared in such classics as* Macbeth *(as one of the Witches),* Much Ado about Nothing *(as Hero), and* The Glass Menagerie *(as Laura).*

She has appeared in television commercials for such companies as American Express, AT&T, Merrill Lynch, Metropolitan Life Insurance, Kellogg's, MCI, and Toys R Us. She said the roles would range from a white collar executive to a mother, or consumer.

She says she is a full time, working actor and points with pride to this. She said she has earned over $15,000 annually. She is in her 30s, married to an Asian American actor. She started in the business in 1983.

How it Started

My family owns a Chinese restaurant in midtown Manhattan. As a way to increase business my father's idea was to feature as entertainment, celebrations of the Chinese New Year and the August Moon Festival. So he enlisted the children's help, my sister, my brother, myself to perform various folk dances and rituals like burning incense. This was at a time when no one in New York was doing anything like this. We opened the restaurant in 1963 and so it was a really good form of advertising for the restaurant.

Karen Tsen Lee

I had been trained in ballet and tap and my father hired teachers to teach us Chinese folk dances so I was like already pre-conditioned. I think dance was a way for me to express myself. This kind of grew into a sense that I wanted to do more, be more expressive.

I still think every once in awhile, who was I, as an Asian American growing up in America? There was a time in my life that I had a big denial of Asian cultural heritage. I maybe performed for the restaurant for my family but because they were first generation I didn't really feel comfortable communicating with them. And I think that happens to a lot of second generation kids when their immigrant family is still speaking Chinese, and they're more fluent in English. So I was trying to find myself in all of this. And acting just led to trying on different shoes to see who I really was.

I took a class in 1983. This particular woman had her own school. So some of us, her loyal followers became like a small theater company. We put on the production, we built the stage, we hung the lights, we did everything as if we owned our own theater company. And that's basically what I did for a good three to four years. This was on the showcase level, it was really not a professional company. For me I was still a novice, I was still learning, but I was learning on my feet.

In the Actor's Equity code the showcase level is a show in which you're not getting paid if you're an equity actor. You might get travel fee, a token, whatever. Fifty bucks for the whole run. And it's an opportunity to showcase your talent. Agents are allowed to come and see it for free; producers, directors, anyone in the business or anyone with a union card. Producers don't generally make any money, in fact they generally lose money in those kinds of productions. But it's a good way for people to get experience, be on their feet in front of a live audience. It's a pretty safe environment for trying experimental stuff.

We did plays by O'Neil, by Tennessee Williams, things I probably would never be cast for. That's another reason why I went into it. Here was an environment where I was being accepted for who I was and not being cast because I was Asian.

After the showcase experience I left and started to take some classes elsewhere with different teachers. Then around 1988 I started auditioning for more commercial venues. And I got an opportunity to work with Pan Asian Repertory. They were probably one of my first commercial opportunities.

I ended up joining the union after doing a radio commercial. And that brought me into AFTRA. I played a Chinese character in a story about a woman who was coming to America for PBS Radio. There were several characters and my friends were also playing parts in it. There weren't a whole lot of us then, so whenever there were people you knew, you would recommend them. That's how I would often get jobs.

I also got into Actors Equity. And through that I was also able to get into SAG, which is Screen Actors Guild.

Getting into the unions is sort of like a Catch 22. You have to get the work to get into the union, but then you have to be in the union in order to get the job. So everyone has his own story about how they got in.

I did a few student films to get my feet wet after that. And around that same time I did an independent film called *Pickles Make Me Cry*.

I ended up doing a little more with Pan Asian Repertory, a production called *Letters to a Student Revolutionary* in 1991 and since that time up until now I've repeated that role on stage. That's a recurring piece that comes up in my life.

I would say that today 90 percent of the calls I get for auditions are in commercials for television. As for theater I would say like three to five percent. Film is maybe one or two percent. But this cycle changes a lot. In the fall it maybe more theater, it maybe more film. And when I speak film, I'm talking not only featured film but I'm also talking television films.

Over the course of my career I would break it down in terms of 50 percent commercials maybe, 35 percent theater, and the rest will be split between industrials and print work—modeling.

In commercials I can be the young mom or the business woman. That's about the two big categories I fall under.

In theater, I've played the mother in *A Doll's House*. In *Letters to a Student Revolutionary* I played the Chinese comrade who wants to come to America, also the lead. In *Macbeth* that I did in Washington, D.C., I played one of the witches. *Macbeth* was nontraditional casting.

PROFESSIONAL REPRESENTATION AND CONTACTS

An actor can be represented by two types of people. Either a manager or an agent, or both. The manager will call me up and say he got a call from an agency. He in turn has gotten a call from a casting director to submit people who are business types. And that's how the chain is. The casting director, the agent, the manager, and me. Sometimes it goes from me directly to the agent. Sometimes it's just the manager and the casting person. But generally there are at least one or two people I end up working through. I work with many agents. But I have only one manager, and am obliged by contract to tell him of any work that I receive.

Managers get anywhere from 10 percent up for commission, then you have the agents. Print agents by the way get 20 percent. There is no regulating company that tells them what they can ask for. So if I get something through an agent, I give ten percent to him and another ten percent to my manager. It ends up that anytime I work, about twenty to thirty percent of the check goes to somebody else.

It's really sad because I look at my check after taxes, and everybody's chewed up a piece of it. Less than half is what I finally get. On a personal level I'd say it's always helpful to have a personal connection with other actors because I feel like there's a support system. It's not really a support system, but the fact that you're kind of feeling that you might be in the loop. Whether that's an illusion or not, that's just a feeling, like you know what's going on. And you can gauge what the industry is doing, and how you're not getting work, and you should be getting work, or it poses a lot of weird questions in your head. So that if everyone's working and I'm not it feels really bad. And you go, mmm, I better work on some things. It says your agent doesn't get you enough work, or your manager isn't pushing you hard enough, or you can just take the attitude well I just wasn't right for it and not go too crazy because like all my friends, being employed is the exception, not the rule. It really is.

On the professional side myself and many actors feel like we are constantly having to improve our contacts in the professional world. That could mean sending photos or cards to agents to remind them you're around and you're available. And you're lucky if they do remember you. Because if you've done jobs for them it's more likely they will remember and try to submit you for other things. It's very easy to slip out of their sight. And there's always an influx of more actors, so they're willing to try new people. So that part is very competitive. And I feel intimidated having to schmooze.

ON OPPORTUNITIES AS AN ASIAN AMERICAN ACTOR

Being an Asian actor I kind of think it affords me some opportunities to work because I'm in a smaller group of people to select from. And because people are now more aware and want to cast more people culturally, they're more likely to pick from the smaller pool so you have a greater chance to get work. At the same time however if they're already narrow-minded and their vision is small you'll never be looked upon to fit in a particular role, just because you are Asian.

For most commercial venues if they're doing a contemporary piece, unless the playwright specifically asks for it an Asian might not get the opportunity to do a Tennessee Williams play because it's by a southern writer writing about life in the South. There aren't too many Asian actors doing Big Daddy, or whatever. So that's the one thing, unless they're going to make it nontraditional casting and then of course the doors are wide open.

Or let's take *A Doll's House*. When Pan Asian Repertory did it, it was a logical thing that they would cast Asian. But if the play was to be done at another theater, such as a major theater on Broadway, it would be very unlikely that I would be cast as the lead. That would be the case with biographies as well.

I try not to think about it too much because it's really frustrating. You always are looking for a job so you try not to let that one lack of opportunity drag you down. What can I say? I'm here. I'm trying to make a living from this. Right now I'm split between trying to make a living and being on unemployment. And I don't want to commit to any other kind of work because in order to be committed to this business you really have to avail yourself a lot and to make the auditions.

I just got two auditions for tomorrow for which I have to be available and I don't even know when they're going to happen. I can get a call at any time to audition. It's only 4:25, and the casting people work until

6; the agents work until 6. I've gotten calls at night to see if I wanted to work the following day. So it's really a kind of crazy, unpredictable business. Some deal with this by limiting what they will do. They might say I only want to do theater and film. And they make do by taking jobs outside of acting. I'm a little more open to opportunities that will give me work. I'm lucky that I have some print work I can do. Industrials I don't pooh, pooh. I play background on work as extras, some people would never do that, and there's a practical side to that. A few years ago I had to go into the hospital for an operation. My husband was covered by SAG from his health benefits so I was covered automatically, and if he wasn't we would have had to lay out $15,000 because I had no health insurance. So for me it's a very pragmatic goal to make my health benefits so that he and I are always covered by health insurance. So my commitment is to take work that I might not normally want to do, but it's just a reality.

The minimum threshold for medical coverage from the Screen Actors Guild is earning $7,500. And that's for one tier. The second tier is $15,000. That's quite a bit of money, given the cycles of this business.

Am I in this business to make a living or is it more than that? I've gone through different phases. I think there have been times that I've enjoyed the opportunities I've had and I've really grown from that; and I may not have been paid well. There are times I make a lot of money and it thrills me I could do it. And that's a different kind of satisfaction.

I have always thought to be an actor I would go to exotic places. I've gone to Philadelphia, El Paso, Minnesota, Singapore, Washington, D.C. My husband has gone to Virginia, Las Vegas, he's gone all over. That side of it, is the adventure side of me—to explore a new city and be paid for it and to do a job. That to me is really exciting. Not everybody gets those chances. This business is so tough only a fractional percent of the union is ever working at one time. So I think I've been actually very fortunate.

I'm in a phase now where I want to find more satisfaction for my artistic side, and it's tough. I'm realizing that I'm having to change gears a little bit and focus on something different.

I think my attitude, my self-confidence has changed over the years. Because I've come of age I see the cycles in my life. There's actually more focus. In the beginning I'd said I'd try anything, see how it feels. Many people used to say to me why are you going in this business? Don't go into acting. And I now say to myself I don't think I would ever say that to someone, but I would warn them of what to look out for. Ultimately the choice is yours to take a piece of work or not. All the managers, agents, and casting people will always tell you to take the job, even if it means selling your soul, because they're going to be making money from you. The question always goes back to you, what do you want to do. Now that I've gone through the experiences I can say this is what I will or won't do.

What is acceptable in a film is a good role that doesn't make me feel stupid; if it's a good script, if I think the roles will be challenging, if I think it would help my career. I'm not put off totally by nudity but then I don't know if anyone would want to see me nude. But the script should be clever, have good writing and a good director involved or it has to be fun somehow. But the opportunities have been very, very rare. One out of twenty, maybe.

I was offered this chance to do a role in a television series called *Homicide* but it meant breaking a contract with a theater company. It was my decision to do that. I had to pay the theater my last two weeks of salary which was not a good thing.

In *Homicide* I got to play someone younger than myself, a college student, who's an American without an accent and who worked in a sleazy motel as a clerk. I thought this would be so much fun to play because I never get cast as this. I had to pay for it. But to me that was a gift. To be cast in a role that I normally don't get seen as—usually I'm the young mother or a business woman. It was a top notch show. The director was fun and the other cast members were really great to work with.

My reputation with the Shakespeare theater is now sullied because I broke this contract. And it's unfortunate because this was another place I would have loved to develop a relationship with to do live theater. I don't have really strong theater classical background but it was just something that I always admired and had done a smattering of.

The Likelihood of Making it as a Big Star

When I see someone like Sharon Stone or Meryl Streep do I ask myself whether I can be a superstar like them or can't I be? The heartbreaking part is that I have asked myself that question. That's the heartbreaking part of this business. If I were to set my goals to be that, I'm in for a real bad time. I know that from the other actors around me. I tell myself how many people do I know who have gone out to California striving for that level and haven't reached it.

Who am I to think that I'm going to be the one? Who am I kidding, myself? I don't want to set myself up for that kind of a fall. If it happens, I would be thrilled. Not only Asian actors but actors of any other race have a similar mentality: if it hits, great, if it doesn't, I'll try to find the opportunities that help keep me going.

It's like any other business. You start out as an entry level person and hope you're going to be the CEO one day. And you work your way up; either those opportunities come along or they don't. What are you going to do? Throw everything out because you never got to be CEO? No I don't think so. There are people who probably think that way though. Especially people in the beginning, because things are so wide open to you, you don't really know what you're up against.

There are some people who are very, very lucky. I've never felt like I was the lucky one. I'm not banking on it. You just learn over time. If you stayed in the business for at least five years, you're going to have that body of experience, and you are going to say okay, this is how it is. Most actors who have been in the business for more than five years will have that attitude as opposed to the expectation of getting there real fast.

Is it possible for an Asian to attain mega-star status? I'd say today yes. Yesterday, maybe not. The international audience has expanded. You have more films being shown here from all over the world so people have a vocabulary. They have an identifying mark of what kind of talent is out there now as opposed to ten years ago.

Would I like to be a star? Sure, why not?

How important is that? It's not a major goal in my life. But I think it might be fun for awhile for somebody to say hey, I saw you in such and such. I always get a kick if they do recognize me from something because I look different in various roles and somehow people don't recognize me much; especially if it's a commercial. My friends who do recognize me are thrilled for me and I love that. And I'm thrilled for them when I recognize them and I tell them and they get thrilled. So that part is very satisfying, it's fun.

Do I dream of having my own TV series or a leading role in a major film? No, I don't fantasize like that. I'm too much of a realist. How do I know I've achieved success? When I'm sitting in Bermuda and somebody calls me up and says hey, come on down we're shooting a film, we want you in the lead; when I can go anywhere and somebody will still ask me to work for them. That I think will be a pretty good indicator that I've been successful. And in a way it's interesting, every once in awhile, even now I'll get a commercial call. My résumé has been on file somewhere and they've requested me. That to me is like an indicator; oh, gee, I must have like stuck in somebody's head. And so to me that's a certain level of recognition. Or when someone knows my work and they recommend me for something. That to me is an indicator that I'm doing okay.

I don't know how long I will stay in the business. It's going to probably get really tough in the next 15 years because we all know how this country loves youth. And I'm getting older by the minute. On the acting end I feel like I'm more limited in terms of time. On the producing end that's still actually very wide open if I ever wanted to produce or direct. I'm pretty optimistic. I'm not a pessimist at heart. I'm a realist when I need to be.

Lia Chang

Lia Chang appears to be in her mid 30s. She was born and raised in San Francisco, and came to New York City in 1981. She is a fourth generation Asian American. She sees herself as both an actor and photojournalist. Over the past 15 years she said she's worked as a petite model for Liz Claiborne, and has worked in both film and television roles. When I met with her she had just returned from a modeling shoot.

WORKING IN NEW YORK CITY

All they were looking for today was to photograph my eyes because that's what they are going to end up blowing up to use; and possibly my lips. It's a pharmaceutical product they were shooting for. I don't know exactly what the product is, but it is going to be a whole montage of different ethnicities, different ages, and I'm sure all kinds of body parts.

This is not the first time that my eyes have been the highlight to a product. When the *Asian New Yorker* put together their new T-shirt the art director wanted to know if they could borrow my eyes for the logo. So they just used my left eye.

Earlier today I also had a casting call for American Express where they wanted me to be hip and trendy which is why I'm dressed this way. And luckily somebody had already done my makeup so I didn't have to worry

Lia Chang

about that. But it turned out to be a massive cattle call. What a cattle call means is, if you're told you have a specific appointment you hope that when you get there, you just get seen. And instead there are like 50 people ahead of you. But it was fine because I got in fairly quickly. I generally don't go on cattle calls anymore. I've been in the business for 15 years, and if there is a cattle call I will ask if I can leave my composite and I'll walk out.

I started out my life in New York as a model in a convention. The modeling agency that first saw me told me you have the best teeth that we saw at the convention, but as a petite model you're not going to be able to make a full time living so you are going to have to get your survival jobs to pay for your pictures, to pay for your rent, all the practical things.

But when I first started pounding the pavement and going to see all these different photographers for print work, they would tell me the price of silver had just gone up, which meant it was very expensive to do what they call testing, which is trading your time for the photographer's pictures. So they were only interested in photographing tall blondes. Not much has changed.

They would tell me to go into TV, because that's where height doesn't matter. So I started taking acting classes. I started taking voice classes. And a model friend introduced me to Jadin Wong [her manager]. She started sending me out. And she only sent me out on a few things. The very first thing she ended up getting for me which was in 1984 was a movie. My very first movie.

I had only been dealing with my acting life for about a year. I hadn't really spent time on movie calls. When I first came to New York to acquaint myself with other Asian actors I was just ushering for a show at Pan Asian Repertory. I was a volunteer. I thought it would be nice to meet some other Asian people.

One day Jadin was sitting in this casting person's office and they were talking about this movie called *The Last Dragon*. They were looking for martial arts women, black, Hispanic, and white. And Jadin said, "What about Asian? For God sakes it's karate." And they said do you have somebody, and yeah, of course I do she said, because she handles like 98 percent of the Asians in New York. Do you have picture book? Of course I have pictures but not in my wallet, I'm not carrying one in my wallet, she said. So, she sent me on the call, and the day I went it was pouring rain. Two days later I found out that I got the movie. It was the same year that I got Liz Claiborne as an account. I was a petite show model for Liz Claiborne for nine years. So that was the start of my acting career. And in the meantime, I was keeping my daytime hours open for modeling and acting appointments, I was going to school at night and working at night. When I first came to New York I worked at a few survival jobs, Barnes and Noble, and night receptionist at an animal medical center. I was also a coat checker and did reservations at the Russian Tea Room. And juggled all this other stuff too.

In 1984 I was in my first movie, and in 1985 I did *Big Trouble in Little China.* When I first was cast in *The Last Dragon,* I was supposed to be one of the bad girls. When I showed up they told me I was too sweet and innocent to be part of a gang of killers so they put me on the good side, as one of the students. So, in my next film I was determined to play a bad girl. And I did. So, the sequence in *Big Trouble in Little China* that I'm in involves two Chinese guys going across a bridge, and Kurt Russell is scaling the side of the bridge. I'm the first one out and I tear gas them, knock their guns out of their hands, fight them across the bridge and then I get knocked out. So, that's my big thing in *Big Trouble in Little China.*

I made my stage debut in 1986 with Robert Goulet and Barbara Eden in *South Pacific.* Ironically Jadin took me to see the musical saying who knows, one day you might have to play the part. I left for San Francisco the next day, but the following day Jadin called me and said Lia you have to come back to New York, the person who was cast in *South Pacific* had gotten a part in *The Last Emperor.* And you have to come and replace her. Well, I didn't sing, and I didn't dance, but I had seen *South Pacific,* the movie. So I ended up coming back to New York that Friday, watched the movie and Jadin trained me in her traditional happy talk method. On Monday I auditioned. On Tuesday I got the job. On Wednesday, I signed the contract. On Thursday I was on a train to Valley Forge, Pennsylvania, to watch the show and a week later I was making my stage debut in Toronto.

I played Leoit, the young girl whose mother, Mary gives her to the Lieutenant and it's her first love. He sings "Younger Than Spring Time." I had my training, but a lot of it was I just was thrown into the field, and luckily I had the right people to lead me on stage, and lead me off.

I consider myself an actor, and I don't actually consider myself a model anymore. Modeling was really my bread and butter. I started modeling in high school. I never dreamed of being a model. The only reason I started in the modeling field at all was because my parents had gotten divorced. I moved in with my dad during the summer and it was really hard when you move to a new town during the summer, because you're not dealing with other kids. So he enrolled me in this modeling class at the local community center, and the woman who ran the class asked me if I wanted to come and work at her school at her agency and take classes in exchange.

So, as far as I was concerned to me it was always a business. I always knew it would be a stepping stone to my other lives. In my last three months of high school, my dad worked for IBM, so he got transferred a lot, so I moved from San Francisco, to San Jose, to Tucson, Arizona. In Tucson, I took a class called modern media, which was working with the camera and studying film. And film is really my first love. And at that time I really thought I was going to be in the journalism world. I had done my first magazine in my sophomore year in high school, but when I came to New York and went to the library and looked up all the things I was interested in doing, I knew I would never make a living, I would never be able to support myself on a broadcast internship. The last film I was in was about four months ago, a short called *Four Out of Five Dentists*. It's a little independent feature, and they are taking it to the film festivals. I played a hooker, but this was very comedic. As I mentioned there was a time when people would not cast me as a bad girl, so we got over that. And there was a time where people would not cast me in anything sexy. They couldn't conceive of me being sexy. So, I did my research and I played my hookers. I don't generally do them; it has to be a major role, or it has to be of high comedic value; and in this case it was because I did her with a Jewish accent. But I currently have running roles on *One Life to Live*, where I play a nurse on TV, and *Another World*, where I play a television reporter.

Do I feel my career is going the way I want it to? Yes. Actually part of my going into my photographic life was because of the lack of control I felt as an artist. When you are in a profession where your job is based on what you look like, it can be quite disconcerting unless you have a lot of other things going on. When people ask me what do you want, or what are you giving up, my answer is generally I don't have to give anything up, I can do it all. Everything is really kind of seasonal. And it's just that some people can do one thing, and I happen to be able to do quite a number of things. And it keeps life interesting. And I'm more in control of where my career is going now compared to three years ago because of the choices I've made in the roles I've chosen to take or not to take. For instance, I decided last year that I was going to give up theater, this was because I was also doing a lot as far as my photography was concerned. So for me to do theater the role either had to be really great, or it had to be a very short run. And luckily enough last year it happened over the course of like two weekends I had four very different roles, two in the same show. They were all leads, major parts, lots of dialogue. Both were in theater. So I had some very well established roles that I could sink my teeth into. It's not enough for me to be in something anymore that is of a stereotypical nature, because I've been in nine movies and most of the films that I've been in have been stereotypical characters, ranging from martial arts, (which I don't do anymore) to hookers, and babes. It started out as gangsters, gun molls, mud wrestlers, those have been my film roles. But then of late I've also played more regular sorts of people—a hotel desk clerk, a shoe sales lady, a nurse, and a reporter. And that's a difference in terms of the roles that I have been getting in film and television.

There was a project so far as TV is concerned that I deliberately chose not to do that was of a stereotypical nature—they wanted me to play a house keeper who didn't speak English and they thought that was funny. So that's what I mean about having more choices today. Also they wanted someone who could speak Chinese, and I can't speak Chinese. It was for a TV pilot and I turned it down for the same reason I'm doing photography, which is to promote the positive images of Asian Americans in the media.

Well, certainly with the *Joy Luck Club* we have come a long way but we haven't. It's very refreshing to see a lot of Asian actors working. It was very refreshing to see a lot of Asian actors who don't have accents play roles they didn't have to do with an accent. But what has to happen is there has to be more Asians writing. The power is in the producing, the directing, and the writing. And that's the direction I'm heading in. I know my colleagues are taking that initiative also. A colleague went back to school and is studying playwriting and she wrote her own play. In one respect it's a headache, on the other hand you can create your own venue for you to be in and to have your voice heard and to have your perspective put across, as opposed to some other ethnicities idealized version of what the Asian American experience is. So I see myself moving in this direction without question.

Do I think it is possible for me to achieve superstar status? Yes. When I tell you about the choices I made as far as the parts I chose to take or not to take, there are a lot of things that I auditioned for in my career that I did not get cast in because I was too pretty, too exotic.

I come from a different era as far as my acting sensibilities. My favorite actresses are of the thirties and forties. You know, Greta Garbo, Betty Davis, Joan Crawford, Audrey Hepburn, when they really had serious roles, or just a whole other sensibility.

What other roles would I like? Doctors, lawyers. Really a lot of the characters I've played have been very stereotypical. So, when you are playing a fully astute character it could be anybody. It could be a next door neighbor but it is at least somebody who is real, rather than a machine gun trigger, on screen for 30 seconds and just one shoot for one day.

Do I feel the screen is color blind? No. But I'm talking about working as a character actress as opposed to just being a pretty young thing.

Look at the Asian American film festivals. More and more, we are adding new voices, new directors, and new talent. So it's happening. Obviously it's not happening quick enough. I understand what you are trying to get at in the questions that you are asking me. I'm fourth generation Chinese American. I was never raised like this is Asian American, you are Asian and this is it. If there is something that I want, I prepare myself, I find a way to get it, and I get it.

How do I measure success? It would entail being in a position to be where you would have to be on the A list. And the A list is usually defined where there is international recognition, as well as compensation, and being offered the parts first before your other contemporaries. But more importantly being offered the parts that have nothing to do with the color of your skin, which is why I went downtown to the experimental theater to begin with, where I was being hired as an actor first and not as Asian.

I think that for me the only way that is going to happen is if I am directing and producing my own stuff. Not necessarily writing it. Or if I have someone who will write, direct, and produce for me, but there is probably less chance of that happening. My interest really is being respected for the work that I do and being compensated for it. Certainly as an artist, you want to be able to make a difference in whatever medium you are working in. It is all the roads we travel that lead us to another road. If for some reason if someone told me tomorrow you can't act anymore I wouldn't lose sleep over it.

Why am I in acting? I was very shy growing up and it's certainly a neat way to express oneself. And whereas maybe I can't be a doctor in real life, a real lawyer in real life, or be a CIA agent, whatever it is, I am able as an actor to be in lots of different worlds, be in lots of different characters, and be in lots of different mindsets, it's just a very well rounded kind of exposure value.

Do I think I would be more or less further along in this business if I were white? You would have to look at the ratio of parts for Asian actors and compare that with parts for white actors. There are going to be more parts for white actors but there are also a lot more white actors. So, I'm actually in a very specialized field. So, I would actually have a greater chance of being cast in something than a white actor would. So, a lot of times it comes down to the luck of the draw.

In some cases it helps you, in some cases it doesn't. I mean obviously, if I go on a commercial call which is very specific, where they want an Asian for that part, or they want a white girl for that part, you know that's that. But, there are times when I have been seen for something and they weren't thinking Asian and they cast me. I get cast for a lot of things. I guess the easiest way to put it—because it would happen in any color, in any job, in any area, in any field—is you need to surround yourself with the right players to do what you need to do.

That's the control factor. I'm not saying that I would necessarily want to produce everything I do, I'm not saying I would want to direct everything I do, but I would say the additional thing of success would be being in the financial position to call all of those shots. Obviously that would not happen in theater for me, but that could happen in television.

I don't think one should ever limit oneself. Be it color, profession, I mean there is so much. I'm not just an actor. I mean, when my photography came to the forefront, it didn't mean that I was giving up my acting, it simply meant that I could really make a difference behind my camera at a time when as an actor I could not. And things changed and they evolve. So, now I'm really coming back into my acting life, and making very specific choices. But, my photography life is burgeoning. And as far as my modeling is concerned, I don't really do runway anymore, unless I feel like it. And it's not about the money aspect. It's just in fact, I am moving much more into my journalism life. I guess a lot of people want to be an anchor person like Connie Chung, but I actually want to have my own interview show on television.

Fay Ann Lee

She appears to be in her mid-twenties. Born and raised in Hong Kong she came to the United States with her family when she was 15. She first lived in Texas then attended the University of Pennsylvania where she earned an MBA. She went into banking in Los Angeles.

The first time she auditioned was as the understudy in the lead role for a production by the East-West Players, a theater company in L.A. When the lead actress left the play Fay took over. She moved to New York in 1992 and soon afterwards landed a position on the chorus of Miss Saigon. *So within two years of her venture into acting she had landed a job on Broadway.*

Getting Started

When I first tried out for roles I had no training. It was just based on what I thought would be good acting, you know? I never took a lesson before in my life. When I was in Los Angeles after I got that show I started taking voice lessons and still not acting lessons yet. But after six months of that I realized this is what I really want to do.

I found some very, very good teachers in New York and I auditioned and I got some summer stock stuff immediately. I quit my job as an account executive for an advertising firm. But before I got a chance to actually do the summer stock I got *Miss Saigon.*

So that's really what started me going and I was very lucky because I was never badly paid for my first job. I never had to struggle really.

In *Miss Saigon* I understudied as one of the leads and I was in the chorus. I actually did the first national tour in Chicago. I opened that company and I was there for seven months and came back to New York, and I did it on

Fay Ann Lee

Broadway for a few more months, and then I left the show to do other projects, but they would call me in all the time to fill in for people, which I did for a period of a year and a half after leaving it for good. So it was on and off for like two to three years.

ABOUT *MISS SAIGON*

I played all the roles. Like almost every single one because when I came back to New York to do it they would swing me in for people that were missing. So I learned everybody's tracks, basically.

I left it because I was really bored and unchallenged. I wasn't crazy about the atmosphere of being a chorus girl. It didn't sit well with me. I know that one has to start somewhere, but I just didn't like that feeling at all, and since then I've never done another chorus part.

In that show I don't think the ensemble people feel like their talent is truly being used. So if you stick with something like for a long time you feel your self-esteem going down a little bit because this isn't what you were trained to do. You can do a lot more, but you're not given that opportunity so I made the decision that I had to leave. I mean that if I want to be an actress, then I need to be acting in many different things. I mean that as long as it runs, I would have had a job, but that's not why I wanted to be an actress.

When I first saw the show, not knowing whether or not I was going to be in it, knowing that I was auditioning for it, I was like, I can't believe this show. I mean this is such a horrible stereotype of Asian women. That's how I felt and I thought if I don't get in this show I'm not going to feel that bad and yet I knew it was my opportunity, so how could I turn it down if I get it.

How did I reconcile this? Well, by the time I got the role and was on stage doing it I felt like, wow, this is a Broadway show. It's a big deal. I'll do it for a little while and then I'll quit which is exactly what I did. I mean it's like get the credit but you don't reconcile the fact that it is a stereotype. You just live with it; you just accept it; you do it; you move on.

We should feel like we're dancers out there moving with choreography, but there were times when there was so little respect from the male company members, that that's what made me really feel like a prostitute. They spoke to me like I was a prostitute on stage; they touched me like I was; the things they were saying. There was so little respect. They were able to get away with it because they said we're in this nightclub and, you know, that's our role. That's what you would have heard if you were a prostitute in Vietnam.

They will say things and because we're running around half naked most of the time it even heightens that atmosphere, and I'm thinking I'm so different from this character I'm playing that it really made me feel bad. The thing is if I were a prostitute in Vietnam I suppose I would be used to this and I could handle it in a certain way. But I'm not. And it's not written dialogue. They're just spewing out on stage as they please.

What you hear as the audience is written dialogue but you can't hear them talking to us on stage; they're mouthing off horrible, filthy things. And you know what, they think it's funny.

That's why I felt cheap. If it were truly just for show, I wouldn't feel that way. But they talk like that backstage too. I just didn't like that atmosphere and I realized that that's not the kind of show that I want to be a part of anyway.

I definitely draw lines about what I do. I mean especially since I'm lucky that my husband is supporting me, that I have a roof over my head and I have food to eat. I don't have to do things I don't want to do.

I think I was extremely lucky to get in the show, but I think that *Miss*

Saigon has given a lot of young Asian actors opportunities like that, where they don't care if as an actor you have experience or not. If they feel you're the right type, if you have potential, if you can sing and dance well enough, and act well enough, you're in. I'm sure a lot of people still can't get in, but the fact is it was an easy in for a lot of new Asian talent. So, I, in that respect, think I'm very lucky.

I will say that was a very important step in my career. Probably the most important step in terms of recognition. And that's the irony of it all because I had the least fun in the most recognized show that I've done. I don't think chorus people are treated that well in general. That's why I don't strive to be a chorus girl. I also don't think you need that much talent to be in *Miss Saigon.* I think the look is more important. Being in the show really didn't help my acting much. I grow so much more doing big roles in smaller theaters.

I think that I started off on the wrong foot with these people because I was too strong for them. They didn't like the fact that I was intelligent and had a brain and could speak my own opinion. I mean I felt like I was being, not that anybody sexually abused me or anything like that, but I felt that they were treating me not like an actress, but like you're lucky to have a job. That kind of attitude. They looked at us like this is a gift to you guys. Without us you won't be working, so you do whatever we tell you to do and you guys don't know anything anyway because you're green, you have no experience. Sometimes I felt like a prostitute and that's why I had to leave. I hated it and I left because of that.

Also I'm a highly competitive person and I don't like to be seen as second best. I mean I hate that about everything that I do. Like I need to be the best. So a lot of it came from the way I was feeling about myself.

I wanted to be the lead. It was partly about that and I knew that I was capable of it and that I was good enough, but they apparently didn't think so at that time, anyway. And they were looking for very specific types of girls, that were very Filipino looking. They were very specific.

I had never taken a singing lesson when I first auditioned. So I wasn't prepared to do it and they saw me that way. They didn't see my growth as an actress or a singer. They saw me as a chorus girl.

That show was my beginning so I don't need to look back. I can prove myself elsewhere.

ROLES AFTER *MISS SAIGON*

After *Miss Saigon* I started doing a lot of regional theater because that's the only other place I could get roles. Maybe I was still too green 'cause there was nothing on my résumé aside from *Miss Saigon* and that one show I did at East-West Players. So I really had to fill out my résumé and no Broadway shows were willing to see me.

I went to Singapore and did some theater there. I did some theater in Pennsylvania and Connecticut. I did some shows for Pan Asian Repertory off-off-Broadway which was great for me because I got to do things other people would never consider me for. Like a Noel Coward play.

I was up for *Rent,* a musical hit on Broadway, but I wasn't the right type. I can't remember the last time I was really up for a big role in television. Actually, I was up for one role for a television show, *New York News.* They were looking for a television reporter and I did very well. It came down to three people, I think. But ultimately they cast someone older. In fact, they didn't want to see me at the beginning because they thought I was too young for that particular role. One of the casting people saw me in a class that I was taking and said oh, you must see Fay for this role 'cause she'd be perfect. And they told my manager, look she is 10 years too young for the role, but we'll see her. And I actually did very well, but ultimately I didn't get it anyway. But that was really the last time I was truly up for something, and of course the show got canceled.

I've done a few things on television. I just haven't been in the market that long. People need to know you before they call you in for things. I did do something for Lifetime Television, which I think is running now and some of my friends saw me, a piece on voting. They encourage women to vote and they had hired some actors to come in and do different segments of the commercial. So, I think that is running now. And I did a sketch spoofing *Nixon* the movie, where I played Mao's interpreter on the *Dana Carvey Show* before it got canceled.

Right now I'm taking two acting classes with two different teachers. One is sort of a method class where we work on sense and memory. And the other class is just purely doing scenes. So, I feel the combination is very good for my acting. And I have to keep up with my voice because I still do musicals, and so I do that. I've been delinquent in my dancing but I should get back into that. I'm not primarily a dancer but I think it's just necessary to be able to dance even though you're not a dancer. It's constant training, like being an athlete and working the muscles.

I've decided that now that I've been in the city for three years and I've done some work—I do have a résumé now—that I should look for an agent. So that's what I'm doing this summer, find a good agent. I don't really think an actress of my caliber at this point needs both a manager and agent. I think it's one or the other. And right now I think an agent would be wiser because they could submit me for everything.

BEING AN ASIAN AMERICAN WOMAN IN ACTING

Because I'm new to the business I don't know what it was really like five or ten years ago even. So what I only know is that it is still very hard. I don't care how much it's improved, it hasn't improved enough. Even regionally. I mean given the credits that I do have now and the things I am capable of doing, this year I've probably been to just like five legit auditions for roles. And that's way too little. How I am supposed to book jobs if I get seen five times in six months? It's ridiculous. It may have improved, but certainly not to the degree that we need to hone our skills. The only way the skills are honed is to get employment.

In regional theater I have done roles that anyone can do. Some of them of course were Asian specific and that's why I got those roles. But I have done roles where they have not been Asian specific. I did a show called *My Name Is Still Alice*, which is a review of women: five actresses ranging in different age groups. I was chosen as one of the five women, and it had nothing to do with being Asian at all. There was no mention in there about being Asian. I think they decided they wanted to go interracial. They hired a black girl, but I think it was written for a black person. So things are happening, but just not enough.

For myself I would say the roles have been 50/50, Asian specific versus general, which is good. But, there again, it's not like I'm constantly working.

ON SUCCESS AS AN ASIAN AMERICAN ACTOR

I enjoy the experience of it. I'm very passionate about wanting to be a good actress; I love learning and the opportunity of doing, playing different people and different roles, assuming personalities that ultimately are not who I am. And that to me is incredibly fun.

I really haven't thought about how long it might take to make it. I think it's really hard to make those decisions because you never know when your time is, you'll never know how you'll feel. I could be totally sick of this in two years as opposed to five. Who knows? But at this point in my life I feel like this is what I want to do. And I want to be very, very successful at this. I don't know if it's going to happen, but I believe I have the skills to make it happen and I need the opportunity. I feel my career track is growing, so I am excited about that. It's still a struggle, in terms of what roles I get seen for. But if things are going to open up then I think I'll be okay, actually. I think within five years I'll know, I think, whether or not I want to stick with it for a few more years or that I just contribute myself in different ways in the industry.

I think that there are opportunities for Asians. It is possible to win a Tony Award as an Asian person. It is possible to get in a big film and maybe even win an Academy Award. I think that those opportunities are possible, but I think that even after you win those awards, they don't guarantee anything because right now the audience is not craving to see Asians on the screen and that's what ultimately makes you popular and makes you a star.

What I would ultimately like to be able to do is have people offer me roles without necessarily auditioning me. I mean I believe in the process of having to go through auditions. I think that's an important process. But in my opinion when you are a star it's a different thing. Auditioning is a different process. It's maybe more of an interview, they want to see who you are, they want to ultimately offer you the role, or even invite you for a special audition. If I can get to a point where I'm on the short list for everything, especially if they're looking for Asians, or even on a short list if they're not looking for Asians in specific roles then I would be very happy with my career I think. I would love to say that, oh I'd love to be as famous as Julia Roberts or Meryl Streep, but I don't think that's going to happen.

I feel like I have the potential to be very good because I work very hard and my acting teachers are very encouraging to me, and they're not that encouraging to everybody. I mean, and I'm not one to be constantly looking for compliments at all. In fact I like it when my acting teachers are hard on me because my goal is to be better. I don't think I'm going to rely on my looks or the fact that I'm Asian, or maybe even the fact that an Asian woman is exotic. And if doing character roles will make me a better actress or will give me more opportunities in the future when I get older or whatever, I'd be much happier to be in that position.

As for succeeding? You have to be lucky to get there. But it's true for a white actress too, I would say because there are millions of them out there. So for anyone who wants to be a "Michelle Pfeiffer" that's a pretty tough goal. And sometimes I think, well maybe as an Asian I'm in a way luckier because my competition is less. There are fewer of us and maybe it's a little bit easier to shine. But then there are so few projects. There are just so few. And being in New York too for television and film, it's tough.

Ultimately you need to find producers who are willing to produce work for Asian actors. I think a lot of time the producers wonder will this bring in my audience? So if it's not commercial enough, maybe we don't do it. And I do believe that we have to write commercial products in order for us to be known in the industry. I'd see stuff that's a lot of fun and extremely challenging but it is not going to be enough.

Commercial products to me means something that middle Americans would watch and not get offended by it. Not necessarily innovative.

I think there's a market for black stars to rise because there's a larger black audience and they like to see movies. They like to be entertained and watch television. I don't think Asians are very good audiences, they don't go see movies very much. And therefore why should producers spend money on Asian actors when their own people won't even go to the movies or won't care about watching television that much? I mean if we had the same support as the black actors did, or even the Hispanic actors did, it's a different story. If there were larger numbers of Asians going to films, we'd have more support.

When you see a black or Hispanic actor on the screen, do you immediately think a black actor, or Hispanic actor? Definitely less so than for Asians, because they're seen much more often and as an audience member you accept that. But whenever you see an Asian person, it's such an anomaly that you say, "Oh, it's an Asian person." But if it wasn't an anomaly you wouldn't say that.

Now the reason why you would see more Asian people in commercials is because I think companies know that Asians have money and if you sprinkle them in commercials it's a ploy to get them to buy the product they're selling. It's all about money-making. But if white producers know that Asians don't really go to movies that much anyway, they might think, why do we need to sprinkle that many Asians on the screen for, because it's all about who's gonna go out there and buy the tickets.

The way I look at it theater is really a great training ground for actors and I believe every actor should do it. But that's not what's going to break ground for Asians either. I think that we need to be seen more on television and in films so that the audience gets used to seeing Asian faces. It's just a matter of getting used to seeing that Asian women can act. They don't have to just be exotic and sexy. They can actually play roles that Michelle Pfeiffer can play. Like they need to look at us and say, "She's an actress," rather than "Oh, but she's Asian." I think the black community has been able to break that ground a little, even the Hispanics. It's been tougher for us because we don't have that kind of backing that other minorities do because I think there are a lot of minority producers who are African American. I don't know about Hispanics that much but Hispanics are being accepted more as well.

I can only hope that I will have the opportunity to break the barrier because I know that I could, if I were given an opportunity to audition for say, an intern or a doctor in the television show *ER*, or a lawyer on some law show I really, truly, believe that I could be just as good as any white person they see. Okay, I can play the part, I look the part, I speak the part, you know. But have I ever been given that opportunity? No. But I'm just hoping that in the next several years that I will be seen for one of those roles and therefore I can break that barrier and then if I can break that barrier for a TV show, then maybe, all of sudden I can break that barrier for film as well. I mean, you can just have to hope that you can do that.

I want to do it all. I want to do TV, I want to do film, I want to do theater. I don't think I would abandon the stage. But the money is not in theater. So to be practical it would be great to get a TV show because then you can really start making some real money. I think if you're good at what you do, you deserve to make real money.

If I want to play a professional woman, I would say the opportunities may be more for me in the next five to ten years as opposed to now because I look younger on screen. I'm still not that believable according to the producers. They still want to see somebody with a few more years on them. So I think that maybe my opportunities will come later. I don't know.

As for playing a hooker, it depends on the project. If it's a truthful character and if it's not written merely, it's not put in there just because the character is Asian, then I think it's okay because some of those roles are great roles. Like the *Taxi Driver* that Jodi Foster was a young prostitute in? If it's a well written role and has meat and you can really sink yourself into it, then I think it's fine. But I have turned down auditions even when I first started in this business, when I was in Los Angeles. An agent saw me and wanted to sign me up immediately in L.A., a very reputable agency. They wanted to see some exotic Asian actress for a Madonna movie, but the Asian actress would have to be naked at some point. I turned it down. I said I can't do that. I didn't know anything about the business, but I knew that I didn't want to do that because it seemed like they just wanted an Asian babe who would look good naked.

On soap operas I've seen Asian women play roles like maids or secretaries. It's definitely getting better because they tried to put Asian storylines in there, and they tried to do that with *The Young and the Restless*. There is a Eurasian girl in *Bold and the Beautiful*, and there was a Eurasian girl in *One Life to Live* at some point, a few years back. But when I see Asian women play little bitty roles, as nurses in shows like *ER* or you know, or the prostitute kind of things I just think, oh typical. Does it offend me? A little bit, and I keep thinking, when are they actually going to put the doctor in there when there are so many Asian doctors in this country. A lot of my family members are doctors and I'm thinking, you know, why is it that they're not in there.

As an Asian it hasn't been that easy for me to get my foot in the door. I mean *Miss Saigon* was easy, yes. It was luck. I had just decided to be in the business when there was a huge demand for Asian actors for that show. Other than that it's been very silent. I would say it's hard for anyone to get in the door. I truly believe that, I don't think it's easier for anybody.

To be realistic I don't think that I will be the next Sharon Stone or Julia Roberts. I don't think that's going to happen. I'll tell you who can be that. I think Eurasian women can be that because they look more white. I don't think a pure Asian person is really, really going to be that.

Like Tia Carrera who's apparently Filipino, but she has very European features and she's very exotic and she's beautiful in the way white people think she's beautiful. And she's tall, she was a model. Those are the people that can, but she's not going to be the next great actress either. I mean she's only being put into the James Bond female role types which isn't what I'm striving to do at all.

I think television is the next step for Asians, if not film. I mean you need to hit the mass media which is television, really. Maybe a show written for an Asian woman, you know, like a comedy. Something that's not that intellectual, and it's not an all–Asian show. An Asian role that people can maybe laugh at also, but to be somewhat American as opposed to typical Asian.

I would love the opportunity to do a good Chinese film; an independent film that could go to a festival, like the Sundance Festival. I just started thinking about this seriously this week, in fact, because I'm thinking, okay, how do I find my opportunities? You know, it's not really in the States at this time. I mean, maybe little roles and if I get lucky, yes, maybe then a big role somewhere. But it's not really happening for anybody, even for the big name Asian actors. So why do I think it would happen for me? I think that you need a different strategy so I'd love to do that, and independent films are really big now.

Actually the female version of Jackie Chan would have a better chance of really making it big because those are the types of films that everybody goes to see. That's where the true mass market is and that could be a worldwide market. Who cares about what the language is or who's saying what anyway. It's all action.

It doesn't matter whether one makes it as a kung fu star as opposed to a theatrical actress, because once you make it you have your choice of what to do. The most important thing is getting your name out there and to be recognized because after that you can do anything. I mean almost anything, especially if you're talented.

Do I think middle America is ready to have an Asian star cast as a hero figure such as an Arnold Schwarzenegger in *Terminator*? No, I don't. That's the problem. I think that this country is still rather racist. And the only reason there are black stars is because of the huge black population that is supportive of that. And if you look at the really big black stars they are very handsome in a white kind of way. Like Denzel Washington. He's lean, he's got a good physique, he looks very African American but somehow he's lighter, not that dark. Those are the realities. You just have to live with it.

MORE SUPPORT WANTED

I was thinking last night when I was watching some of the Olympics that what Asian American theater needs is a training center. You know how there's this great gymnastic training center in Houston and these kids go there and they train and train and train for the Olympics. That's what Pan Asian Repertory should be for us. They should be training us, making us do the classics, bring in the best directors to help us along. The thing is if you have a very well respected Asian theater company, I think at least New York audiences will come and support the theater if it produces top quality work every single time. Part of the problem now is that we're not getting the big training that we're supposed to be getting. I can take as many acting classes as I want but if I'm not in a good production it's not worth that much. You need to be out there performing in front of an audience and doing good work. And to be seen.

I think that when your quality of work is consistently high, then producers would be more willing to take a chance. I mean, it's all about perception, right? How can you be a star unless you're seen? It's impossible. But I do believe in the notion that if you have a goal and if you strive really hard to get there you can, somehow. But you've got to figure out a way to do it. We're not going to get those calls by sitting back and waiting.

ON CASTING

I recently auditioned for a Broadway show that's coming up and the reason I got into this audition was because I knew the writer. Okay, it's not an Asian show at all and he had never even seen my work but he was told by some other people that they thought I was really good, I can sing, I can act, you know, that he really should give me the opportunity to audition. He's a famous writer in New York. He made sure I had the opportunity and I went in. They saw several hundred people that week.

But it was an invited call requested by the writers and the director, and the director's from England and it's a very white show. I don't know of any of my Asian friends that got invited. I got invited because in this case I had a connection, you know, and he called me the next day and said, Fay you did extremely well, you're on the callback list. I don't know if I got one of the key parts. But I guarantee you I'm on the callback list for a chorus spot.

I'm saying that even with a very strong connection in this case—and I know that I nailed the audition, so I know that I deserved the callback, and the callback was not a favor because even though he does have a lot of say in this project, he does have two other people to deal with—I'm saying that even with the connection, I'm only seen for a chorus position, because I'm Asian.

But can I blame them? No, because it's not an Asian project and it would be a little odd to cast me in one of the roles. It would be very nontraditional casting. So what do you do? If I'm writing an Asian show, would I cast a white person in it just to be nontraditional? How do you answer that? I mean that's what we're asking people to do but for specific shows.

So what keeps me going? The love of acting. The passion.

2
Veteran Actors

Jadin Wong

She is in her 80s and has been in entertainment since high school. She went out to Hollywood in the 1930s and appeared in a few Charlie Chan films, she said. But it was difficult getting work so she returned to San Francisco to study ballet and dance. Her first national exposure was in Life *magazine, where she was featured in a full page photo as a dancer for the Forbidden City, a nightclub in San Francisco, December 20, 1940. Four years later she came to New York City and danced at the China Doll nightclub until it closed in the 1950s. She went to Europe for five years where she found work as a dancer and entertainer (part of that was entertaining the American Armed Forces) then returned to the United States. She went to Las Vegas where she danced and did standup comedy. When she could no longer find work as a dancer she worked as a comedian for about 15 years in the Poconos. She started her talent agency 22 years ago. Today she says she's worked with over 600 Asian American actors mostly of Chinese and Japanese descent.*

She is about 5' 4", spry, and in what appears to be good health. She is slim, has short white hair and says she still does her exercises on her bar in front of the mirror every day. She said she's had training in ballet and tap. She still acts and will be doing the role of a shrill old lady in an upcoming film.

She was wearing a red mesh pullover top and beige slacks the first time we met. Our interview took place in her apartment which also serves as her office. Her one-bedroom apartment is crammed with furniture. At one end there is a desk at which her assistant Barney sits answering calls. Throughout our interview the phone rings or he's calling up actors for "go sees." Barney is 25, according to Jadin, very smart and wants to be an actor. She is apparently also his manager and coaches him before he goes to an audition. On the side of the desk is a cabinet stuffed with a row of clipboards. Barney says those are various calls for certain projects: films, commercials, theater.

On the wall in the hall between the bathroom and bedroom are photos of Jadin in her 20s: seated with Humphrey Bogart and Lauren Bacall; dressed in a Chinese dress, her waist length hair swept up in a tight pony tail adorned with flowers. There is also a shot of herself and her husband seated next to the Shuberts. She explained that her husband Ed Dowling used to be a producer for the Shuberts. Next to that are autographed photos of Frank Sinatra and Bob Hope. She said she's worked with both of them.

HER EARLY YEARS

I started singing in Stockton when I was about 8 or 9 years old. I went to a music store one day with my mother to buy music. So I look around and see some lights flashing on and off. I go and look. The fellow asks can you sing little girl. And I said well I guess so. So I sang a song. They were broadcasting a live radio show on the air and he gave me $50. My mother couldn't believe it when I told her. She loved music and sang to me all the time. She was born in San Francisco. I'm second generation.

I kept on dancing even through high school. During that time we didn't have too much money. I skipped lunch so I could take singing and dancing lessons. That's the story of my life, I was always skipping food so I could have lessons.

When I graduated I went to Hollywood with a girlfriend, we didn't know anything. Everybody goes to Hollywood. That's where all the motion pictures are. It was the mid 1930s. We almost starved to death because we were both very young and had no idea. When you're young you have no fear, you don't know. We were so poor, I didn't have regular shoes to wear. I was wearing tap shoes. Walking down Hollywood Boulevard, clop, clop, clop. A man stopped us and said, "Hello girls, I can use you in a movie."

I said well, I would like to work, so he said come over to this address at 7 o'clock. I'm not that stupid, I brought my girlfriend—who knew if he was on the level? I figured there would be the two of us. When we got there and knocked Claudette Colbert came to the door. They knew we were hungry and offered us food. We ate everything. Potato chips, everything. I got to work on Charlie Chan pictures as one of the daughters. We just said a few dumb words, like "Hi, pop."

Did I find it hard to break in as an Asian woman in Hollywood in the 1930s? I just got homesick, I went home. And I was a little smarter, I know you can get very hungry if you don't have food, you have to pay rent. From Hollywood I went back to Stockton, because there wasn't any other work and I got tired of being hungry. I even studied with the San Francisco Opera Ballet for a while and then got a scholarship in San Francisco with a dance trainer. I studied from 9 to 6 everyday. Being an Asian woman in show business I really had to be as good if not better than a Caucasian. If I was in a ballet I would be the only Asian. If I didn't do well I would stand out more so than if I were like everybody else.

THE FORBIDDEN CITY AND BEYOND

When the Forbidden City nightclub opened in San Francisco it was the first of its kind. The club was exquisitely beautiful, all Chinese paintings and screens. When you think nightclub—you think of something cheap. But this place was like a museum. It was gorgeous. They watched me do the dance I'm known for called the Moon Goddess. I gave it that name, I don't know why. I was the first act in that show. The money was good. Instead of milk and tuna fish sandwiches I was having fillet mignon and champagne. I kind of liked it. I stayed. It paid our rent and I could eat properly. Then *Life* magazine came to the Forbidden City to take pictures and changed my whole life. It was right after Pearl Harbor.

After the article appeared I had all kinds of offers from all over the world. I was too young and too stupid to know the value of it. When that came out I got two or three sacks of mail every week from all over the world.

But strangely enough those of us who performed at the Forbidden City were not accepted by the Chinese. We were looked down upon. They thought we were not much better than whores, because it's unheard of, Chinese dancing girls, people singing in a Chinese nightclub. They had never seen one; they just believed it was immoral. I used to say to them we're not whores because if we were we would make a lot of money; we wouldn't be working eight or nine hours a day and getting $25. It took two years for the Chinese to accept us. The Caucasians accepted us immediately but the Chinese people were very practical and the arts—which I could understand as I grew up—were seen as a very precarious way of life.

After about four years at the Forbidden City I came to New York and performed at a club called the China Doll, sort of a duplicate of the Forbidden City. I stayed there until 1951. I remember that very well because the door was padlocked one day when I went to work as the owner didn't pay the taxes.

In those days 1946–51, seeing an Asian woman on stage was quite startling. People like Walter Winchell took me out because he had never seen an Asian woman entertainer and I was taught to wear my hair up with bangs and I had the long-sleeved Chinese dresses so I was the belle of the ball.

And from there by accident I ended up in Paris. My roommate asked me to take some pictures up to the William Morris Agency and as I was walking off someone said, "Can you come back here a minute." They offered me a chance to do some work on the Riviera. The China Doll just closed and so I went to Paris.

I stayed in Europe for five years. I spent part of that time entertaining the Armed Forces and doing Air Force shows for GIs.

After I returned from Europe the nightclubs were gone. Television had replaced them. I was able to make like $1,500 a week doing acts in Las Vegas but that did not last forever. I was in my 30s by now. After awhile there was no place for me to dance.

Show business was the only thing I knew how to do. I always had a sense of humor. So I became a comedian. But nobody would hire me. They would say, Jadin you are a beautiful dancer but you can't do comedy. Chinese women don't do comedy. I'd say don't tell me that. I know what I have to put up with as a comedian.

Everything I tried to do professionally everybody said I couldn't do because I was an Asian woman. Comedy was the worst. No one wanted to use me. An agent said, Jadin, in the last show at twelve o'clock you're going to be dealing with drunks, and they're going to insult you, your race, the way you're built and everything else. What are you going to do, run off and cry? I said no. If a Caucasian woman can do it I can do it too. Some drunk will really scream at you, he said. I said, so I'll scream back.

Finally I told him I've been coming here and asking for work for eight months, give me a booking. He's says okay, Chinese New Year I'll give you a shot. But I said do you give a shot to a Jewish comic on a Jewish New Year? An Italian comic on an Italian New Year? I said if I have to wait for Chinese New Year for you to give me a shot, what do I do for the rest of the year?

He said if you're so funny, say something funny then. I said fuck you and I turned around and walked out. Then he said come back here, I'll give you a booking. He aggravated me to a point just to see what I would do.

I learned to handle hecklers no matter what they said to me and I can insult people in a ladylike way. I played the Poconos on and off for 15–20 years. I made a lot of money. I was very good. I wrote my own humor.

Did I want to go into films at this point in my life? Whatever happens to me in my life, happens. You cannot make things happen. You cannot.

A MANAGER OF ASIAN TALENT

When I started this business of managing actors, they said the business would eat me alive, that I wouldn't last two months. She's a woman, subservient, nonvocal, they'd say. What I'm in is a very tough business. These same people are now kissing my tush to get my work.

I am an actor's representative. I've sent out about 600 actors for jobs. I work with Asians, South Pacific Islanders, American Indians. Anything except round-eyed Caucasians. I have nothing against them, I just want to specialize. I deal with Asians because no one else really cares.

We send actors out on casting calls on a color blind basis [meaning race is not an issue] unless color is part of the storyline. I mean if it's a black family, I can't put him [pointing to her assistant who is also an actor she manages] in there. But if it is a chauffeur, a doctor or a lawyer then I send Asian actors.

As a manager of Asian talent I work with people on a nonexclusive freelance basis. But I do have three or four actors who are signed to me.

This how it works: someone calls me and says I want to see an actor for the new musical *Rent*. I send them a bunch of pictures and they in turn tell me whether they'd like to see so and so. There are far more opportunities now. It's much better than when I started.

Today I teach my actors to fight. They will complain to me, "When we went to a job last night, we started at 5 o'clock and they didn't give us any food until 12 o'clock. We didn't get any water and it was cold and we didn't have good bathroom facilities." Well, they're supposed to be fed every six hours.

On the phone I'd tell the employer off. Because I'm a woman they would say she's a tough cookie, don't fool around with her. I said I resent that. And I tell them to pay my actors according to all the rules in the union. I said if you don't I'll bring charges up against you. You don't do that to my people. Just because Chinese are nonvocal. I said if we were another minority group we would have bombed your office by now, so just be content. I'm asking you to pay them for what they deserve. But afterwards they respect me because I'm not making unreasonable demands.

Could there be an Asian American superstar with the status of Tom Cruise? I believe so, if he looked good and could act. But there aren't that many around with those combined qualities. It comes right down to talent.

There are far more roles for Asians today than in the past. Much more. Fifteen years ago you wouldn't have a Chinese judge or an Asian judge. We do today, in film and TV. Asian jurors, Asian doctors. Thank heavens for Judge Ito. We have a lot of calls for Asian judges. It just takes someone to start it, you know.

There are still a lot of calls for stereotypical Asian characters like a waiter, but not so many gangsters anymore—maybe businessmen. Or it might be they play a geek who is usually very bright in computers, but otherwise is a helpless Asian who wears glasses.

Recently I had a fellow who played a Korean taxi driver. The character goes crazy driving a cab because everybody's telling him where to go and how to drive it. He jumps on the hood of his car, and is going to blow his brains out. So the roles are not as limited. It's just like with Italian people. They say why are we always made the gangsters. But there are also a lot of roles for Italians that are not gangsters.

As for Asian American women actors they've played doctors, lawyers, they even do Shakespeare in the park. I have a fat, a heavy set Japanese lady who's done Shakespeare in the park and another Japanese girl has done Joan of Arc.

When I first started in this business there weren't this many calls for Asians. Generally we're busy all day long until the evening. In a given day I might get anywhere from 50 to 80 calls, for theater, films, television commercials, everything. Things have gotten much better.

ASIAN AMERICANS AND ACTING

Today it doesn't matter if you're black, green, or yellow. If they want someone for the job and you can fill it, you do it.

In acting all Asians think there should be more Asian parts. But I say you're living in America. It's American consumption. It's the same thing as Caucasians in China. Why don't they have more parts for Caucasians? Because it is China.

In casting an actor for a particular film it's also the name value. If they make a ten million dollar movie they want a Caucasian who's a name to draw the people in the theater. They make movies to make money, not to give someone a part.

And the reason why they don't use an Asian man or woman is because they can't draw the people in. You mention John Lone [star in *The Last Emperor*]. You know his name, I know his name, every Asian probably does too. But when I talk to non–Asians and I say John Lone, they ask who's he? A name means when you put that name on the marquee people from all over will go see him. They don't make movies to give actors a job, they make movies to make money. People want to see stars.

You ask, if one don't get cast in those key roles how can one get a name for oneself? Actors don't get leading roles in the beginning. It doesn't work that way. You have to earn it. You just don't get cast in a major role out of the clear blue sky.

Also as a writer for film and theater you have to write what people would pay to see. But there's no explanation for what's going to be successful and what's not. It's a very unpredictable business. If it weren't everything would be a hit.

The most important thing is who is going to come and see this production whether it be a film or a movie. If it's about blacks there are far more blacks and they buy tickets to many things. You don't ever see an Asian in line to buy anything. Or they don't even go see the shows on Broadway. I go a lot. I always look around and see that I'm the only Asian. That's why the Asians don't get the great parts, because many Asians don't support the arts.

Also our lifestyles and cultures are different. It is difficult for Asians to be singers or dancers, because in an American home they sing "Happy Birthday," "Easter Parade," "Merry Christmas." The blacks have gospel; the Filipinos, the Spanish part of them, they play guitar and sing. But in most Chinese homes you don't even see a piano. We don't sing anything at home.

I will soon be in a film where I am cast as a Chinese woman who owns a restaurant or art shop. I play a very feisty character because they wanted a female who's funny. I get to swear at them in Chinese. I would rather play a funny old lady than a subservient one. Because some Chinese old ladies are very funny. Of course it's not a starring role; they can't have a little old Chinese lady doing a starring role.

One thing I learned with the Shuberts, if your show has a message, don't use our theaters, use Western Union. We don't want shows with messages; we go to theaters to enjoy, relax and laugh. My husband was a producer for them. That's why I understand the nature of show business.

The Pan Asian Repertory Theater

According to its promotional literature Pan Asian Repertory Theater is considered to be the largest Asian American theater in the nation. It specializes in intercultural productions and new Asian American plays. Its home is a one flight walk up creaky wooden stairs inside a rather shabby looking building at 47 Jones Street in New York City. The building is owned by La Mama, and Pan Asian Rep has been housed here for the past 20 years. The office is an open space with high ceilings crammed with the hallmarks of a hectic office. Two college-age assistants are working at phones and computers on desks facing each other along opposite sides of the wall. There are piles of costumes against a corner, a fan going in another and to the side is a table surface propped up by six large garbage cans. Stacks of flyers and brochures cover the tabletop and news releases paper the room. The light is naked white neon suspended from the ceiling. At the center are two overstuffed couches where I waited for Tisa Chang, artistic director, as she talked on the phone. Her desk is at the far side. There are no walls here for privacy. Conversations and all activity are conducted in completely open space.

She is dressed in tan shorts, heeled sandals, a blue top. Her hair is cut short, and her physique is that of someone who works out.

Tisa Chang

> *Tisa Chang is the artistic/producing director of Pan Asian Repertory Theater, which she founded in 1977. Tisa came to the United States with her family in the 1950s. She grew up in New York City and led an active career as an actress and dancer on Broadway in the 1970s. She appeared in the Broadway musical* Lovely Ladies Kind Gentlemen *and in* The Basic Training of Pavlo Hummel *at the Longacre Theater opposite Al Pacino. Her TV and film appearances include* The Year of the Dragon, Ambush Bay, *and* Escape from Iran.

IN THE BEGINNING

Even as a child I was interested in acting. I directed and starred in a production of Cinderella in my kitchen when I was 7 or 8. I'd always been mesmerized by the magic of theater and the arts. It's a window into

Tisa Chang

another world where we can project our deepest yearnings. So using the arts to make a difference is what I chose. That included all kinds of training in piano, ballet, Chinese dance. I was a very quiet child, very skilled. I never spoke in public school until the 5th grade. I was really, really shy. One was because English is not my native language. Two, at that time being extraordinarily shy, perhaps we find recourse or meaning in other worlds. I went to the High School of Performing Arts which meant I was a music major. I didn't date, I had lots of dreams. I'm a sort of perfectionist. I have very high ideals and very high standards. I started dancing professionally in summer stock while I was in high school.

After one year of college at Barnard, I was cast in a film, *Ambush Bay*, opposite Hugh O'Brian, so I really never graduated, although I received a Medal of Distinction for Excellence from Barnard in 1991. So I went into show business. In those days because of my youth and because I was really a very shy and withdrawn person, I was ill-equipped, and not prepared to meet some of the challenges, intense pressures, and the socialization that came with theater and film. Therefore I feel that I did not maximize my opportunities. I found Hollywood overwhelming.

I was out in Hollywood for auditions, to meet producers, and promotions. *Ambush Bay* was filmed abroad, in the Philippines. We made personal appearances in connection with the film and even went to some military bases. To be 19 and have all of this was very intimidating at that time.

I did all of those expected public relations kind of things and pro-

moting. But I didn't move to Hollywood. My mother was very supportive, but my father thought it was just a lark, a little experiment. I don't
regret anything except that I think I could really have become a serious
film actress if I stayed in Hollywood. I think I have the charisma, I think
I have the commitment. But my personality is very strong, my character
is very strong. I am too strong perhaps to be overly accommodating with
Hollywood producers, and agents. I found it so repugnant when one agent
said to me, "What kind of men do you like?" You know, there were some
expectations. I found that a little frightening. I don't think in those days
we were quite so sexually active. I thought that Hollywood values were
very superficial. Also the horror stories about the casting couch—part of
that was true. I've had guys chase me around a table, literally.

Nowadays, everything is PC. With the sexual revolution now, women
are simply more aware earlier and people are very sophisticated and can
handle themselves. Today a 19 year old would think nothing of being able
to handle herself. I've become strong because of confidence and awareness.
In those days I didn't know, so I had to learn the hard way. My producers also told me I had to get my nose fixed, my teeth fixed. For films you
have to be so perfect. Also, the camera favors a certain type.

I came back to New York. I also got into the Broadway shows, *Lovely
Ladies, Kind Gentlemen (1972)*; *The King and I*; *Jones Beach*. So, I would be
constantly dancing, acting, working.

Auditioning was a wearying process because of the disappointments,
the abuse and rudeness that actors would experience in constantly going
to auditions and interviews, and modeling interviews. In those days we
were very often either hired or rejected based on our "type." It was not
talent.

There weren't many opportunities to do major roles on Broadway,
unless it was an Asian theme show, like the musical *Teahouse of the August
Moon*. They wouldn't really consider you, and you couldn't really audition.
It just wasn't even in their consciousness. I remember when Medea was
being staged at Circle in the Square. I waited in line five hours to audition with my photo and résumé, but I was not asked to audition—just to
hand in my photo and résumé. In those days—the early '70s—the consciousness was not there to even give minorities a chance to audition.

Although we never got opportunities to do Shakespeare or the Greek
tragedies I studied with the great actress-teacher Uta Hagen. Seldom
would we even audition for Shakespeare. They would more or less, as the
case is now, look for a type. They needed an Oriental type. I played a lot
of Vietnamese prostitutes and ghosts of Asian women who were killed in
Vietnam. Now, roles are somewhat better, but not by much. Also, because

I think I was very attractive and a good dancer back then (I had extremely long legs—God gave me a great body and I try to maintain it, so I'm very fortunate in that sense), that's why I probably got quite a few opportunities. I did summer productions of *Sweet Charity* and *Flower Drum Song*. I was in the National Company Tour of *Pacific Overtures*. I was on Broadway with Al Pacino in *The Basic Training of Pavlo Hummel*, which is by David Rabe. It was with the earnings from six months on Broadway with *Pavlo Hummel* that I subsidized Pan Asian's first season. We were also at La Mama, so I benefited from Ellen Stewart's patronage. I was married at La Mama Theater.

I have to say that while I've been very lucky and quite productive, there were those weeks and months when I was very lonely. Didn't know where money was coming in from, collecting unemployment. Fortunately, I always had a home, but I think that's what young people do. Go for broke. I was in my early 20s and so I also worked doing other things. I was at the UN part-time as a guide. I mean, you do everything. You learn to be resourceful. I always said that an aspiring actor, a serious one, an aspiring actor is as resourceful as the guys in the military or the secret service. You can't sort of sit there and say, "I don't know what to do." You always say, "Hey, what can I do about it?" I have never sat back.

Of course, my mother's death was very, very, very traumatic. My grieving for her took such an emotional, psychological toll that it also shaped and formulated some of my resolve to create from that. We create beauty from tragedy. So after two weeks of intense, lonely mourning, I was able to turn it into a play. And I adapted the Peking opera *Return of the Phoenix* using five actors only. We opened at La Mama, on July 4th weekend in 1973. We got a wonderful notice in *The New York Times*. CBS saw it. We also talk about luck. I very much believe in mystical powers. I believe that my connection with my mother spiritually is so strong. Yes, her spirit has always helped to guide me because that little original piece, my first directing effort as a creator, was bought by CBS to be the very first premier of their Festival for Lively Arts for young people, so it was a very nice bonus. I didn't get paid a great deal in those days, but I guess $6,000 was pretty good for a beginner at that time. I gave a third of it to La Mama. I wasn't obligated to, but I did. That is called honor, that I called repaying, because she backed me. And it is that kind of, I think, respect and way of operating that has always stood me in stead.

Perhaps my ultra-focus in my work has denied me certain other interests—what one would say are the practical applications of life. I don't own a home, I don't own property. Middle class values are not important to me. I just want another path. With my son, of course, and his educational needs, I have learned to be much more practical. Running a company, definitely you learn about being practical. I actually have a very good business acumen, otherwise I think Pan Asian wouldn't be so robust; and thrift I learned from my mother. With Pan Asian, it is very important that we are responsible—fiscally stabilized so that I can proceed and plan. I have to say that I learned an awful lot about being an adult, a responsible adult, from managing the company.

ON RUNNING PAN ASIAN REPERTORY

I didn't know anything about marketing when I started Pan Asian. I didn't believe in that. My father really impressed upon us the Confucian virtues of self-reliance. You do it on your own. Never go through the back door, because you always end up somehow paying for it in another way that you don't want, or you'll end up owing somebody. Always do it so that way you don't owe anybody. So to this day, some people will find me a little bit brusque, a little bit cold or a little remote simply because it's a danger to be in a producing-directing position and to get too close to your actors in case anyone says, "Oh, it's partisanship, or nepotism, or favoritism, or backdoor-ism" or whatever it is. I try to be a very objective, impartial leader because I think respect is another virtue my parents instilled. My mother meant that in a sexual, personal sense. My father meant it in a professional, moral, ethical sense. Because Chinese philosophy is so ingrained in everyday life, it becomes part of the culture. I used a lot of the old stories from Chinese novels and poetry in my early plays.

People think it was easier back then. It wasn't. It meant being on unemployment half the time, working at night when other people were finished with their jobs. It meant being a pretty organized boss. I did everything. As a director-producer I was financially responsible. I put my own Broadway earnings into Pan Asian's early productions.

I'd been performing for quite a few years before I started directing. That first directing job, *Return of the Phoenix*, was a turning point in my life. I love directing, not because I'm bossy and have natural leadership tendencies. It allowed me to do something directly that would have impact on the field. You see, as an actor, it's sort of a passive profession. You're waiting for someone else to hire you. As a director and producer, you are the mover and you take control of the reins. You plow that path, you're in the driver's seat. That is so important and Ellen Stewart's La Mama allowed me to do that. I love being in the driver's seat. I love the interest of marketing, ticket sales, PR. It's that sense of over-curiosity about everything. When I adapt and write, create my own works as a director, that is the creative part of it. I also consider producing and being a leader very creative. You have to constantly talk other people into sharing your dream and doing what you want them to do.

I think I'm successful and have achieved what I have because I'm fortunate to have a receptive environment. I do not think I would have had that receptive environment in Hollywood. I didn't like their values, I didn't like their operating tactics. You ask the actors who go out there. It's a totally different environment and they become very changed people. When they deal with you, it's always testing you, it's never a straight answer to your proposal. If you want to do something, they see what they can get out of it. It's turf, it's constant jockeying. This is something that saddens me, and disheartens me about a lot of the younger actors, even in New York. They have learned a whole vocabulary of superficial values and tactics; so much so that I don't know who I'm dealing with sometimes. I'm learning all the time but it's very, very debilitating and very disheartening. I like to think of a young inquiring mind with aspirations, with artistic meanings. Someone who's genuine and honest. I hate people bowing out of our theater productions. We do not pay like Broadway or TV productions. Yet, all of the actors make a commitment to me for two months or more and they stick to it. I've had one or two instances where they've bowed out but they don't come back and work here. The point is, you're an adult, you're a professional. You know your schedule. Can you make a commitment? A creative, artistic commitment in life. As a professional, discipline is high at Pan Asian, commitment is high. Of course there are extenuating circumstances. There are certain values that I think most actors see come straight from the top. Most artists say, "You don't know how hard Tisa works." And they say, "You know, you can not begrudge whatever she has achieved." People say, "Oh she gets big grants." I get big grants because the work is extraordinarily good. I work so hard to maintain that caliber of excellence. I don't allow people to slack off. I used to be at the theater every night taking notes and watching.

In 1983, we'd only been incorporated five years, we were young. I took the chance of taking *Yellow Fever* [a play] and moving it to off Broadway, and running it for six months. That experiment, that exploration, that professional risk-taking garnered for us many new audiences, much PR attention. We were reviewed by all the publications. It was newsworthy. But we took such a financial bath because of it. For us, at that time, a $36,000 deficit was a very big thing, our budget was so small. It was a calculated risk. It was not foolhardy. But I did something foolish. I sold a family piece of jewelry, a diamond. So that is my one major regret: that I was pushed into a corner like that.

We had to live that deficit. Live it for many years. Yes, I very much want to take Pan Asian to the next level of producership—of impact. I very much need the community to help as workers, leaders, donors, volunteer committee heads so we can grow into the 21st century as a major force. I pride myself in that Pan Asian is now nurturing the next generation of artist managers: young people who are coming out of the colleges—Vassar, NYU, Columbia—with graduate degrees as well as professional interest in the arts. But they are also very committed to doing all the slog work in an office. They're computer literate, they write well, which is very critical. So, it is different than when I started. This younger generation, the good side of it is they are much better prepared to meet the demands of what it means to be in the arts.

As for integrating with the commercial aspect, in 1990 Pan Asian had a major setback in terms of public relations because of the *Miss Saigon* controversy. I was right in the eye of the storm. Unfortunately I was vilified for being so forceful and so clear in my objections to the misrepresentation about the casting issue of the engineer in *Miss Saigon*. I had seen the show in London—so when I spoke about it I spoke from qualified experience. I saw Jonathan Pryce in the role with grotesque makeup [playing an Asian]. So that is what I was speaking about. I felt that I was totally misrepresented. Pan Asian and Tisa Chang were misquoted in the newspapers, in the mainstream press. I feel Pan Asian's image in the commercial world was eroded at the time. Yet the Asian Pacific Organization in Los Angeles gave me an award in March of 1991 because of my stand on *Miss Saigon*. But, there were also some in New York who said, "Tisa did it for PR value." I said, "Maybe that is part of being in this position called leadership."

ON CHANGES IN OPPORTUNITIES FOR ASIAN AMERICAN ACTORS

Over my 25 years of directing I've probably worked with hundreds of actors in over 70 productions.

The opportunities have definitely changed. My professional parameters were defined by my own experiences and by the icons of the people in my generation. Nowadays, many younger artists tend to work more experimentally; they tend to work more solo or duo; they don't need an ensemble to create work. Many of the actors, dancers tend to write or choreograph their own work and then perform it. They are also very business-wise and sophisticated. These are 24 year olds who are earning their own way, and renting apartments on their own, like my staffers.

I think it's easier being an Asian American actor today. So many avenues are open. Younger actors being better trained and having access to knowledge they can use to climb, to do film, television. The steps are to try to get a theater world award, do a Broadway show, go into a TV series, then to movies. It's like, strategized all the way. There is also a trend that more and more Asian performers now are Amerasians. I think in the 21st century I expect many more intermarriages. So that the delineation of the traditional, ethnic definitions may be expanded. These Amerasians can then assimilate, interface much more. You're seeing it on television. So I think that this is a new trend. It's perhaps good for them, for the younger people. For myself and my work, I've always been culturally specific or dictated by certain specific interests, whether it's geographic, ethnic, artistic. And I believe in that and I think it's all for the good because it gives me selectivity.

I do think things have changed. Actors don't say this very often; they don't think this is so. That is because if you're a serious, dramatic actor, the trouble with the whole theater industry, whether it's commercial or not-for-profit, is that no one is supporting ensembles. They are not supporting the classical work. It is just heartbreaking that serious, well-trained actors have to go to TV to do fluff in order to make a living. For Asian American actors, I think it's still very difficult because they're caught somewhat between that dilemma of, "Am I more an Asian type?" and "Oh, we need some Asians for a TV commercial." That's very specific. But to go beyond that and just as an actor attempt to do the lead in Shakespeare. Would they be considered for that? I don't know.

We have now six albums of photos in my office of Asian American actors. Unfortunately, except for a handful of Asian American actors who are in film or TV or theater on Broadway, many of them also have to have other sidelines. I think everybody now does do two or three jobs. I mean, that's what an aspiring actor used to do. You know, you're auditioning for dance, theater, Broadway, off Broadway, summer stock, and mopping. I mean, I did everything. I think what is unfortunate is that Pan Asian is just one of four in the nation, and I can't serve these 600 actors and others to the maximum. Anyone who sends me a photo gets into our albums, they are really filed. I truly draw upon it as a resource. But I don't feel we're doing a good enough job. It's very frustrating because I cannot showcase and utilize more actors.

On any given show the audience tends to be more mainstream and diverse. Asian Americans are smaller percentage-wise. When I started, it was much more than 50 percent Asian Americans. I think along with the success and the growing competition, and the graying of our audiences, things have changed. It's a plus because I enjoy newer audiences, which is wonderful. I really want to be very, very relevant and very meaningful to the Asian American community, and that's still fairly small in this city. With funding and everything else predicated on statistics, Asian Americans come out behind everybody else.

Why do I continue doing this? I find it very invigorating. I like adversity and challenges. I will never grow old, I will never get gray hair. I find it very energizing.

I want to expand opportunities and stabilize the company financially. Once that is accomplished I would like to able to learn more about TV, and film production. I actually would like Pan Asian to host our own cable TV show. As an expansion of what we do, that's something I really want to explore. I could do it well, professionally, I can do some very interesting programming and interviews; talk about expanding the impact of Asian American theater. So I have to do some exploration as to what it would cost, but that's a little secret dream I have.

Peter Kwong

Peter Kwong has been an actor for 22 years. The bulk of his work has been in television. He's appeared in over 70 television shows and 12 feature films in a variety of roles, from gangsters to a young professional. He moved to Los Angeles in the early 1970s and has been in acting ever since. He appears to be in his mid 40s.

Aside from his work as an actor he also sees himself as an activist for actors' rights. He is on the National Board of Directors for the Screen Actors Guild; he's a member of the Asian Pacific Alliance for Creative Equality, board member of the American Federation of Television and Radio Artists, and a member of the Academy of Motion Picture Arts and Sciences.

Peter was born in Sacramento and is a first generation Chinese American. He originally studied biological science but said he was motivated to go into theater because of a need to communicate. He studied at the American Conservatory Theater in San Francisco for one summer and graduated with a degree in theater arts.

CHOOSING ACTING

In college there were many things about the media that came out in the '70s. One book that influenced me greatly was Marshall McLuhan's

Peter Kwong

Understanding Media and his statement that the medium is the message. I felt that in film and TV you can impact people visually in one fraction of a second and touch many thousands, millions of people's lives through emotional response. That to me was one way to impose a lasting memory. I was thinking how can we use this to deal with the impressions of Chinese Americans.

I finished my degree in theater arts and decided to choose between New York and Los Angeles, since those were the two hubs of artistic expression in the media. I chose Los Angeles because it was closer to home. I packed up all my things and started knocking on doors.

THE PRESENT VERSUS THE PAST

Going back 20 years there were far fewer role models in terms of actors. There are a lot more Asian actors today. Before, you'd say there's not a chance for Asians to make a living, it was a real long shot. Now it's not. People even have aspirations to be successful in the business. You find a few successful actors in acting. You find a lot of working actors. I'm not necessarily talking about major stars but you find a lot of working Asian actors in this business.

Let's look at the overall odds. They're in the statistics. There is approximately 3 percent Asians in the Screen Actors Guild and on any given day actors across the country, (not talking racial background) 85 percent of them are unemployed. Approximately 10 or 15 percent are above the poverty line and making a living from it, so those are the realities. You can take further odds from that. People reach for their rainbows.

In terms of changing images and perspectives in America I see a lot more changes now than before. Certainly we're not where we would like to be. Just working from the numbers aspect I've slowly seen an increase but it seems like the roles are the same. In some areas we're making a difference but all of a sudden we're seeing a backlash of racial injustice and racial crimes and sometimes it doesn't make sense. How did we get set back after 20–30 years of slowly working at it?

Are there glass ceilings? I certainly can't answer that in terms of the corporate studios. But things aren't completely open. I think that if there is a pecking order of choosing ethnic performers, say like for example I have a role that is open to any ethnic person, (let's not go with white this time let's open it up) then most likely especially in Los Angeles it would first go to a black for consideration and then it would probably go to a Hispanic because 40 percent of Los Angeles' population is Hispanic and then it would go to others. Maybe an Asian, Asian female, then it might go to a Native American at the tail end. So if anything we are not at the bottom of the totem pole.

I do acknowledge the difference between the opportunities between Asian females and Asian males. Commercially in television ads Asian females work more than Asian males.

But I think in films and TV they are pretty much neck and neck in terms of employment possibilities. I can't even say that those fall into any racial stereotypical roles such as May Ling, the heroine who needs to be rescued by Mr. White Hero, or the sidekick Chang that is the chauffeur, or Kang the ultimate evil guy who's fighting the ultimate White Hero. Things like that. We have those general stereotypes but work doesn't fall necessarily into these categories anymore. Today we kind of have the Asian group flavor of the month. For a while it was Japanese, then Chinese, then Vietnamese, now we are seeing a lot more Koreans. What's hitting the news. So who knows maybe in the near future it will go back to the overseas Chinese. It's like you see issues that come up in real life and the media have a tendency to want to mirror that.

Personal Struggles

I think one of the things my parents instilled in me was that real sense of freedom and choice in America. And as an American I will not be denied and that's why I'll face obstacles with great odds because I know that I won't be denied my personal freedoms whether my choice is wrong or right; and who's there to judge me at the end but God.

In different aspects of my career I faced certain obstacles that I felt were racial.

About 15 or 20 years ago I was hired for a commercial to do a role playing the number one son to Charlie Chan. The Charlie Chan they hired was Caucasian and the first thing I did was to take the job but report the incident of the hiring of the Caucasian guy to the Ethnic Equal Opportunities Committee of the Screen Actors Guild. I did not take the role after I landed it. So, there were some personal sacrifices there.

Now I see I have more input as an established actor and depending on where you are you can make certain suggestions. I do feel there is more sensitivity at the casting level but it is an ongoing thing you have to remind people. People forget far too easily.

One of the things that I acknowledge is the racial and political things that I face everyday. That is one of the reasons why I decided to actively participate in certain institutions within the film industry. I want to see if I can make a difference on the contractual end, in the wages and working conditions.

One of the things that started me with that was a protest. I was on the set of *Mr. T and Tina*. This was auditioning for a television series in the 1970s. Pat Morita was the star and this casting director was auditioning for Asian people and they were looking specifically for Japanese Americans, but they had brought me to the interview. They asked me my national heritage. Of course that's not legal in California or the United States to ask your national background, and I brought it to his attention, and he said, "Well what are you?" I said Chinese American. He said thank you, we won't be interviewing because we are looking specifically for Japanese American. Well, I brought a case before the California EEOC as well as the United States Civil Rights Commission and won both cases. The compensation was that they were supposed to cast me in a role in *Mr. T and Tina*. But unfortunately the series was short-lived and that never happened. I was blacklisted for a little while too so in that aspect I don't leave things alone when certain injustices go on and that's one of the reasons why I joined the Ethnic Equal Opportunities Committee of the Screen Actors Guild, and AFTRA.

Situations that happened 20 years ago when I started in this business are slightly different than today. There used to be when I first started covert racial things that happened on the set. Small examples would be the issue of separate dressing rooms for guest stars. But even though some Asians would have guest star roles they would be coupled in with other actors, while Caucasian actors who were guest star actors had their own separate rooms. Minor things like that slowly changed over the years and are now fairly nonexistent in that regard, but there are other covert racial things that go on.

The Possibility of Asian American Superstars

I think it's real right now. I don't believe in the trickle down theory or waiting our turn. I think right now is the time; because of the financial situations with the studios you see a lot of independent films come up at Cannes. A lot of independent filmmakers are out there pushing through the doors. You see an influx of films from Japan; America acknowledging Chinese films from China, Taiwan, Hong Kong; a flood of directors and producers that are coming from Hong Kong and Taiwan.

I think that we're getting more and more global and we're seeing quite a change. Before you used to see a tremendous gap between Asian American actors and foreign based Asian actors.

Take for example the last Academy Awards. You're talking about star quality and that's when all of Hollywood comes out. Look at it this way: we may not be there right this second, but acknowledge the fact that Jackie Chan was on the podium. I don't care by what method, or how you come in the door—just as long as you're in the party. So whether it's through his martial arts expertise or this door from Hong Kong, the fact that he was in Hollywood at the Academy Awards, you know, really made a statement.

We're seeing a lot more of that happening. He is in his own right a superstar, when you're talking about a multi-million dollar grossing film. That's where the pocket book meets the box office, and that's where you make a difference in Hollywood. Eventually that's going to make headway and turn into role models and change how the American audiences and the Caucasian and blacks and Hispanics perceive us.

This is a wedge. If you want to use martial arts, if you want to use *The Last Emperor* as a means for hitting through I'll take it whatever way it comes. But just realize the blacks started with the black exploitation films back in the '60s and so we have to start from the place of our own and be more global in our acceptance. We cannot think only in terms of Asian American. We have to think in more global aspects and we wind up helping each other.

Independent filmmakers from Asia—they're going to pitch in an international market, then they're going to pitch to video distribution and then they're going to get domestic and international releases. So that's what it comes down to—the global financial pocket book. If you can make the difference there then you can talk about acceptance across the board. The mention of superstar: superstar is about money. It's not about art.

In joining the Academy of Motion Picture Arts and Sciences you think on one hand it's an artistic move, but it's actually a political move too because I was able to as quickly as possible join the foreign film committee. I'm in there among 300 voting members screaming my head off for Asian films. A couple of years ago we wound up with three Asian films among the five finalists. It was an accomplishment that I haven't seen in years prior. When I joined the Screen Actors Guild in the very beginning it was Ingmar Bergman films, films from France. We didn't have a chance even getting on the books.

Just look at our past and you'll see the gradations in the arena. How many years of film and TV have there been? Compare that with the reality that it was only 20–30 years ago that more Asians started getting into the business. We saw two or three stars back then who broke the barrier (names such as Anna May Wong) who said I am not just an Asian icon I'm a universal icon. Now we see more in this generation and there will be more in the next generation so I don't see limitations in that regard. You're asking when are we going to make it? Are we not on that road now?

Imagine if you will freeing our minds from the limitations and saying it's not how difficult it is to get into show business, but a question of when will I achieve it. Imagine if you will a flood of, instead of doctors and lawyers and pharmacists and those kind of professions that most Asians get pushed into—that if everybody changed their endeavor and changed their mental focus towards the pursuit of arts. It would flood the arenas in film, TV, stage and go well beyond that artistically. We are doing that now in music, in visual arts and if you open up your *New York Times*, your *L.A. Times* you'll see that change right in the calendar section. It's a very exciting time for us.

So mine is to acknowledge the reality that's out there, the obstacles before me, but don't let them stand in the way. I'm an optimist in that regard. If you put your heart and mind to it you can achieve anything.

Romantic Roles and the Guy Next Door

Beyond the action films are there certain roles Asian American males are closed off to? It exists to some degree. But I don't think it's totally closed off. I think it is opening and to cite an example: Russell Wong in the television series *Vanishing Son* had the opportunity to play a romantic lead; and not only a romantic lead within his own race, but with a Caucasian woman. Jason Scott Lee was able to open doors in several of his feature films playing opposite Caucasian women. Not to say that playing opposite Caucasian women is the end all, or the goal of Asian actors per se. But at least it says that an Asian is good enough for anybody.

Let's just say for instance a major studio head says to me, "Peter you will not play anybody but an Asian villain—bad guy—in my films." That's his limitation; that may be a reality that's forced in my face from just that one perspective. But that doesn't mean I can't do an independent film and blow him away and make a million dollars and just come in the back door.

But as for being cast as the guy next door, there is a reality we have to face: that as long as we are a minority in this country it's hard to perceive of us as the guy next door because the odds of being that is still very small; as ninety percent is still going to be whatever the U.S. population is. So if people of Asian backgrounds think in those terms the wall is not that tough. If we can get our ten percent in, if we can get the guy next door ten percent of the time then we are just right on the button. And the only perspective that we would really want is that perspective; that and the perspective that we are accepted as human beings and not generalities and stereotypes. And if we can achieve that then we've achieved our piece of the pie—our nirvana if you will.

Defining Success

I see it in two aspects. One is success within your own spirit: that is, are you happy in doing the things you do whatever the financial condition. Then there are the other measures of success that other people put upon you, which are superstar status and the financial considerations. There might be constant work in this business, as there are many lags in-between, so it is really how you evaluate yourself.

I think that's where fortunately I have come full circle, in that to come to a peaceful place with myself is the idea of success. If I can bring in a paycheck, if people tap me on the shoulder and say, "Can I have your autograph?" I say thank you. They may even mistake me for another actor which sometimes happens. I kind of chuckle at that but there is certainly many rewards that this business has given me.

I've been able to go places and do things that many people cannot do ever in their lives. But there are certain things I cannot do because I am financially limited, so to me it's a trade off. I've been blessed to have traveled to many different countries and visit dignitaries in V.I.P. situations that many people cannot do. But at the same time, will I buy a first class ticket for myself to go overseas? I don't think so. I can't afford that, unless a company will pay for me first class.

If you want something, strive for it and if you're successful you might have to make certain sacrifices along the way. I can't say I have the guaranteed income of $50–$60,000 a year, a regular paycheck, and a nine to five job, but I have the freedom to do certain things that other people don't get to do.

I have a lot of faith in things, and it's withstood the test of time. Initially you may be scared of certain things like the lack of success; you wonder whether you can pay the rent, and then later on whether you can pay the mortgage.

You live in a place for over eight years and you don't miss a mortgage payment; you know you're o.k.—you've got a roof over your head, food on the table, you're able to feed yourself and your loved ones. That's all you need in that regard. You say well maybe God doesn't want me to see life as a paycheck, as a month to month salary. It's like can you continue to survive and live well? Then if everything else works, what is the quality of life? Is it brand names, or is it just needing a quantity of food, fresh healthy things that nurture your body?

There are the personal aspects of what makes my life rewarding. Moments. Blessings. It's like the circumstance of me going to Sammy Davis, Jr.'s, funeral was a gift. Sammy Davis, Jr., was in his time a living treasure. When he died I went there among the masses but could not get in. All the celebrities went in, I stood there in the rain. Someone said there were only a handful of people who got vouchers to get in. Some had been waiting there since 6 o'clock in the morning. I arrived there late and didn't think I had a chance of getting in. But a stranger turned to me and said "Would you like my ticket? I'm not going in." Three people begged for it. The person who handed it to me was a black person and the people who were begging to me were black people and he just looked at me and said, "Well, do you want to go in or not?" It was an acknowledgment that I'm not limited by my race and that somewhere out there they wanted me to be in there. I was really inspired by the people who were there.

In a nutshell there are different reasons why I stay in acting: It's God's blessing to me that I was given this talent. I also have a great desire to communicate on a mass media level. It's part of my determination to break down barriers not only for myself but for other Asian Americans.

I think the industry has proven itself to be very moving, flowing. Sure you are going to have your preconceived ideas, your prejudice, but then don't let that stand as a total block to your creativity.

You see a kid in a ghetto, whatever ghetto—it could be Hispanic, black, Asian—the person is stuck there, but it is the mind and the spirit that is stuck before the physical being. And if we can get beyond and release the spirit then it simply cannot stay within the vessel because it will permeate through the limitations of the walls.

Pat Suzuki

Pat Suzuki starred in the Broadway version of Flower
Drum Song *in 1958. She has been in and out of show business for
several decades. I saw her in a 1996 staged reading of* Knock Off
Balance, *by Cherylene Lee.*

THE BEGINNING

I had seen a write-up about *Tea House of the August Moon* in *Life* magazine and I thought it was the most incredible thing imaginable. It was playing on Broadway. I came to New York after I got out of college and managed to get a walk-on part in it. There were maybe seven people, and we went on with mud on our faces, and I could speak enough Japanese so it sounded like I was one of the natives in Okinawa, because that's where the setting was. It was just a gaggle of fun. We toured the country for several months—Kansas City, St. Louis, Los Angeles, Seattle—I jumped ship in Seattle.

That's where I met my manager. He had a supper club, and was a producer of jazz shows. He said hey, you can sing, you want to stay here? I'll pay you. I said, yeah, why not, I'd rather do that. So they let me leave the show and I sang—within six months I recorded with RCA—mostly Broadway kind of music. This was in 1956. I guess in about three years I was on Broadway—maybe it was less than that. By 1958 I was rehearsing for *Flower Drum Song.*

It was fun, I mean, naturally I was nervous because I had to show up on time and had to do all the disciplines. I was serious about it when I worked at it but it isn't as if I sat at home, read a play and thought of that as the next project I wished to do. Today I love art—it's a way of life for me. I see a lot of Broadway shows. I like to be excited, to see the best of it. But back then, I had a lot of luck. I was in my twenties. I starred in *Flower Drum Song* for two years, then left and got married and had a child.

I stayed home for a few years, then I did some appearances in Las Vegas. Then there was a huge period, maybe 13, 14 years where I didn't work. I just think that the sources had dried up, there were no music rooms and of course the momentum of doing a Broadway show had died down. Back then I guess I never thought of myself as a serious actress. I didn't think that it would be a long term engagement. I just assumed that it would be like any kind of thing that you go into—whether it be going on a binge or seeing a lot of movies, you know—let's just have some fun.

I quit twice, one time, not as long as this last time, which was a good 13, 14 years as I said. I never considered myself an actor per se, so I didn't try out for things or I wasn't asked to do a lot of stuff.

On Being Asian

I remember one television show. At that time, it was bigger than all television shows were big, and they wanted me to sing. It was a year before *Flower Drum* opened. They wanted me to do a skit that had some cornball thing where one guy was supposed to make lasagna or some cockamamie thing and she wanted me to do an Asian song and I said, what do you mean Asian? I know one song, it's a Second World War Japanese wartime song. She said, no, no, no—don't you know something that's like—whatever—and I said no, no, I was born and raised in Cressey, California. It was the first time that being Asian came up in that context. If you want to talk about how fun it is to be a giggly girl singer, I think I can do that, but don't ask about serious wartime experiences because it was a royal difficult time for me as a kid. So I said, no I can't do that. I don't know what you want me to sing, I sing what I sing, I can't do it. So I got kicked off the show the night before. My dad was with me at the time. We just said, well, that's that, and I think I got a new dress to celebrate it.

My family was in a camp in Colorado during the war. I was there until the end of grade school.

As for marketability—my distinctness as an Asian relative to non–Asians—I certainly hope there was a certain amount of attractiveness about that, because I tell you I think it's a hell of a lot more fun than looking like every face on the street. I particularly liked being me.

In terms of my career—at times I thought oh, hell, I've just been phased out and I'll have to be a good sport until I kick over; I know a lot of people who are still involved not so much in performing but as people who handle the stuff now. They usually invite me to see the latest plays, the musicals, because it's part of my interest. I was a pretty bored cookie myself, lots of times. The important thing is that you generate a kind of bliss, of your own, otherwise it does get lonesome because you're your own best fan.

At one point I thought that my sources had pretty much dried up, especially when my then-manager moved. I looked around and I didn't like the selection in management available to me.

I always wanted to have one body between me and the market because two heads are better than one, and I certainly did not like working without an ally. So that's what made me just give it up at one point. I felt if I could not have a conspirator who if I said, I got hurt out there tonight, he'd say yeah, yeah, but look you still have two arms and one leg, or whatever—just some way to be able to stand a kind of diminished market or whatever,—I simply could not withstand doing much of that myself. I had friends who talked me into doing older parts, which was okay, but for some reason, totally, the taste for it was gone. I just had my feet and arms against the door jam and I said screw it. I said I will not take any more body damage. To hell with it, I will just choose to become an interested citizen.

I did do the TV sitcom *Mr. T and Tina*, in 1979. They sent for me and I read the book and I said it was lousy. I said I wouldn't do that, but they said no, it's been rewritten, come out. Try out, and you'll have a round-trip ticket. You can visit a couple of days with your pals. So I went and tried out. First they put me in a gray wig because I was supposed to play the guy's [Pat Morita's] aunt. Then they decided to make me his sister. At 1:30 in the morning they called me and said, welcome aboard, we'd like you to show up tomorrow morning at 11 for costumes. I said, what are you talking about? I'd never heard the expression, welcome aboard, because I had obviously never done a series. He said, we'd like you to play the part of Pat's sister. I said you have got to be kidding me. You actually want me in this thing? And they said, yeah, we'll just do six shows and you'll love it. We did six shows and then it died. As for accents—I would act like English wasn't the easiest language for me. It was a huge budget show, though.

Talent? A lot of times you really have to push it. I mean I was so lucky at the beginning I was spoiled.

Would I go back to acting? *Knock Off Balance*, which you saw me in the other night is the only thing they've asked me to do in how many years, but I don't know.

Have I had fun in my career? I don't even think of it as a career yet. It's so new in just thinking well, maybe I'll go do some singing. I'd love to do anything. I think I'll go back to show business so I can have more friends—make friends.

3

Talent Brokers

From the actors' perspective there are those who represent them in finding work: managers and agents, and then there are the people who do the actual hiring, namely casting directors and producers.

Narratives of Donna DeSeta and Michael Amato provide the perspectives of two individuals who have been in the talent brokering business for decades. Donna DeSeta is a casting agent whom I contacted through Michael Amato's suggestion. Michael Amato is Billy Chang's manager and was at one time Ray Moy's agent.

These are but two individual voices of experience. They do not represent the entire views of the industry. Their views add further insight to the Asian American acting experience.

Michael Amato: Agent and Manager

Michael Amato's office is on Broadway in the heart of Times Square. The building lobby identifies his office as the Michael Amato Talent Agency. Off the elevator into the 3rd floor hallway it is dark, cool and quiet, in stark contrast to the heat and noise outside in the street. There are metal plated locks on many doors as I walk down the hall, attesting to a keen awareness for security. Michael's door is bolted tight. I knock with no answer. I knock again. This time a man in his 20s opens the door halfway. He is dressed in a tee shirt, has long hair, and asks me what I want. I said I had a 3 P.M. appointment with Michael. He lets me in, then locks the door. The front office is roughly 10 feet by 20 feet. The carpet is brownish, setting off the yellow and tan wall. The man resumes his reading after telling me Michael should be back but he doesn't know when.

Two facing sides of the wall are covered with photos of faces—many with smiles, some looking glamorous—most the kinds of photos that are passed out to agents for jobs. A framed photo of a bare shouldered brunette draped in black with a slight pout on her lips reads:

My Dear Mike, I'll never forget what a sweatheart [sic] you are, and what you've done for me when I was nothing. Love, Aina.

The corner of the photo is labeled: Cover Photo "From Russia Without Love," NY, May 11, 1987.

Close by there is a photo twice the size, of a half nude Asian male, wearing a black leather jacket, leather pants, and a belt buckle with a serpent-like clasp. It reads: To Mike: You've been an agent and a friend and like a father to me. Wherever we end up, we'll get there together. Billy Chang.

An unautographed black and white photo of John Wayne, almost poster size, hangs next to Billy's.

Another knock.

A young man in his 20s is at the door. He says he wants to see Michael. He is dressed in jeans, has a clean cut appearance, and looks to me like someone who might be seen modeling polo shirts for JC Penney ads. The receptionist asks if he has a picture with him. The young man pulls out a wallet-size color photo. "You have nothing else?" asked the receptionist.

The young man shakes his head, and appears to me a bit nervous. The receptionist tells him to wait outside in the hall.

Michael walks in about 10 minutes later. He agrees to see the young man in his inner office. Parts of the conversation come filtering out of the half open door: "You want to get into modeling?" asked Michael. "You want to model?"

The young man says it is something he has been thinking about, and since he is visiting New York, he thought he would take a chance and pass his picture around, to see if he could get started.

Michael tells him to leave his name and number and go home. Michael suggests he do some reading about the business and says he will get back to him if something opens up. The young man walks out. It is my turn to see him.

Michael is about 5' 8", has white hair, a slim white mustache, and speaks with a heavy New York accent. He said he's been doing this for 25 years. His job is to find talent and to represent them. Most of the time he will call his clients for possible auditions if he feels the role is a good match.

He started out in entertainment as a member of the singing group the Duprees. Then he managed a singing group and he's been in the business ever since. He's known in the industry for representing "ethnics" and says he gets calls when casting directors want a certain ethnic type.

He says he sees little change for Asian American actors, and in films and television the roles haven't gotten any better. In fact roles have been drying up for Asians. Everything in the business is about money, he says, and the producers and the directors don't want to take a chance on casting an Asian in a role. They want to make money, and to do that they want to use stars. Someone has to be brave and smart enough to take a chance.

As a talent agent his job is to find talent and to act as an agent, representing his talent. And the client he constantly talks about is Billy Chang.

STARTING OUT

I thought many years ago like everybody else did that I wanted to be a full pro actor. When you're young you think it's easy but then you find out it's not easy. I tried being an actor, then sang with some groups in the '50s; even had a couple hit records with a singing group called the Duprees.

I was in the background going doo wops. The group broke up, then I fell into managing. I'm not sure how I started. I can't really say what I did.

Nobody really traces his life, no one has a direction. I believe things happen for the best. As far as an education, I am not embarrassed to say I have none.

No education. No high school. No grammar school. My father always told me you learn as you do. You know, you want something bad enough, you learn about that particular thing. That is your education. If I wanted to be a banker, I'd go to college. If I wanted to be a doctor I'd go to college. I want to be in show business. What education do you need in show business? You have the talent.

I came from a very poor family when we were young, about seven kids, eight kids, so all we knew was we had to go out and work. I had no education. Today they call it welfare. I mean when I was a kid they called it relief. So we were on relief. I was very young. I was born in '32.

What an agent really does is find talent and places them. To me I'm also a talent scout. It's the same thing.

I found a few singing groups when I was young. A group called Ronnie and the Highlights; they were from New Jersey. But I was young and stupid. I made them money but it was taken away, you know, that's it. You trust people. All I gained at it was a sense that I know talent real well. That's my gift—finding talent and placing it.

Michael Amato

ON BEING A TALENT AGENT

In my lifetime I've worked with about 1,500 actors, but not on an exclusive basis. I don't believe in signing people.

Eventually they might go on to bigger agencies. I'm only a stepping stone. I'm a small agent. It's like going to grammar school to high school, to college.

I have an active list of 20–25 people I work with in a week. Of those I might have four to five actors actually on a job.

Everybody wants to be a star. The people come in here and I'll say why do you want to be an actor? They say, it's a lot of money. I say what? Forget about it. There's no money in this business. Not when you're starting out.

Eventually most switch to agencies. They want to better themselves. You can't blame them. A lot of big agencies like William Morris, ICM, they have package deals. Package deals mean a company will say we want to use Rod Steiger. The agency handling Rod Steiger will say okay, if you want to use Rod Steiger, then you'll have to use Billy Chang or so and so as well. So that's the package deal. That's how they make their money. They have to double up what they sell. I don't have package deals.

I get ten percent when I send someone on a job.

Ten years ago, eight years ago, a lot of agencies were making a lot of money whether it be for print, commercials, movies, but the economy really brought everything down.

There's not that much work out there. It's not as much as I want in the movie industry. All the movies are mainly shot in California. Some are shot here but they're cast before they get to New York so they give all the dribs and drabs to the actors in New York. So, how can you make money like that. Unless you work with a heavy celebrity then you'll make some money. But, you know, if Billy gets $1,000 a day, what I make is $150. That's no money. The big agencies, they work on big scales.

Commercials have quieted down too. So have pilots and series. A lot of it quieted it down. The government, the president says the economy is in great shape, we don't see it. Maybe for him. But we don't see it.

You see a lot of films coming out but we get all the leftovers. Let's say you're doing a movie. Let's say you're a star and you say we are going to do it this way: I want my brother in it, or my sister in it, or my friend in it. The actor casts the movie with the friends that he knows. Then there are the leftovers.

Everything is politics. Which makes sense, I would probably do the same thing. When Al Pacino casts a movie he uses a lot of his friends all the time. A lot of his friends.

Stallone the same way. It's all cast beforehand. So they give all the bits and pieces to other people. It's very rare if they want an Asian, to have to go looking for that particular Asian.

On Billy Chang

There are a lot of scam artists out there. Billy gave a guy $800–$900 to represent him. But the guy didn't do anything for him. The guy is so stupid he didn't stop to think that Billy had talent. Then someone told Billy to see me, so he came here. That was about five years ago. We had a contract but now we work on the handshake basis because he's very loyal and I'm loyal to him.

When he first came in he wanted to be an actor like everybody else. Like that kid who just walked in here. Billy's first movie was a nonunion feature film shot in New York, shown in Hong Kong or China. And when I saw him I thought this boy can act. So that made me excited, I thought he was just another pretty model.

I've been sending him a lot to auditions. He did *Kung Fu: The Legend Continues* with David Carradine. He played the role of Clarence. He's on his seventh episode. So if they don't kill him off that means they want him back. David Carradine loves him.

He just went up for a TV pilot. It was a comedy for Time Warner.

Billy wants to be a movie actor. He doesn't want to be a stage actor. That's it. He loves the screen. And he just turned down the chance to be an understudy in *The King and I*. He also turned down a cigarette ad for Camels. It would have given him $1,200 a day. He has his own business on the side as a real estate agent. But his heart is really into being a film actor.

When a role comes in—let's say a role calls for a college student 25–27 years old, but it says Caucasian. I submit Billy's picture. I say, why can't the role be played by an Asian. I don't always go by what they ask for in a breakdown [a sheet circulated to agents describing a role to be cast]. If they ask for a Caucasian I might put a black in there or an Asian.

They may not buy it cause they have no imagination in this business. But why not? Why can't the character be Asian or black? It's up to the producers to say "yes" let's go with him, or let's not go with him. He may not get the job but at least they've seen his face.

The TV series *ER*, Billy would love to be on there. There is no Asian on that show, why not? I contacted them. They said that's a good idea. We'll keep it in mind. But they're not ready for it. I don't know why. There are a lot of Asian doctors. How come there aren't any Asian doctors on the TV show?

I even contacted my friend at *All My Children* [soap opera]. I say, you know, this Asian actor you got to see, he's sexy, he's good looking, he's a great actor, you got to see him. He says, "Alright Mike. I'll send some material over for him." But you hear nothing. You keep calling and calling.

It's aggravating because the scripts don't call for an Asian. They make these scripts up and they don't throw the Asian in there. All they see is Caucasian and black, Caucasian and black, that's all they know today. They don't spread their wings. Let's take a chance.

The networks, the money people are afraid to take chances, I don't know why. They're afraid the public's not going to buy Asians, I don't know why. Asians are here to stay, you know what I mean.

I think they just don't focus on Asians. It's mind boggling. Why can't Billy be a college student? Why does a certain character have to be a black man? Why does he have to be this or that? I don't understand that.

Placing Asian Americans

I place ethnics. Are they hard to place? No, because relatively speaking there are so many more Caucasians out there.

I look at breakdowns—they come from other agencies and they list roles that will be cast. We get them everyday and we pay for them, we don't get them for free.

If they're looking for Caucasian actors I leave that to William Morris and a lot of other big agencies. I go for the ethnics. Ethnics are easier for me to book. A lot of people know through the years that Michael Amato specializes in ethnics. They don't say it but that's what they know is so.

I submit the photos and then they go by the photos, and then they say we want to see so and so for this particular role. That's how it's done. That's a "go see."

Everything in this business is about looks. Looks are very important. Say in the breakdown they want an ugly fat Italian. You want a Mafia looking person, heavy. They specify what they want. Denzel Washington has great features, he's an attractive man. Does he play a bad man? He always plays a nice guy. See, 'cause of his features, that's what he's selling. Then you get the black man, the street type, who plays a bad man. So you have different types.

When the breakdown calls for an ethnic, what kinds of roles are there? Well the African American right away—classify them as the drug dealer, the bad guy; the Italians, Mafia. Everybody is stereotyped already. The Asians are the grocery man, the bad guy, the gang members. Billy always plays the bad guy.

He hasn't played a good guy. Not yet. But I like him playing the bad guy. And he doesn't mind. He loves it.

I've been in the business for over 25 years and I haven't seen the roles for Asians change very much over that time. There aren't that many roles for Asians. It could be five to seven percent of Asian actors that are working today.

You got Jackie Chan who is coming in now. I'm hoping that he expands the Asian market here. There are a lot of Asian movies made, but not in the United States, in Hong Kong, China, but I'm hoping Jackie Chan opens up the Asian market here.

Why do I think it's been so limited? Because I think this country is still prejudiced. The networks are afraid to take chances. Archie Bunker was a good show because what happens to people was related in the Archie Bunker series. Everybody's a racist one way or another in this country. They say that they're not, but they are. Rosanne, she's a nut to me, I call her another, a female Archie Bunker in a roundabout way. The average housewife relates to her because the housewife, I'm not saying they're all fat slobs, when they get married they let themselves go and this is why they relate to her. You follow me? She's a typical housewife. I don't know how she got there but she did. You can't knock success.

There isn't that much work out there even for blacks though the black market opened up awhile. Actually it opened up a lot because they fought. It makes a difference. They fought and they're still fighting.

The casting directors and the producers have the power in this business. Let's say Time Warner hires a casting person to work on a project. It leaves the casting in that person's hands. In other words the producer and the network will always use their own discretion but they'll always listen to the casting person too.

A lot of times I'll go directly to the producers themselves, rather than go through the casting person because a lot of casting people, excuse my language, don't know their ass from their elbow. They're all kids today. They're all young people today.

ACTORS, MOVIE STARS, AND HOW ASIAN AMERICANS FIT IN

They don't look for talent no more. It's money, yes, it was always money. Back in the twenties and the forties it was always money but at least the studios MGM, Warner Bros., they nurtured their talent. They made stars. They're the ones that made legends, the Joan Crawfords, the Lana Turners, the Joan Fontaines, the James Stewarts, the Marilyn Monroes. But that era is gone. Today they hire an actor and they give him what he wants. They do not nurture his career; here is your money, good-bye and go. If you want publicity then do it yourself. They hire you for your talent, that's it.

It aggravates me when you watch let's say *Good Morning America* and they put on a guy or girl who has starred in a new movie to promote it. The news talent asks "How does it feel to be a movie star?" Like, oh God. A movie star? The person did one damn movie and suddenly he's a star. That's a big word. You got to work for that word. You are not a movie star. You're an actor.

A movie star is a star that delivers. What is a movie star? I can never find that definition. I don't know. I guess Judy Garland was a movie star, Lana Turner was a movie star, Marilyn Monroe was a movie star. I think Sharon Stone is a movie star today. She commands at the box office. That's a movie star.

Do I think there can be a big Asian movie star in this country right now? Of course, why not? I would love to see it happen. Why hasn't it happened? Because they're not ready yet.

The networks, the producers, they're not ready to back an Asian yet. There is an old saying, if you want something done you got to do it yourself. And I believe Asians have to market themselves and push themselves more agressively.

You can see through the breakdowns that come in everyday. There aren't that many Asian roles. There are a lot more for blacks and Caucasians.

The kinds of roles Asians get to play, they are basically as a vegetable person, a professional, or a criminal. The opportunities haven't changed that I could see.

It's not the audience that is the problem. It's the people behind the scenes. It's the big honchos, the big business people and they're not ready to produce Asian people yet. They'll throw them in but that's it. But they'll never give them a major role, and there are a lot of great Asian actors out there.

So why do I represent minorities if I feel they're hard to place? I just always did. In a way I think its easier to push minorities.

Casting agents when they call me up say, Mike I need African American men or what have you. They call me because they want the ethnics and they know I specialize in ethnics. They'll say send me the ethnics you got, but don't send me too much white because I got a lot of white, I don't need that. So they'll depend on me to send the ethnics, see.

I work with motion pictures, TV, commercials, pilots, series, no stage. Of the four categories very little has opened up for Asians. Day in, day out, seven days a week I see this.

We get more calls for Asian men than Asian women for films. I think it goes back to the idea that they want the bad guy.

There is less for Asian women, from what I've seen. Unless it's a commercial or something like that. As far as movies there are more things happening for men.

Connie Chung did open up the market for anchor women. They took a chance, the network. Then the others followed. The thinking is she's going to get all the Asian audiences, so we'd better move in.

You see commercials using Asians now and then but it really hasn't opened up, no. If an Asian opened up his own casting agency maybe that will have an effect on the market. We have no casting agents who are Asians. I'm talking about a casting agent who gets on the phone and starts calling up all the damn companies around and says "listen!" It's like politics, you know. You have to get out there and sell the Asian market. You can't wait for them to call you and say we need an Asian person.

Then there is the problem of limited scripts. You see that box full of scripts [pointing to the cabinet by the wall], I bet you there's not one Asian in those damn movies written into those scripts there in those boxes.

Is there any hope for an Asian to become a big star? I hope I see it. Why? Billy Chang is such a great actor, I really can't explain why this person isn't there yet. It hurts me. He knows it bothers me everyday. He says, Mike, don't worry about it. He's always scared that I'm going to give up the business and I said Billy I will never leave you. As long as I'm alive I will work with you. You're loyal.

You have to see him on the screen.

It's tough all the way around. It's tough for the Caucasians, the blacks, and the Italians. But it's also politics. So everybody suffers, but the Asian market suffers more because they're not opening up the door for them. The black market has opened up, the Caucasian market has always been open. There's a lot of work out there for Italians too. But the Asian market is very tough.

It's all taking chances. Nobody wants to take a chance.

Donna DeSeta: Casting Director

Donna DeSeta also has an office on Broadway, but near Spring Street in lower Manhattan. As a casting director Donna specializes in casting for films, theater, and commercials. She's been in this business for 17 years. Her outer office is a softly lit waiting area with a pinkish hue. There are benches along each side of the wall stretching far enough so that it could accommodate at least ten people on each side. Two receptionists sat at the entry way at a glass partitioned desk. Both looked to be about college age. Michael Amato gave me her name after I mentioned that I wanted to speak with a casting director. It took me nine phone calls and two faxes over a space of three weeks to get an appointment with Donna.

Donna's office overlooked a busy corner of Broadway and Spring Street and during the course of the interview the honking of horns, street conversations in English and various foreign languages floated up into the room. The large windows gave the small room a very airy, professional feel. A wall lamp shaped as abstract sculpture adorned the bare stucco wall. There were no pictures of stars here. She said the industry has changed along with the cultural mix of society. Just take a walk outside in the street, she said. What she sees are a lot more Asians, more people from different cultures. That's being reflected in the industry.

She is about 5' tall, and looks to be in her 30s. She says she has cast about 20 films, including two with Jackie Chan. She has also cast 10–15 off Broadway plays and has just completed casting for an upcoming Broadway show produced by Andrew Lloyd Webber and directed by Hal Prince. As for her work she says a lot is contacts—meeting people, getting the right connections to score the casting jobs. She said she has to please producers, directors, and the writers. She also told me she has cast Asians in roles which were not written for an Asian. She says today Asians are seen as professionals; there are the green grocer and gangster roles, but Asians are now also doctors and businessmen. What they are not, are the next door neighbor types. You don't see them as regular people living next door.

On Casting

In theater I am hired by the directors, the composers, the writers and usually it's a decision made by all three. In advertising it could be the production company, the director, or maybe the advertising agency. In film it's almost always the director's decision along with the producer who's been working on the project.

With a commercial they will give you storyboards, you interpret them, you talk to the director and he gives you his take on it plus the agency gives you their take on it and you try to come out with something that everybody will be happy with.

In theater you do the same thing. Hopefully the director and composer are in the same room when you're doing this so if there are any disagreements you can find out where your problems lie right away.

I generally cast the whole project. I will do the main players to keep the look of the film intact, but not necessarily the extras. If it's a commercial I usually cast the extras. If it's a film I don't necessarily do the extras. If you're talking about 200 extras to fill the stadium, there are other people who do that. That's more of a payroll business. The whole business is structured differently.

Most of my work is commercials, then film, then theater. Except the balance is changing now because we're doing more major theater. We do things for Asia, for Europe, we do Levi spots, Dr. Pepper spots; we just did Gillette, so we do commercials all the time.

I believe my suggestions are important. Ultimately the decision ends up with the director. But suggestions are always made by someone in my position. And I have found they are not totally ignored. Sometimes they get shot down, and they're not always agreed with, whatever I suggest, but they get heard. So you make them when suitable.

Do much of my feelings enter in the way I approach a project? Yes. I think it should. Part of who you are and what you do should come through. I have passed on projects which I did not support. But when you're doing a film project, you read it and you can see all kinds of things on the page, the colors and personalities that would go into it and the kinds of things that would come out of it—what they should look like, how they should move, how they behave—all that comes out of how I perceive the world. What I see. And because of what I do I know I look at people a lot and watch them in the street—the behavior. I pay attention to it.

CASTING ASIAN AMERICANS

I have seen a direct increase in the amount of Asian American actors available to me, and work available to them, and I think fortunately it's happened based on how the population has grown. Which if I look at it makes perfect sense. Because in advertising certainly you have more dollars being spent from the Asian community so there's more advertising geared towards the Asian community. Years ago when I was instructed to cast an Asian actor the pool was very limited. I think in Los Angeles the pool was larger but here in New York the talent pool was very limited. This was not that long ago, 5–10 years. And the reason is because of supply and demand. There wasn't that much work for the minority or ethnic actors so there weren't that many people coming into the field. Now there seems to be more work available to them so you have more people trying to do this as a profession.

I have also found that because the Asian population is growing I find more Asians working behind the scenes. Executives, art directors that I'm working with—more than I remember in the past. I see this across the board, but particularly in advertising because there is a direct response—there is a dollar to be spent so we'll advertise to it. That's why you see an increase.

I find that people are very open to suggestions—when you have a lawyer, a doctor's role whatever—to cast a wonderful actor regardless of the ethnicity, changes the storyline, give the storyline more interest, color, and reality.

Are Asians more likely to be cast in certain roles? Well there is the perception that Asian Americans are well educated—except for the obvious things, such as the Korean green grocer.

We were doing a Dime Savings commercial and there was an Asian actress here for something else and I just threw her into the mix, and the producers liked her. A young yuppie type person.

I know I have cast Asians but I'm trying to remember what roles they've been in. I've cast a young Asian woman as a working woman when it could have been anybody chosen. I do it as much as I can. Because I think it makes it a far more interesting role. It's more interesting to look at and it's not so boring. Often we're told by the director we need a man of a certain age, and the background doesn't make a difference. And they certainly want to see people of every ethnic background.

In films it's similar because we see more people in all walks of life so you can cast them more—you can cast them as doctors and lawyers, as gang members, as street people—they're visible, they're evident.

How do I respond to the idea that Asians may be getting in at the filler levels, but not at the big star levels? I don't place them at that level yet, because aside from your John Lone's, your B.D. Wong's, your Joan Chen's—you could name them—that pool to me hasn't built up yet. Because this has just started. Five–ten years is not a long time. And before that there was nothing. And now we're getting to this point. So I think you have a dearth of them at that level. I think that will change. But that hasn't happened yet.

That's not to say there isn't an Asian male somewhere who has the energy or personality to be a superstar. It just may be that he is doing something else, and all of that energy and power is going somewhere else. That's why I say I don't think the profession has attracted those people yet.

Also there hasn't been a great demand or work available so there hasn't been that many people who have chosen this as their profession. The more work there is in films the more it will attract a body of quality actors.

Is there such a thing as a stereotypical Asian American? Not any more. At one point there was. What changed? I think life changed and people realized it was wrong and not necessarily the case where—I remember one time I called up this Chinese American actor. He said he didn't mind playing a gangster—he had no problem with that. But he didn't want to play a laundryman, a restaurant owner, or a waiter. I understood perfectly why he would find that offensive. So those are the stereotypical things that used to go on, but I don't see that very much at all anymore.

I don't see much of Asians being cast as gangsters either. Unless it is a specific subject, like tong wars. I don't see it any more than I would in a Scorsese film where I see stereotypical things going on. Or in black exploitation films where you have stereotypes. Those things, yes. They exist. Certainly. But I think our perception of the Asian Americans—which may be just as stereotypical by the way—we see Asian Americans as being very educated, working very hard to get ahead, certainly in the medical profession. That's what I think the American perception of Asian Americans is. The Japanese industrialist is another stereotypical image—I don't know if that's as wrong—it may be.

How about the guy next door? That's where you don't have it so often. That's the barrier that has to be crossed or broken down. You don't necessarily see it where you would have a multicultural neighborhood—you do see it sometimes—but not as much as perhaps you would like to see that, or the way we see it in real life. You will see it if you're seeing an urban sitcom, or the situation where the girl upstairs is an Asian girl. You do see that.

As for roles for Asian men versus Asian women I don't think there are any less or more for either gender. I think women in general have a problem getting to play lead roles. But not in the lesser roles, because there are always women in everything.

Defining a Star

It has to do with an inner charisma that they bring with them, a person who has an inner strength that makes people want to watch them. In an actor it's someone who commands the stage. You can't help but watch him even if he's sitting still in the chair. He may be doing nothing on the screen but your eyes will go there. As far as it applies to Asian people you certainly see it in the Asian community. Did you see the Jackie Chan film? God knows he's got it. He walks in and the whole room lights up. There is no other way to describe that. I've always said that when I'm casting and an unknown person walks into the room, and the person has it, you know when you're in the presence of a star. That person is going to go far.

I don't think ethnicity is a factor in that. Jackie Chan is a star. Denzel Washington is a star.

But you've got to get someone to have the courage to cast a Russell Wong in a Denzel Washington type role. 'Cause it's all economics. The bottom line is it's all economics. The producer might say I've now spent so many millions of dollars on the film I've got to get at least so many millions back. So I have to have the ticket buyer. So you've got to have someone who's willing to take the chance to say yeah, I think they'll pay it to see Russell Wong. But you don't know that. I know as a casting person I find it very frustrating sometimes when I want to present somebody new. Forget ethnic. Just somebody new. Somebody no one knows. They'd say, yeah, but I don't know if I'd want to go see him. Nobody wants to see him in a movie. So there's that issue too. It's economics in the long run.

Broadway has changed. The theatrical event has now become the event. It wasn't always that way. Now they want the big names who can draw the audience. It used to be people would spend money to see the show, and it would be whoever was in the show.

There is some value to the producers to having big names—at least in the beginning. It's a question of selling tickets. Once the show gets its own momentum then people go to see the show.

If ethnics don't have the opportunity to be in movies how can they become stars? The point is that is true for all of us. Nobody was born with a SAG [Screen Actors Guild] card. You gotta make these opportunities. You just do. I have people coming in here and saying, but if nobody gives me a chance to work, how do I start? Well, everybody's been there at one point. Most of us are not born with the opportunities given to us. You gotta make it. I was some dumb kid from Queens. I started my business. Nobody gave me this. I made it myself. Yes, it's a struggle, and people make some inroads, and then they make it easier for people who come behind us. That's been true forever and that's been true for every ethnic group coming to this country I know of.

As for succeeding it isn't just if you know somebody. You better be damn well up to the work. I mean one is always more apt to hire someone one knows if for no other reason but that one knows what to expect from that person. Say you have two equal situations where two people come in to read. They're both right for the job. One would think the director would hire the person he's worked with before if he likes him, because he knows exactly what will happen during the rehearsal period, and what he's going to get.

What do I say to the belief that the big films Hollywood is making today are action films with the white man as the hero? It's true. It's annoying, but true. But what is happening is you get the smaller films being made through other venues such as independents, and even with that they don't have women starring in them. So yeah that's true. But that's obviously what people are paying money to see. When they make other films they don't do as well. So it's not so much a comment on Hollywood as it is a comment on society. Do people want to look at stars who are male and white, I guess they do and I guess it's what people identify with, for most of the population is that, so they identify with that.

But I do think anybody can be a star, and it's not an issue of race. However I think there is less work for ethnic groups, people who are minorities—at every level. You know there aren't as many star roles, so there won't be as many for blacks or Asians as there are for whites. There are more for men than there are for women. We know that. That's something we have to work on 'cause that's a fact.

In choosing a particular person for a film or theater piece normally it involves the producer, the director, then your writers. So there are three to four people to satisfy.

It is done collectively. Sometimes some in the group will like a person, and others will not. What you have to do is bring in the person that everybody responds to by saying, ah, perfect. That's the one. They all have to agree.

FUTURE FOR ASIAN AMERICAN ACTORS

It can only get better. As you have more Asian American writers you're going to have more Asian American actors working. As you have more Asian American producers and directors you're going to have more Asian American actors working. As you have more Asian Americans in the populace you're going to have more of those people. So it's going to be better.

Will there be the day where there will be an Asian of superstar status of the level of Tom Cruise? Yes, but in my lifetime, as long as I'm doing this? I don't know. I think it will happen. I haven't really thought this through. The question has never come up before in my mind. Will he be an Asian American? Maybe. Will he be an Asian, like what Jackie Chan is trying to do? There's a language problem right there, so it gets in the way. So more than likely it will be an Asian American. Will it be a woman or a man? I don't know.

In casting of Asian Americans I see things changing, the momentum picking up, where there was nothing, to a couple of things, to much more.

The Conflicting Perceptions

Michael Amato and Donna DeSeta appear to have very different perspectives about the state of the industry as it relates to Asian Americans actors. What they appear to have in common is an awareness that Asian American actors can and do make contributions to film, television, and theater. Where they greatly differ is in the amount of progress or inroads Asian American actors have made in recent years.

One assertion made by Donna DeSeta is that Asians are being cast in more films and commercials. She does not see the lack of roles for Asians to be linked in any way to racism. According to Michael Amato the amount of work available to Asian American actors has not increased but has decreased. Furthermore the types of roles for Asians have not changed much. He sees this as part of a larger issue of racism, as related to how producers and those in positions of power perceive of Asians in general.

Michael Amato feels that in film a high percentage of roles for Asian male actors are still tied to certain characterizations, such as the gangster or bad guy. As for Asian American women the numbers of roles are even fewer. Donna DeSeta says this is not the case; her perception is that Asians, both men and women, are being cast more and more in professional roles as doctors or lawyers. This is especially the case in television commercials, and somewhat the case in films.

Michael Amato repeatedly asserted that those in power, "the big honchos," won't take a chance to place an Asian American in a leading role because this was a "money business" where decisions are made for reasons of profit.

Donna DeSeta also acknowledged the issue is one of economics, saying that producers want to make sure they can cover their million dollar investments at the box office.

What both seem to believe in varying degrees is that the chance of an Asian American actor achieving superstar status is there, despite the profit-making priorities of television, film and theater. This may appear contradictory in that superstar status is determined in the box office, where Asians are still a minority playing to a predominantly white majority.

But Donna DeSeta reasons that superstardom is also a by-product of inner charisma, and inner charisma is what the audience will be drawn to, whatever the ethnicity of an actor. All that is needed is for the right actor to come along. So far that actor hasn't emerged.

Michael Amato's rationale is that Asian American actors already have the talent and ability but what needs to happen is for those in control to take the chance to cast Asian Americans in leading roles. Amato feels the issue is tied to race; DeSeta says it is not.

The purpose of including the talent brokers' perspectives in this study was to provide a glimpse of how those on different sides of the industry perceive opportunities of success for Asian American actors. The narratives of Michael Amato and Donna DeSeta reflect only their individual experiences within the industry. Their responses cannot be generalized to reflect any sort of broad overview about how Asian American actors are perceived in the business.

4

Summary of Interviews with New York Asian American Actors

The previous chapters have focused on how Asian American actors see themselves and also included perspectives from two talent brokers. Certain generalities about the overall state of Asian American roles emerged through the research. One, is that more and more Asian Americans are going into acting and things are opening up, especially in television and commercials.

But there remain certain walls: Asians are seen as playing filler roles for the most part. The leading roles are still closed to them especially in non–Asian specific films. This is especially true for Asian men as romantic leads.

Superstardom in motion pictures is tied to box office revenues. Thus the actors acknowledge their potential to succeed is limited because of relatively small numbers of Asians (as compared to Caucasians and blacks) who support the arts.

Outside of Asian specific films such as *The Joy Luck Club* the appearance of Asians on screen are regarded as anomalies, often regarded as the "other." If they do appear it is often as part of the cultural landscape tied to stereotypical roles such as gangsters, grocers, rather than as a focal point of narrative.

An exception to this may be the action film genre where an Asian male with skills in martial arts has played the lead role. This is especially ironic in that many of the big budget Hollywood action films made today tend to be some form of a "single white man saves the world" formula (*Die Hard* [1988], *The Terminator* [1984], *First Blood* [1982], *Batman* [1989], *Superman* [1978], to name a few).

Paradoxically, while Asian men have breached the action film genre barrier in leading roles (Jackie Chan in *Rumble in the Bronx* [1996], and Bruce Lee over twenty years ago in *Enter the Dragon* [1973]), the role of "the guy next door" (a part not based on race-specific characteristics) is still out of reach for Billy Chang and Ray Moy. For the most part their opportunities for work are still race specific: the Chinese gangster, the immigrant, the green grocer. Donna DeSeta indicated that Asians are gradually being cast in cross-over roles of the professional, such as doctor, lawyer or businessman, but these tend to be fillers rather than substantial roles.

Asian women apparently have more opportunities to work in television commercials than Asian men. This was echoed in the narratives with Peter Kwong, Ray Moy and confirmed by Karen Lee's and Lia Chang's accounting of their overall work portfolio. They have appeared in a range of roles for commercials: as professional business women, students, and mothers. Both Karen Lee and Fay Ann Lee said they have been called to audition for the role of a woman reporter. Karen has played a nurse as well as a gangster moll, while, as Fay Ann revealed, the role of an Asian woman as exotic and sexually available still prevails in certain areas.

From all aspiring actors there is an acknowledgment of the money driven realities of the business. Fay Ann Lee, Karen Lee and Donna DeSeta all registered a sense that Asians were being cast in more and more television commercials, but again, this was not supported in so far as Asian males were concerned by Mel Gionson, Billy Chang, Ray Moy or Michael Amato.

In film Fay Ann even suggested that maybe women should think of becoming a female Jackie Chan to make it in the mass market.

Broadway shows offer opportunities but primarily for race-specific roles. The actors point to *Miss Saigon* and *The King and I* as examples where Asians can get work. However it is to regional and off-off-Broadway theater where the Asian American actors are likely to turn to hone their acting skills. Mel, Lia, Karen, Fay Ann, and Ray have all performed in local theater and they say the opportunities to perform are greater with regional theater in nontraditional casting roles than on the screen or television.

Nontraditional casting in public theater has provided opportunities for Karen and Mel to play classical parts in Shakespearean works. Additionally Asian American acting companies such as the Pan Asian Repertory provide cultural outlets for Asian American works as well as nurture budding talent. In short, regional theater, where actors can do parts derived from nontraditional casting, appears to offer greater chances for aspiring Asian actors to hone their skills than in television or film.

Coping Strategies

Their narratives reflect a set of strategies among the actors for coping with being Asian in an industry that is predominantly white. Limitations are framed in terms of several perspectives about the industry and their rationale for choosing and staying in it. With the exceptions of Fay Ann Lee, Ray Moy and Peter Kwong, references to issues of racism tended to be couched primarily in terms of explaining the limitations of the industry based on economic realities and the fact that in film, theater and television Asians for the most part play to a non–Asian audience. Interestingly, the actors for the most part did not wish to confront the issue of race and preferred to explain constraints in terms other than racial ones. What is not clear is whether they made a conscious decision to do this because they did not want to go on record as being critical about the industry or whether they preferred (either consciously or subconsciously) not to acknowledge race as a factor in the potential for success. This latter view was certainly expressed by Donna DeSeta but hers is the view of a non–Asian. Karen Lee handled the question by called herself a "realist" when discussing her outlook on the limitations of mega stardom for herself; Jadin Wong said the reality is that film, theater and television play to American consumption and Asian actors cannot expect to be stars here, just as American stars cannot expect to be cast in major roles in China.

All I spoke with said they truly enjoy acting, and felt they were very good actors. Some even said they were blessed with a talent. Their reasons for remaining as actors—even though as Asians superstar status is not a reality in America at this time—are revealed through recurring themes which emerged. One is rationalizing in terms of past conditions: Things are much better for Asian American actors today than several decades ago. There are more parts and it's possible to even support oneself as an Asian American actor. Given the globalization of media as business there is a sense that things can happen for an Asian actor (this was shared by all but Ray Moy).

Another is the belief that there is actually more opportunity for

Asians than whites: As competitive as things are, there is a sense that there are fewer Asians competing for Asian roles than whites for white roles. The chances of getting a part therefore are actually better because one is Asian.

Most felt it is possible to be a superstar if the right break came along. Acting as a career is sort of a gamble, where success is dependent on chance and luck. It is a business of money with decisions based not on race so much as the profitability factor. Therefore if Asians as actors aren't making it big at the box office then there needs to be more support from Asian audiences for the arts.

Given the realities of the profit factor they set their sights not so much on being a Hollywood superstar, as having opportunities to play significant roles. They say supporting themselves as full time actors is an achievement they are proud of.

Ways to Enhance Opportunities

All the actors talked about the need to develop their own material as a way to showcase their abilities as well as for control and power, because they feel the opportunities to do big roles are very limited in film and television.

Furthermore if the public gets more used to seeing Asians on screen they may not perceive Asian actors as anomalies. As Fay Ann Lee and Lia Chang said, Asians appearing more in television and films might change public perception of Asians as actors.

But the reality is that Asians have become the fastest growing ethnic segment in an increasingly diverse America, and comprise roughly four percent of the population in the United States. As Peter Kwong pointed out, even if we can't play the guy next door all the time, ten percent of the time would be right on the money. But for now many of the screen roles in which Asian American actors appear—and can be employed—are not as the guy next door, but tend towards repeated characterizations such as villains, gangsters and immigrants or filler roles such as professionals, or side kick to the leading role. Asian specific roles are fine, the actors say. But there is little opportunity to go beyond that.

—PART II —

Asian American Actors in San Francisco and Los Angeles

5

Aspiring Actors in California

Greg Watanabe

Greg Watanabe lives in San Francisco and has been an actor for eight years. Much of his work has been in theater: the Asian American Theater Company, Berkeley Repertory Theater, Theaterworks–Palo Alto, Seattle Repertory, and the Idaho Shakespeare Festival. He has also done work in children's theater, sketch comedy, commercials and industrial videos. He has appeared in several films, and on television in the series Nash Bridges *and CBS Movie of the Week* Web of Intrigue.

AUDITIONING AND ROLES

Most of my experience is in theater. I'd like to do film but living in San Francisco, there's not that much that you can get a chance to audition for. I've also done videos and CD-ROMS.

As far as auditions go, theater for me is getting called in by various casting directors, people who know me because I've auditioned a lot for them. It's nice because it reduces the number of cattle calls I have to do. Other times I'll go to certain calls and I know I'm being just considered for smaller, spirit carrier roles because when I look around everybody's white. I'll go in for the engineer or the goofy Asian guy and I look around

Greg Watanabe

and you always see the same guys. They're really nice, so we always hang out, talk to each other; that's sort of a small circle of actors.

In my experience I usually get sent on Asian specific roles. Usually that means in the context of a media gig [such as industrial videos]; they just need spokespeople, consumers, or technicians that meet their demographics profiles. All the characters are pretty dry usually because they're entirely informational.

When it's for a movie for television it's like a gangster or somebody with a heavy accent—that kind of harsh stereotype thing where you're playing something like that. Sometimes you get stuff where it's just the police guy, state trooper, the number two, and it just happens to be that I'm Asian and we do it, but then it's only one or two lines. There's no real character involved; you're just in the background. I'd say in the last year I worked about 22 weeks, much of that in theater.

In the last film I was in, I played a gangster. The roles for Asian males in films right now suck. Ever since *The Joy Luck Club* it seems like Asian women have been able to cross it better.

The *Joy Luck* women are all doing pretty good. They've all got TV series, television movies, or they've had pilots and things like that but none of the Asian males seem to have been able to hit. I think it's entirely because it's still a white male vibe, so Asian females sort of tuck quite nicely into the armpit of the white male lead. The Asian males are good [for roles] as neutered, evil guys. Or as the emasculated nerdy, and ineffectual guy; we see that type a lot. For Asian males it's also a kung fu thing but they're never at the center of the story, just the periphery.

I doubt that things will change in my lifetime, though it is possible. The thing is you can put up whatever you want, you can present whatever you want. Let's say within the Asian American community a whole bunch of money is pooled and everybody gets down to produce a project. You have really talented people who all get together, who do some tremendous piece of art. But that still will not necessarily change the hearts and minds of everyone in America, and ultimately that's whose minds we have to change. Maybe that's sort of a cynical attitude but I kind of feel that's the way it is.

You can't blame those making the movies. Who are we to tell them what kind of movie they should make, or how they should cast it. If they're white and they want to cast it that way, then that's fine. They should tell their story. But if it's going to have a bunch of racist garbage in it, then take the racist garbage out. The Asian American community should be able to have that much power. It's incumbent upon us as a community to support monetarily things of value; to tell our story, to tell things from our perspective—not just go see the paradise which is definitely from the white guy's point of view.

Ultimately the change has to come from within the Asian American community. All Asian Americans have to have a sense of themselves as a political, activist body. It's a place of power. It's a consumer coat. It's also a political umbrella that protects a certain quantity of people. It also means that when a Korean American artist comes up and says this is a great story, I have to tell it, that other Asian Americans say, "I support that artist because he's Asian American, not just because he's Korean." In that way we can pool our resources and seek out benefactors and support from Asian American businesses, perhaps to ultimately win over and change the mindset of movie companies which don't produce anything with Asians or with any positive Asian roles.

GOALS AND ASIAN AMERICAN IDENTITY

My hopes? I would like to be an actor that can be good enough and be able to have the opportunity to make a living in film and to do roles that are interesting to me that have qualities to allow me to explore what it's all about. I'm really hoping that I can work on Asian projects though, I mean, just because that's where I'm at right now. There are a lot of independent guys now coming up now and so they have a lot of stories to tell and it'd be nice to work with them.

I just sort of assume I'm going to do this for the rest of my life, unless I can't stand it anymore. I think it's a matter of emotional need, to perform, to get into somebody else's life, to express somebody else's feelings. Ultimately these feelings come from me but to be truthful to the character I get to do all these dynamic things and get to explore all these relationships with other people. I guess in a lot of ways I'm very quiet, introverted. I go from that to being very extroverted and then I sort of go back in my shell. I think it's probably just where I grew up, in Orange County.

I went to UC–Santa Cruz, and then I dropped out there, went back home and then I went to UC–Berkeley. I was studying English literature and was kind of lost there. I wasn't really enjoying school. Then I took one acting class and from that one acting class my interest grew until I changed my major. I got more and more involved in theater studies and then finally I got a job with a children's theater and I dropped out of school.

Asian American activism is important for me personally because I grew up feeling very shut down, even in my body posture. Everything was just sort of crumpled in, and not feeling comfortable. I can't tell whether that was just normal adolescent insecurity or whether that had anything to do with being Asian and growing up in a place where people called you chink. Taking acting classes was a way to shed that a little bit for me. I had a lot of anger although at the time that didn't occur to me. That's the first thing I got in touch with—that it was okay to be that angry on stage because you were in a character.

I discovered slowly through the course of working with the Asian American ensemble and then going to see plays like *Mission to Buddha*, *FOB*, *Yankee Dawg You Die*, then doing a play that I worked on with a friend, that there was this whole level of my own experience. There were some sort of specific points of view about being Asian American, about being Asian in this country.

When I saw an Asian character on stage I thought, that's what this is all about; so it was very important to me at that time just on that level. Later on I spent more time with the Asian American theater volunteering, and then I did a play there. I realized how good I felt, and how important it was that I was on stage and that Asian Americans would come in and see me; they would see my face and to a certain degree I was telling a story that they could own, that was part of them.

I was starting to see that this was really what I wanted to be in terms of being a conduit for the words of the playwright. I was wishing that I could go back to Orange County and do a show. There's this whole intolerant vibe there like you don't belong, like you're the outsider. One example my father gave me: when you take a rat and put it boiling water it will try to get out. But if you put a rat in warm water and heat it up slowly it will die because it doesn't know that's it's boiling. And I think that growing up in Orange County is like being in warm water and having it heat up slowly, because when you're a baby, what do you know. But if you come from the outside and you go there you think, "My god, how can Asian Americans live in this place." Unless they have their own community today, and I haven't been back there so I don't know how things have changed.

I would say for the longest time when I grew up (there was a tremendous level of denial) I never called myself Asian. I have to put words in my mouth that I didn't have back then but I have to assume that that was a feeling inside me—not wanting to be Asian in this community.

It's the whole coming into the kind of militant vibe and then into a more accepting vibe so that I've now crested out. I see all these other Asian Americans leading their lives as well adjusted human beings as well as others who are as far as I can tell, sort of trapped then getting saved by more Asian American consciousness. It's very much to me a whole community.

There's a level of Asian American consciousness that's hooked up to Asian American Theater. The content of this stuff means as much as the experience of acting. It's becoming more and more true for me. I don't think that it's necessarily true for other Asian American actors. I know that for the Asian American actors I work with in the comedy group that's definitely true to a greater or lesser degree.

But then I remember a session at American Conservatory Theater where there were some Asian Americans. They pretty much universally subscribed to a vibe of, well I don't want to be pigeon-holed as an Asian American. I want to be free to do whatever I want because there's a kind of idealism about theater and acting; the purity of the acting process. I thought, these people are also in theater for an escape and it's also a relief to them to be in this character. But they're also going to be in for a rude awakening. The reality is that everyone will always see your face on stage, and your face tells a story in itself. So you have to have that consciousness, and I find that more and more. Which is why I enjoy doing Asian American things because it gives me more freedom in terms of my own comfort level of what I portray.

For me, I can't just disappear into my role and just be an actor. Boy does my face tell a story. I think that's part of the whole stereotype thing. The higher level you go the less input the actor has. Asian American acting ensemble we have a lot; the Asian American Theater we have a little more; white theaters you have a little less.

It's hard to say what roles I won't do because I've already played a gangster on the TV series *Nash Bridges*. On one of the short movies I played another gangster and there were no other Asian Americans in that.

Being cast as buckteeth and nerdy—I would never do that. Being the kowtowing guy, I would never do that. Being cast as something just totally humiliating to me as an Asian American is out.

Do I think things are getting better or worse? I think they're about the same. I think that it might have improved some because of things like *Joy Luck Club* and the repercussions of Asian films crossing over to the art scene. I think that that has helped us. I think it's gotten better for Asians in the movies. Then there's Garret Wang. He's a guy who is on *Voyager* so he's a regular on a television series. But it's cool because he's not doing anything offensive and he's just one of the guys. He's in there doing his thing and he's on the show all the time and so that's cool. I think though that the immediate thing has gotten better for Asian American women but I think it's pretty hard for men.

Do I think an Asian American will get the opportunity to be a mega star in my lifetime? I don't think it'll happen but I'd like to think that it could happen within the next ten to twenty years; that someone with that kind of magnetic personality can lead middle America and the mainstream into accepting Asian American faces as being able to carry a movie and tell a story without always having to have a reason why. Someone like Jackie Chan maybe.

An opportunity to break in, for all of us to sort of march in line and reach that level of acceptance where there's an Asian American sitcom once every ten years, and there's a pilot as the norm. I use African Americans as an example. Guys like Wesley Snipes or Denzel Washington can do movies that to a certain degree were probably written by a white guy. As it comes up to whoever is going to play this Denzel's name crops up and he fits it. It's beautiful because he's a growing actor, but it's also because people will accept that. It'd be nice if that happened but I think it's going take a Spike Lee sort of guy with similar perspectives for Asians.

I would say right now that ethnic theater, Asian American theater is on the margins. I think that it's on the margins because Asian Americans in general are on the margins. I think that's the problem. We have great stories to tell. If I had seventy, eighty million dollars I could make a movie, but I don't know if people would come to see it. I mean, our image is pretty bad. The stereotypes that work against us are that of poor, disempowered people; disenfranchised, illiterate immigrants, people on welfare, taking away jobs. You know, you're always the engineer guy who's getting in under affirmative action and you're taking away my slot at Yale. It seems pervasive. I think race will always have a story on stage. But that's not necessarily a bad thing.

Still, I enjoy being an actor. Being a part of a great show, doing a play that means a lot to me personally, and doing an A performance that people enjoy. That means they got the story. That means a lot to me.

Sharon Omi

Sharon Omi is a third generation Japanese American, born in California. She has appeared with the American Conservatory Theater and in numerous stage productions for such groups as the Asian American Theater Company, Berkeley Repertory Theater, East West Players, the Eureka Theater Company and the San Francisco Shakespeare Festival. She also teaches acting at the American Conservatory Theater.

ACTING AND THE ASIAN AMERICAN EXPERIENCE

I grew up in the Bay area, in a predominantly white neighborhood. The reason I originally got involved in theater was because I just felt so different on the inside than what I felt like I was perceived as—as an Asian American growing up in an all-white community. I always felt a little bit outside of things and I think inside, I felt a lot more daring and bold than I could actually be when I was growing up. Theater was an opportunity for me to be something that I didn't feel I could quite fill the bill in real life.

I started acting when I was 12. I got bitten by the bug in middle school and got heavily involved in high school. We had an ensemble. We directed them and produced them ourselves. We were very serious about it. And that went on for a couple of years, and then I went off to college at Santa Cruz and I was full of myself.

I thought I was really talented and really deserved to be in acting. I went in and auditioned for a couple of shows and couldn't get cast. It was a huge disappointment, and also shocking to me, because I had all this confidence and I thought for sure, I'm going to do this. It was the first time I started to feel the edge of racism in theater.

I felt racism before, but not in theater. The great thing about theater was that you could be whoever you wanted to be, and people would just buy that—which was the liberating thing about it.

The first show I auditioned for was by Federico Garcia Lorca, a Latin playwright. So I thought they'd definitely cast whoever they wanted in this because they're not going to get a fully Spanish production. So I was disappointed not to get cast in these shows. And it kept happening.

Sharon Omi

I would audition for show after show, and just wasn't getting cast in anything. Then I'd go see these shows, and they were all white. And I started to feel really discriminated against, so even though I had decided to declare a major in theater, I thought, based on the experience I was having, I would have to start thinking more in terms of teaching acting, than actually becoming an actor.

So I applied for my major in my second or third year in college. But they turned me down because they felt they couldn't fulfill what I was looking for in the program, because they didn't cater to teachers. And I was outraged because, well, it's not like I didn't want to be an actor. I only wanted to teach because what I saw in the realistic world was that I can't even get cast on a college level in these productions. They would always cast white. I was so mad, I was like, "You people are so racist!" When I got the verdict I went back and petitioned against them and had this totally emotional confrontation with one of the advisers there. And I just accused this department of racism and let them know what I thought of their casting policies. This was in 1975 at UC–Santa Cruz, which was considered a very progressive college.

I felt I was hitting this brick wall in a way that I had never hit it before in high school. Because my high school was totally open.

So I called all that stuff on the table. And that stuff is hard to accuse people of because in the back of your mind, you always feel, well, it could possibly be you. But when forced to react, I did, and basically, the argument was, well, the only reason I wanted to teach was because I was not being given the opportunity to do anything else, and I want to stay in the field. So this is my choice, as an Asian actress.

And based on that—they accepted me. But by that point I was so devastated I just said, "I just don't want to do this anymore, I quit."

I studied cultural anthropology and that's what I graduated majoring in. I came out of school and got a great job as a export manager for a frozen food company. I was making all this money, but it was really empty for me.

I still thought about doing theater and finally after three years of that, I started taking classes again at the Asian American theater. But that was really kind of an eye-opening experience for me. Wow! They turned out to be a really close-knit group too, you know. They had actors they worked with, so it wasn't like you could just float in. It was really the first time I had actually seen the Asian American Theater Company. People were talking about issues that you grow up with, but don't articulate for yourself. Issues like what it's like to grow up feeling like you don't quite fit in, really putting racism on the table instead of hiding it as something that's kind of embarrassing to talk about. Which I think, growing up in an all-white suburb, that's what you tended to do. It was like coming home and it was really wonderful. Learning also that there was a common language. The shared experience, the good things, as well as the racism, and finding that there is a language—that it's specific to your experience. It really seemed to celebrate that; a language of culture, and of common understanding as an Asian American, as a Japanese American.

Asian American Theater Company was sort of my home even when I played in other productions. Whenever I'd go back there, it was always this feeling of, like, putting on gloves that fit. All of a sudden, the characters just flowed out of you and there is an understanding. It was always a great experience.

In theater I feel really lucky to be Asian American because of that identification, there was a slot for me to fall into where people were writing what I cared about.

Conversely film and television are terrible. I mean, if I had to live for that, I would get out of the business. You know, I think it's gotten worse. You watch TV, and at first, when I got down to Los Angeles I felt badly because I went, "God, I'm not getting called for very much." Then I would start watching TV and I would go, "Nobody is getting called because there's nobody here representing Asian Americans on TV." They're just not casting that way.

Part of the thing is you don't even get the calls. You just go in for these smaller parts. By the time you're called in, they've decided to dole that little part to an Asian American or a black. Usually, it's like, "Oh, this is the rainbow part," so you go in and there's like, four or five other ethnic types in there. So that seems racist to me. It's like the little pulled-out part that they placed their little rainbow coalition on. It's never for the larger parts.

Sometimes I've been told that I'm a little too American for what their stereotype is, for what they would accept. You know, be quiet, a little more demure, soft-spoken. All the gross stereotypes—a little bit of an accent or subservience. But they're not me. I can't even do that when I'm asked to do it. My nature is just a little more out in the open and straightforward. But I don't judge other people for doing that. I mean, some Asian Americans really are like that, and those are the ones that will get those roles.

I have a black actor friend of mine—he's a bit goofy-looking—and he gets asked a lot to do this shuffling black dopey guy. He goes, "God, the directors asked me to do that, and what I try to do is pretend I'm giving everything I can, but I always try to not give them that really horrible take. Because if they get it, they'll use it." So it becomes this kind of negotiation thing that he does—doing enough so they think he is doing it but not enough so that he's going to humiliate his race.

I'm a type. I get confronted with it all the time. The thing that kills me about theater is that I should be able to play anything. They're suspending belief by walking into a room and looking into a stage. They're not where they really are. It's not cinema or a film.

People still have a problem stretching their imaginations enough to get their minds around an Asian American in a part they think should be European. I definitely think I should have a lot more opportunity in theater than I'm getting. TV and film, it's like even more so.

The last audition I went on was for a TV show, and it was for an Eskimo woman, and it was hard, because she was a little bit of a stereotype, you know what I mean? When you see Eskimo women, you go, "Oh no, what are they going to do with this?" She's kind of repressed sexually and ends up totally jumping the bones of some handsome executive at one point. So it was really difficult to do because it had no basis in reality or for me. It was embarrassing. I didn't get the role.

This last year, I think I probably worked—film and TV, including small kind of nonprofit type projects—maybe two weeks. Out of the whole year, including readings and the stuff we did—maybe two or three weeks. And then, I have this two-month gig with ACT.

I mean, I feel like I probably get my share of stuff. I think there are definitely tiers and I would say there's the top tier, and then there's another tier under that, and I would say if you had five tiers, then I'm about in the middle tier.

When I first got down to L.A. I met certain Asian American actors that had found a certain amount of notoriety in the business, that had done the bigger roles, you know, *The Joy Luck Club* or the high profile things.

And they were not as small a boat as I was, but they were, you know, sitting around waiting for the phone to ring in a way that a white actor of the same talents and abilities would not have to. Anybody that had that kind of experience that was white would be on an A-list or a B-list.

I also would be working for a production company in development, and they would have these lists of A-list and B-list actors, and 50 percent of these B-list actors you had never heard of, but none of them were Asian. I think John Lone and Joan Chen were on the A-list, and that was it.

And then, the rest of these people, some of them are really high profile, but a lot of these white actors were people who couldn't even act, so there is definitely an intense prejudice. And I don't even think people are aware of it—it's just kind of the unspoken rule.

My secret hunch is that there is a prejudice out there that Asian Americans can't act. That's my secret hunch, because it's too blatant. I just think that there is, and then it feeds on itself. A few people thought this, and now because they thought this, nobody's being given the opportunity, and because nobody's given the opportunity, nobody's given a chance to prove themselves.

So it's just a self-perpetuating cycle, and I think, my outlook is that the only way it gets broken is if people start really seriously developing and producing their own movies. Because there's no way you can change Hollywood.

The Joy Luck Club was a really beautiful movie, but it was also a kind of Hollywood vehicle. It was really sugared down to a way they liked to portray Asian Americans. I'm thinking more along independent lines, like *Chan Is Missing*. Something that shows Asian Americans in their milieu instead of some kind of historical, traditional vehicle.

I think the bottom line in Hollywood (which is why you don't even want to play that game) is that "Will it sell tickets?" or "Can I get people into the theater?" It's responsible for bastardizing things, you know.

In theater there is no money in it. People who are in theater are there purely for the joy of expressing what's in their soul, because there's no monetary payoff.

Your best gig as an actor, you're going to get paid maybe $800 a week. But that's not what you get all year round. You get that for the run of your show. It's always a labor of love, and because of that, it's fueled by how people feel, and not how they think they're going to make money.

What I'd like to say is if I had my choice, whether to be an Asian-American or white actor, I would choose Asian American in a minute, because what being an actor has always meant for me is the opportunity to express something that I feel. I always have a home. There are always people writing things that are close to my heart. There's always East-West Players [in Los Angeles] that are a source of tremendous comfort.

We have a lot of white friends that just are adrift, because all they deal with is the Hollywood world. They have no place to land, no place to call their own in terms of their artistry, and that's what East-West offers the actors.

Do I feel that as an Asian American artist, my challenges are different than those of a white actor's? Totally, I don't even know how to define that. It's so different, what we're dealing in. I mean, I think the adage is true. I think Asian American actors must be better than their white counterparts to even get their foot in the door.

When I got to Los Angeles I was amazed by the talent level of Asian American actors. They're really phenomenal actors, but they don't work.

The other thing that happens with Asian American actors is you see a lot of fallout. You get to 40 to 50, and there are fewer and fewer actors, because maybe what happens is people walk in with a dream of making it in Hollywood, and after a few years they go, "Oh, if that's why I'm in it, that's not going to happen."

On the other hand, I also think that the frustration people feel will start to fuel itself. The East-West Players do more on volunteer hours than any theater I've ever seen—the actors go in and do everything for free. And they're going to change that, they're going to become an equity theater. This tremendous outpouring of energy, because it's so thwarted in other media will begin to fuel some kind of film development. That has to be the next thing.

Would I choose a film or theater role? It would depend on the role. If you were to say, you would play some great role at an Asian American play for the next six months, or do a couple of weeks at a movie where you'd probably make about three times as much money but it wasn't a very good—some kind of stereotypical—role, I'd do the theater gig. I'd always look at it that way.

ASIAN AMERICANS AND VISIBILITY, SUCCESS, FUTURE

Asian Americans are totally invisible in the film and television industry and it's not going to change unless we change it. It has to be through self-production and writing. People are really starting to write movies in the same way that maybe Asian American Theater started twenty years ago. I think it's starting to happen. You know there's a lot of young filmmakers that are starting to do that. Still, maybe I'm a pessimist, but I just don't see any way that it's going to happen soon.

I've only been in L.A. for three years. So I have nothing to compare as to whether things have gotten better or worse. I guess I would say it's probably gotten worse. Because even when I was here in San Francisco, like, ten years ago, you would occasionally see someone like Rosalind Chao land a regular role in a TV series.

Since I've been in L.A. they've had *All-American Girl*, but that was never right. Like Hollywood totally manipulated this thing. It was stupid. And so I guess I would say it's probably worse.

Success for me? At this point I'd say it would be starring in and making a movie with my husband. He's got a couple of things that he's written up that I really love. That would be it.

I guess that's one thing that's changed for me. When I first started out, success was acting all the time, having gig after gig after gig, being part of a repertory company. But nobody does that anymore. They don't keep a stable of actors.

So lately, what it's become about is balance. Like being able to maintain my family and my outlook and to still do the TV and film jobs when they come along, and be involved in theater, without it destroying me personally when I'm not working.

I have a friend that just was nominated for an Emmy on the television series *ER*, and what she's doing right now is trying to start a production company, so she has some way of maintaining her longevity in the business. It can be here today and gone tomorrow. So you have to be able to enjoy what comes your way when it comes your way, and not destroy yourself when you're not getting it. I guess it's about staying in the business and staying balanced.

I really do see myself doing this for the rest of my life. There's been a lot of different paths for me. This summer for instance for the American Conservatory Theater I'm teaching two hours a day, four days a week, with the same group of 15 actors, which is the hardest thing I've ever done in my entire life.

As for how I transcend the barriers I've talked about, I don't think about it. But I guess my personal perspective has always been to see it but not to let it destroy me. To keep enough of a perspective on it so that we can do something about it. Lately, I'm trying to get more involved in this development company that I'm working for. I'm just trying to set my sights a little higher in terms of being higher on the chain of command than just an actor, because that's the only way I can see things begin to happen.

Ken Narasaki

Ken Narasaki is a fourth generation Japanese American in his late 30s. Raised in a suburb outside of Seattle, Washington, he started acting in the mid–1970s. He has appeared in numerous Asian American Theater Company productions in San Francisco where he lived for about 15 years. He relocated with his family to Los Angeles several years ago. He is married to Sharon Omi. He has appeared on Chicago Hope, The Jamie Foxx Show, America's Most Wanted *and many other film and television productions.*

OPENING THOUGHTS

I really love the act of doing it, I love walking onto a set, I love getting the call saying you've got the job. I actually like auditioning believe it or not, because sometimes that's the most acting I'm going to get to do in a given month. And most of all, I love coming back to a set more than once. I love going back and knowing where everything is. I love doing theater, I love the feeling of being in front of people, and performing, and I honestly believe that I have something unique to offer. Which I think you have to have—you have to at least believe that, because if you don't, you probably should get out. Then it's just something you're doing because you have to do it.

It's still the only work that makes me happy.

HOW IT BEGAN

In 1979, I went to the Summer Congress sponsored at the American Conservatory Theater (ACT) in San Francisco. I met up with a few actors who were part of the Asian-American Theater Workshop. I went to see this play there and it was love at first sight, because I really loved the work they were doing. The show was *A Play by Bill Yamasaki*, and it was about an Asian American writer who was having a hard time getting his stuff produced, so he writes something for white actors, a white play, rather than an Asian-American play. His friend just blasts him for selling out, for turning back on his people, basically.

I was wowed by that because I grew up in a mainly white suburb near Seattle. There were some Japanese Americans but you know, back then, people would say, "Gee, I don't even think of you as an Asian." I would take that as a compliment. I was going to a mainly white school and I was learning about Robert Benedetti and all these obscure theater people that were European. And my Asian friends were going like, "You think you're gonna be able to walk onto the white's man stage and be an actor? Like, you're a fool." They said I was selling out to whitey, and just kissing whitey's ass, and all this stuff.

I thought if I really trained hard enough I would be able to work at the Seattle Repertory. At the Empty Space Theater there was a play that took place in Arizona in the fifties, and it was this sort of odd character who walked with a limp and talked to himself all the time. I actually got cast in that part, but then when I went to the first reading, there was me and somebody else.

They said, "Well, we're just going to trade off, you read one scene, and the other guy reads the other scene, and just trade…" and it was just really odd. I just didn't understand what was going on.

Ken Narasaki

And then afterwards, the director said, "Look, I'm getting pressure from my artistic director. It doesn't make any sense. We can't really explain what this Japanese guy is doing in Arizona in the fifties, and so we had to go with the other guy."

So that's when I started realizing, gee, maybe my friends were right. You know, maybe it's just not going to happen.

And then I did a show at Cornish, where I attended school. It was called *The Italian Straw Hat*, and I had the lead. It was this guy on his wedding day, running around, bad things are happening left and right, disasters … and finally, the happy ending. All the misunderstandings are straightened out and I kiss my bride-to-be. After the first performance, they cut the kiss because she was white, and apparently, her parents complained. I had people tell me, "Wow, it's just kind of funny, you know, you're supposed to be in Italy and you're—you're a Chinaman!" People would think nothing of saying that kind of stuff right to my face.

So I started realizing maybe my more radical separatist friends were right. To make a long story short, when I went down to San Francisco to ACT, I discovered the Asian American Theater Company and saw all these actors in their twenties who all really believed that by sheer force of will they were going to change things with their theater because they had something to say.

At that time, it was really well respected by the San Francisco press and they had some really good actors. That was 1979. They were cranking out six shows a year. Nobody was getting paid, but everyone was in their early twenties, and people just basically lived there. They'd work their jobs and then go to rehearsal at night, and if they weren't rehearsing, they were building sets or hanging lights, or you know, doing whatever it took to get the press out. It was an exciting time. I just loved these people because for the first time I felt like, these are the people I've been looking for all my life, because they were idealistic, they were political, and they were serious actors. I found my home.

I went back to Seattle at the end of the summer when the Congress was over, and just basically worked as a painter and tried to make as much money as I could, so I could move to San Francisco. Which I did six months later. I ended up moving here in 1980 and I stayed here for almost fifteen years.

RACE AND ROLES

In acting sometimes it's good to be Asian, and other times it's like, "Uh, Asian—we don't know what to do with you. We have a Chinatown episode coming up soon—do you know any martial arts?"

And other times, it's a plus. But by and large, if you're trying to break into films or television, it's a serious handicap, just because most writers are white, most producers are white; most studios are basically run by white people. If you go to L.A. you start to see how stratified it is down there; it's really much more than New York or San Francisco. I'm sure all these people live in a world where everyone they talk to, everyone they meet is white, except for maybe their maids, their nannies, and their gardeners. Maybe they have to meet some people from Sony, but they're wealthy Japanese people. So you can sort of understand why it never occurs to them to put people of color in their films, unless it's like a stereotypical role. Because that's the world they live in.

As an actor sometimes you have to make choices—whether or not you want to perpetuate those stereotypes, which sounds like an easy choice, but there's usually a big gray area, and everyone's line of what he'll step over and what he won't is different. For instance, early on, I got cast in a commercial for a stereo company. I was going to be dressed up as a samurai, and I was going to cut a price tag in half with a sword. I turned it down, because I thought, "God, people are going to see this."

The older I get, the more I think some of this stuff is just stupid and I don't want to have any part of it. But I don't fault the actors that take the jobs because I realize everyone's situation is different, and you can get seduced so easily and totally blind yourself with what you're doing because you're so excited.

Race is a reality in the industry. I mean, that's the thing about being an actor. It's like you can't run away from it and it's in your face all the time. You have to find a way of accepting it and doing battle with it and sometimes use it to your advantage by saying to directors, "Hey, why don't you make the guy Asian?" When we were living here in San Francisco, my wife and I made most of our money doing industrial films, corporate videos, even though we were mainly stage actors. The great thing about them was all these businesses wanted a cast that would reflect their companies, which surprisingly enough, was kind of enlightened compared to Hollywood. They would say, I need an Asian, I need an African American, I need a Hispanic, I need women." And they weren't doing it because they were such enlightened people, but because they needed to produce training films that would actually connect with their employees.

I kind of wish Hollywood would get there. I'm hopeful that at some point they will. Commercials are starting to go that way, just because they're going, "Hey, there are Asians out there that buy things! There are Hispanics out there that buy things!" So they're starting to get more conscious about how they cast things. In that sense, it's a plus because you fit a demographic that fifteen years ago, wasn't acknowledged at all.

There is progress in L.A. in some ways. But there's always going to be racist stuff, and I think after 20 years of doing this, I'm realizing that I don't think that will ever change.

When I started off, I really did think in my lifetime, that the kind of racism we're facing now would be pretty much gone. That it wouldn't be what it is today, which I think in some ways is worse than when I was growing up. I'm talking about more than Hollywood.

For one, I think there's more outright resentment towards people of color. You hear it on radio talk shows all the time. The whole term "politically correct" is really just a way for white people to say, "Don't make me feel guilty, because I refuse. You're trying to—don't make me talk a certain way, don't make me think a certain way, because if I want to call you a gook, it's my right as a red-blooded American to call you a gook. It's my First Amendment right."

In that way, it's worse. I think all the things that are happening politically with the anti-immigration proposition, and related welfare cutting, mainly affects people of color. A lot of the legislation that's going down is anti–people of color.

As for opportunities for an Asian actor versus a white actor, it's hard to say. I have actor friends who are white who just say, "Well, you know, don't complain to me, all right? Because I'm really having a rough time too." It's kind of a numbers game.

But the difference is there are just so few meaningful roles, and they're almost never in a studio film or a TV show. For Asians the only time there's a meaningful role is when you're either a villain or if you're doing an independent film for Wayne Wang or an Asian American filmmaker, basically. That may change with the popularity of Jackie Chan and the Hong Kong action style which is becoming so popular. That might actually change people's sense of who can be a hero and who can be a love interest and that sort of thing.

Can an Asian male be a hero or a love interest right now? I think it's possible. Look at *Vanishing Son*. It wasn't great TV but hey, Russell Wong—he was handsome, he was an action hero. I thought, "Well, it can be done."

So I think it's possible. It's going to come down to money, always. If Jackie Chan opened some doors, or someone like him, if they start doing knockoffs and start wanting, "Oh, give me a younger, handsomer Jackie Chan," studios might say, "Okay, maybe we can make some money off this." Or they just might go, "Let's get Nicolas Cage, and he'll do Jackie Chan." I mean, that's the more logical and more probable way they're going to go, but I think an Asian male can be a hero or a love interest. It's just a matter of how it's going to happen. It might happen that some independent film might launch somebody. It could be like some full-on Asian Keanu Reeves who just happens to be really sexy. Sells tickets because of that.

Race is obviously also one of the factors, and that's the one to overcome. Like getting people to think of Asians as heroic, or Asian males as sexy, which obviously, that is a whole other can of worms which I think is a huge hurdle to overcome.

Right now I think Asian men are still pretty much relegated to villains and flunkies. That's when you see them, which is not often.

Why the invisibility? I think a lot of the writers come from the East Coast, and they're still thinking in black and white. They're thinking white, and if there's some sort of racial angle, they think, "Oh, get a black guy," you know. They're not thinking Asians. When they do, they're thinking underground Chinatown, some weird mummies are being smuggled in, and they got deer horn drugs, you know, just weird, out there, bizarre, exotic things they can use to spice up their program.

I think part of the reason for this is the Asian Americans' standing in the culture. For whatever reasons, we're just not as visible. Part of it is just numbers. It's also the glass ceiling we all run into. Then there's the philosophy of "Let us keep quiet and work quietly behind the scenes," which has its plusses and minuses as tactics of a subculture trying to get into the mainstream; it keeps us less visible.

I'm not bitter, just disappointed that we made such little progress in twenty years. But we have made some progress, so that makes me hopeful. It makes me really respect all the men and women out there struggling, because I realize, you have to be a real cockeyed optimist to think it's going to change.

It has to change and continue to get better, and I think it will. I work at the East-West Players as their literary manager mainly. But for that reason I'm there a lot and I see all these young actors—guys and women in their twenties who are really good. And there's got to be a place for them. I think by sheer numbers, things will have to improve.

For now, things are still a struggle. Just the fact that there are no Asian American actors that are considered A-list. When you see the list circulating around Hollywood on who the three hundred stars are that you might choose as the lead in films, none of them are Asian. That, I think, is shocking to me, especially when you have actors like John Lone, Joan Chen or Rosalind Chao. Remember the actors in *Joy Luck Club*? None of them really took off. Here there was this major motion picture that left this huge imprint on people, yet their careers haven't taken off. None of them are considered stars, and that I think is shocking.

The kinds of roles I run up against? I go out for a fair share of deliveryman for Chinese restaurants. I can't believe I'm reading for these; the lack of opportunities and the continued stereotypical roles that are out there.

If you look at *Seinfeld*, and all the Asians you've seen in *Seinfeld* over this past season, they are Chinese, they work at a Chinese restaurant; they are the Chinese delivery boy, or the Japanese tourists hanging out with

Kramer in some madcap episode. That's it, there are no guy next door types. They're just funny people. It isn't said, but the fact is roles for Asians are still mainly stereotypical, with the opportunities few and far between. There are no Asians on the A-list. The A-list is sort of like the industry buzz on who's hot. Producers and casting directors circulate the notes amongst themselves when they're casting a film. And it's constantly changing—it's not an official list or anything.

I'll give you an example. I did a treatment on a script development project for this really small production company. It was based on this Native American myth. The first thing the producer said was, "Too many Native Americans. Really, we just need one. The guy, he's Native American. Everyone else—too many—too many."

And I made his love interest this Asian American. You wanted to have somebody in there who was Asian American, and the whole idea was that they're kind of thrown together by circumstance and they start to realize they have something in common, which is like, not being a part of the culture at large. Their very difference has brought them to this place in their lives, and when they meet, they start to realize how much they have in common. Because that's something that struck me as an actor. You kind of meet Latino actors and African-American actors, and we all, like, bitch about the same things.

But they said, "You know what, the Native American guy—he has to be Native American, so we can't have a star as the lead. So the love interest has to be a star. But there are no Asian American stars. You have to make her white." Boom. It was just cut and dry. But we're talking about a low-budget picture, and this really rinky-dink operation, and they're thinking, "We need a star, we need a name. There are no Asian American names, boom, so she's no longer Asian American, she's white." And I had nothing to say about it.

I'm sure that scenario is duplicated all the time. For any screenwriter who makes one of the principals Asian American, there's going to be a producer who's going to say, "Who're we going to cast? No, sorry."

So that's why you always see buddy pictures, one guy can be black but the star is going to be white. And they're never Asian American.

The way the world is going, with more and more focus on the Pacific Rim, things will change. Every Asian American that gets out there and does something, I think, in the culture at large, will help things for Asian American actors. For every Lance Ito, there will be some Asian judges now on TV, because they saw a real one.

Right after the first O.J. trial, I went out for a couple of judge roles, and thought, "Okay, I hope this lasts for a while."

This in some ways was capitalizing on the O.J. trial. So obviously there is some conscious connection to what is happening in reality. But in reality, you had an Asian American judge, an Asian American detective, an Asian American forensics guy, you had an Indian expert witness, you had a lot of African American principals involved.

When the show does try to capture that ethnic range—like a lot of the science fiction shows will try to do that—they're laughed at, as being politically correct. It's not politically correct. Ninety percent of TV is politically incorrect, you know, that's why that stands out! It's actually trying to reflect reality, which is a laudable thing.

I think one of the dangers that the right has been able to accomplish is to take the discourse on race and just mock it with a single phrase. You can't have any serious discussion about race and color and entertainment, because all anyone has to do is say, "Aw, politically correct," and that's the end of the discussion. You're immediately pigeonholed as some "morals cop," when what you're really trying to do is say, "Hey, the world is not completely white."

WORK AND GOALS

Last year as an actor I probably worked a total of about a week. I had a few days on a sitcom as a sushi chef. I was a paramedic on *Chicago Hope*—twice, I think. I did a commercial for an auto parts company. I was a respiratory therapist assisting in a delivery of a premature baby on a soap opera, and that was pretty much it. But I also did a couple of low budget features; one didn't pay at all. I was a homicide detective. And I think I had about three or four days on it, and another one that paid $99. I think I ultimately got pretty much cut out of it because all my lines were in Korean and my Korean was so bad, so, that was it. The most gratifying stuff is the low budget stuff, and I like playing, you know, the character types.

It's hard to compare this to others because I know plenty of white actors who work as little or less than I. And I know an actor of color—an African American actor—who works almost more than anyone else I know. I know a white actress who's a regular on *ER*, but it's like, so crazy, because who do you compare that with?

All of us have got relatively similar amounts of experience, and have been in L.A. varying lengths of time, which do make a difference. Altogether I have about twenty years of experience. I think screen experience, about ten. I've been a member of SAG for about ten years.

We work probably, still after three years in Los Angeles, less down there than we were working in San Francisco. But the conventional wisdom is that you have to be in L.A. five years before you really start to work, because you're still meeting the casting directors, you're still getting their numbers. There are hundreds of casting directors. In San Francisco there are like three or four.

It's really different in L.A. You go out for a lot of stuff where it's just one or two lines, and it's a lot more of a crapshoot. On the other hand, it's actually possible to have friends who are actors, because you realize there are so many up for the same thing.

In San Francisco, the opportunities are so seldom that you go up for these roles with your friends. You go like, "If he gets it, then I don't get it." In L.A. there's enough stuff—even though it's just one line or two lines. Talent doesn't have a lot to do with it, and whether or not you're a better schmoozer doesn't necessarily have anything to do with it either. It's, do you look like who they imagine this character is like?

It's actually easier to network with Asian American actors because you all kind of hope that you're the person who does well. I don't know if that's true across the board, but I know a lot of guys who were always really happy when the other guy got the job. It's like, "Oh, God, someone did it. Somebody I know and like. A good person got it." That's a big plus, I think, about a big place like L.A. It's kind of the opposite of what I thought it would be, because I was under the impression that it was going to be a lot more competitive in a real gamesmanship way.

People try to psych you out. Like I've been in situations where I'd say, "Where are the sides for this character? They should be on the table." [Sides are the few pages of the script that one uses to audition with.] Someone says, "You'll get it when it's your turn. They're floating around somewhere." And it turns out that one of the other actors was sitting on, like, six of them, so no one else can look at them. I've seen stuff like that, or people try to psych each other out by saying, "Oh yeah, well, this director, we've worked together so many times, we're such good friends. He'll just ask me to read, you know, to make it fair."

So you're going like, "Oh, God, I don't have a chance! Oh no! What am I doing here? I'm wasting my time!"

There is some of that, but mainly, there are a lot of actors who just realize it's a long, long, hard road, and you don't want to burn any bridges because we all need as many friends as we can get.

As for lines, I had a lot of big roles on stage, but on film, I really haven't had much. I played a supporting character in *The Wash*, a PBS production, and that was in about three or four scenes.

Only in Asian American projects have I had anything of real substance.

And this cop flick I did last year. It's about three or four scenes in which I had several lines.

So, I've been a principal a couple of times in Asian American projects, supporting roles. Most everything else I've had has been pretty much feature—just a few lines.

Do I want to stay in this field? I think so, and believe me, there are a lot of nights where I just wake up and I go, "What am I doing with my life? I can't believe I'm still going on for one-liners and hoping to get them." I question it a lot, more and more as I get older, but when I do act, I'm so happy.

I've written a screenplay for a film for my wife and I, hoping to sort of jumpstart things, and give us something to do of substance. Somehow, we're going to raise money to do that, because I think we're going to have to produce it independently. After two or three years of shopping it around we realize we're just going to have to come up with $150,000 and do it as cheaply as we can do. There are a lot of other things I'd like to do. But as far as being an actor, I want to continue. To this day, nothing makes me happier.

Making it to me would mean working regularly enough to continue to raise a family. Whatever form that would take—whether it be a TV series or just being able to do two or three films a year. Believe me, that's hoping for a lot.

But that's what making it would be, because I have no desire even to be a star. I don't think that I'm that deluded to think that someday I'll be a star. I just want to work regularly. If that's setting my sights too low, then so be it. It's really what I want.

Was this always what I wanted? When I came into this, was there this belief that anyone can be a star, regardless of race? Yes. I really thought that that was possible; even if it wasn't possible in 1976 when I first started out, I just believed that it would be possible say, in 1985—way in the future. Now I realize, "Jeez, it's a huge hurdle." But I still believe that it's possible.

I just don't desire that for myself. I just don't think that it's what I really am doing this for. I would like to be able to be financially secure, and to work enough to feel like, at the end of the day, I'm tired. At the end of the year, I feel, "Oh, man, I need a vacation." I would love to do that.

Do I think the industry is ready for an Asian version of Bruce Willis or Nicolas Cage? I think that the industry is ready for it, but I don't think the industry knows that it's ready for it. I think there are still a lot of people in decision-making positions who will say, "Why's he Asian? No one knows who that guy is! You know, forget it."

But I think it's going to happen. And that's how it's going to happen, too. I think it's going to be a Nicolas Cage or Bruce Willis type. Just someone quirky and odd, but who has that star quality; that thing that makes you want to watch them.

We moved to L.A. to make enough money to raise a family. I mean, that was just impossible in San Francisco. Sharon and I were doing pretty well to be able to sort of act—I mean, acting was our main source of money. That was saying a lot. For that, we felt really fortunately, but then, we were really scraping by. There was no way we could even think of saving money, much less saving money for college and retirement.

In L.A. it is possible. That's a reachable goal—to actually make enough money. To put a kid through college you have to be doing well, and we're nowhere near that level yet. But that's why we moved there.

How much does race play in success as an actor? It's everything, really. That's not to say if you're really, really beautiful or handsome, you can automatically make it. If you go to LA, everyone is really beautiful and really handsome, and still unknown.

And that's not to say if you're really funny-looking you're not going to make, because if you look at all the stars, obviously that's not so. There's a whole range of people who we consider stars.

But, when they're looking at you, that's all they're looking at, really. So it is everything, and it's one of the reasons why race is such a hurdle because you're defined by the way you look. If you have black hair and you have Asian eyes, that makes a visual statement. To whoever's casting a film, you're playing right into their racist baggage, stereotypical baggage. So yeah, appearance is everything.

I really don't think you'll be able to change the industry, because it's a monolith. Hollywood is just run purely on money, and so the only way you're going to change it is by making it financially more attractive to cast in a more enlightened way.

It has to be fought on many fronts. The main thing, I think, is independent films. You have to support the directors and writers out there who're making Asian American films. The bottom line is we have to go out and see these films, and I think at the same time, we have to protest when, you believe like, okay, "There were no Asians at all on TV last year except for the guy who ran the laundromat that got killed in that episode of *ER*." You know, whatever.

And I think community leaders and media watchdogs have to say, "Hey, look, how come we have two hospital shows and not a single regular is Asian on these hospital shows, which if you go to any hospital in any major city, much of the staff is Asian."

We have to exert political pressure. We have to make noise, but we also have to do all our own stuff.

Will it change in my daughter's lifetime? I hope so. I didn't expect things to be this bad in my lifetime. I just thought things were always going to get better. But I think so. I think there's a number of forces happening at the same time. So it's really hard to say. On the one hand, I think my daughter's going to be smarter about who she is. She hopefully, will not feel the same thing I felt when I was growing up, which was, "I want to be like everybody else!"

I don't think I really experienced self-hatred, but I certainly wasn't interested in exploring my Asian roots. My daughter already is, so I think that's good. My wife and I are both really conscious of what it's like to grow up in a white world and not really understand what's happening to you—not recognizing racism when it's coming at you and not realizing until you're 20, looking back and going, "Ooh, God! That's why that girl wouldn't go out with me! That's why no one would pick me for the base-ball team! That's why those kids wanted to beat me up! Oh, I didn't know—I just thought they just wanted to beat me up! I just didn't get it!"

Hopefully her own inner strength will help her with that. It's one of the reasons why I'm doing what I'm doing. Hopefully people will see an articulate Asian American male rather than someone who is stereotypical, struggling with the language. Every time I do something it will be nonstereotypical.

Linda Chuan

Linda Chuan appears to be in her mid 20s. She was born in Taiwan and immigrated with her family to the United States when she was eight years old. She has appeared in the film Golden Girl, *has performed on stage, and has done various commercials and industrials.*

Opening Thoughts

Being Asian does limit my potential, but hasn't stopped me from wanting to break through. All I need is that one shot. All I need is someone to believe in me that one time. But to have that one time happen in your lifetime is very difficult.

I'm originally from Taiwan. My father's Shanghainese, and my mother is native Taiwanese. My first language was Taiwanese, and I learned

Linda Chuan

Mandarin when I went to elementary school. When I came to the U.S., I had to learn English, and when I moved to California, I picked up Cantonese. We've also lived in the East Coast. But if people asked me where I grew up, I'd say, Arkansas. Little Rock. Clinton country.

My father is a chef. He opens restaurants. He partnered up with his friends who have better English skills. His friends would manage the front, dining room area, and he would take care of the kitchen. They would specifically target locations—residential areas and suburbs where there aren't a lot of Asian people—where there's not a lot of competition in terms of restaurants. They would specifically cater to the Caucasian market. To the extent that there was no other competition, they made out pretty good.

We used to move at least once or twice a year, because my father moved around that much, partnering with different people. It wasn't until we got to Little Rock, Arkansas, that we stayed for a long enough period whereby I could settle down a little bit in terms of my growth. We stayed from the eighth grade until I graduated high school. That was the first place that we stayed long enough to make friends.

I always performed in high school, in Arkansas. I was the only Asian in the school and felt racially challenged to go out for things. For example, I auditioned for cheerleading, not because I knew what it was originally, but because an African American classmate just said, "Hey, Linda, are you going to audition?" I said, "No, I don't know what it's about," and they would say something like, "Oh, you chinks don't know how to do that."

Not only did I have to deal with the boy-girl issue in my adolescence, I also had to deal with the racial tension between the blacks and whites in my school. It was a black majority school, and the ten percent who were white students were very snotty types who came from pretty well-to-do families. They got their own cars by 15.

Looking back, had I not been challenged in that way, my personality might not have developed the way it is today. Luckily all those challenges turned out positive.

I graduated December 1991 from SMU [Southern Methodist University]. I hated it, all Southern, racial tension, whatever, so I moved down here to California. I felt more at home here because of the Asian population. People just seemed to be a little bit more culturally diverse, and a bit more open-minded, and a little bit more international. Intelligent, I guess. So I felt it was better for my growth in terms of a career.

I didn't even think about trying to pursue acting seriously at first. Looking back I wished I had started earlier, but as an immigrant there were certain obligations and responsibilities I felt I had to fulfill first— like getting my degree in accounting. It was more for my parents than anything else. They grew up during the Second World War. For me to complete my education, be the first one in their entire generations of people, of families, to have had this opportunity—because they never had it—was almost a burden. Then I went through the whole CPA public accounting thing. I worked four years. I felt like, okay, I've sort of done what I was supposed to do for my parents and what they expected of me, so now, I can do what I want to do. I completed what I felt was my responsibility. Then I started venturing into areas I felt I would be interested in. In a sense, though, I always performed, even in high school. Even on the plane coming over to the United States. I was very young, and my sisters and I sang TV theme songs. Flying on the plane, we were the entertainment, the three of us. There was always something with performing, whether it be singing or dancing or acting in front of people. In a way, I had felt that the whole culture and tradition thing restricted me because I didn't feel I could do what I was interested in. I put myself through school, I sent the money home, I helped support the family, the whole entire tradition thing. Being the oldest too. If I hadn't had all that to worry about, I probably wouldn't have even gone into accounting.

I've been in acting about seven years or so. I sort of chanced upon my first role. There was an auditioning for the film "Golden Gate." That was like three or four years ago. Friends who knew me, who knew that I performed and danced called me up and said, "Oh, Linda, there's this casting call for this movie. Why don't you go?"

So I went. I got the principal role, and that was before I even started taking acting seriously. Then I got yet another call about an audition, through another friend of a friend, for an in-house video that a medical company was doing. But I had to do it in Cantonese—a language that I do not speak very well. So I sort of had to learn it on the spot. That all happened before I took any serious acting classes.

In terms of casting, unless the script specifically says, "This character, Maria, has to be an Asian person," a majority of the time—I would say 97–98% of the time—the casting directors and even our own talent agents will not send us to these auditions.

In the Bay area, opportunities for theater—musical or dramatic theater, given the community theaters out here—are getting a little better, because in their audition calls, it would specifically say, "Nontraditional casting, ethnic minorities encouraged." However, in terms of Hollywood, film, commercialism, big times, mainstream, it's still very restrictive unless a role specifically says Asian.

Typically most Asian women starting out get roles such as street hookers, prostitutes, down-and-out types, or the beautiful, good-looking mistress of someone rich. I've been pretty lucky, or I have that certain look. In the movie *Golden Gate* I played a student, which was my biggest role so far. That was in 1992–93. Then in an industrial film for a medical company I was the host, and I had to talk about scary things like caesarians. The director said, because I had a friendly face, I can talk about scary things and not intimidate people. So far no one has asked me to play a prostitute, or somebody's rich mistress.

Now, even with my fifty to sixty hour full-time job during the day, I try to take acting classes when I can, Saturday morning, weekends, or at nights, six to ten. I used to take classes at the Asian American Theater Company. I continued my training at the American Conservatory Theater. In high school, I had trained at the Arkansas Academy of Performing Arts. I'm planning on taking voice classes. You have to keep your instrument sharp. You have to just continue it even though you're not working on a paying job. A lot of times those of us who are starving artists will do a play—an original work—just for the experience. Even if the job is not paying, we do it to add to our résumé and to show that we have some experience other than just the training.

On top of that, I'm currently a member of the Eighteen Mighty Mountain Warriors which is an all–Asian comedy troupe. It's supposed to sound funny. There aren't 18 of us, only 9 to 10 Asian American actors. There's a stage manager and a sound and lighting person.

Some of us have Chinese backgrounds, Japanese backgrounds; there are Koreans, and one person who's half Thai and half Filipino. As a group, we found a niche for ourselves. We create our own materials, and present skits as they relate to every day socioeconomic, political, and racial issues. It's done in a comedic manner and people come to see our show and enjoy it as a form of entertainment. But we also have the audience thinking about what message are we trying to convey.

Not only do we deal with the usual racial tensions and issues of anti–Asian violence—we even focus on intraracial problems, within our cultures. We had a skit with Taiwanese and Hong Kong people on how they always sort of hate each other. And we had a skit whereby the Japanese and the Koreans are always fighting, that kind of thing. We explore dysfunctional relationships within the Asian community—within the Asian races ourselves—between the males and females; all the stereotypes and dealing with them. We're based in San Francisco. Some of us are immigrants, some are third- or fourth-generation Asian Americans. When we're putting on a new show, with new material, we put in a good thirty to forty hours a week, rehearsing four or five days a week after work from 7:30 to 10:30, weeknights, and another four or five hours on the weekends. In that sense, because work for Asians is so hard to find, we're able to create our venue, our own way of presenting what we want to present. It's still acting, and it's a lot of work. Right now, we're not making any money. But you know, to be an Asian actor especially, I think you have to do it more—you can't be doing it for the fame, or for wealth—you really have to love it, because of all the hard work.

We've performed at San Francisco State. We've toured the country, to a lot of the major universities who celebrate Asian-Pacific Week. We've performed in Chicago and Albany. We've been to Hong Kong. We're different, kind of on the edge with our material because we're pretty much like, in your face. Sort of *Saturday Night Live* mixed in with *In Living Color*, Monty Python style but from an Asian perspective. We take that up a notch, in terms of being on the edge.

But I try to venture out and audition also. I actually did a musical *Sayonara*, which is a Bay area premiere of the play. They're talking about bringing it on tour, but what I found was that, had this not been an Asian-based musical, it would have been very hard for an Asian person to get cast in it.

I got into a huge debate with the casting director about it. She was trying to encourage more ethnic minorities to come out and audition. Even for her, when she was casting for *Sayonara*, she had some difficulties finding candidates. And I said, "Well, that's because there's a lot of advance work in terms of invested time, preparing for a theater audition, monologue, songs." Usually for me, I'd like to think I have a pretty good chance of getting something, and if not, why even waste your time?

That same theater was doing *Man of La Mancha*, and I said, "I can almost guarantee no Asians are going to come out for that one." She claimed it was nontraditional casting. That's what we debated about. She said not enough Asians or not enough ethnic minorities audition—and I said but, at the same time, we as ethnic minorities would venture out and audition, but the percentages of getting something are so bad, we're sort of conditioned not to do it. I even told her that I wouldn't have auditioned for *Sayonara* unless it was Asian-based. I knew that if they had to have Asian performers, at least I would have a chance of getting in.

And of course she said, "That's not true, you're talented enough. I would have cast you in another show and blah blah blah."

So we got into a huge debate of what comes first. It's hard enough to get ethnic minorities to audition for mainstream material; but then the other side of it is Asian Americans don't see a lot of ethnic minorities cast in what would traditionally be white roles, so they don't go and audition. It's like the whole chicken and the egg issue—what comes first.

Unless the script breakdown for the characters specifically says Asian, I normally would not even get a chance to go in and audition for the role. However, that hasn't stopped me if I see casting calls on the Internet for movies or projects I think I would be good for. It hasn't prevented me from sending in my résumé for consideration, in hopes that nontraditional casting would become more and more of the norm rather than the exception.

Outside of my comedy troupe I say I probably worked a maximum of three to four weeks last year. But I performed a lot with my comedy troupe so I don't know if it's a matter of not having time outside of that. But yet, there really wasn't anything around.

Beyond San Francisco

I was told that if I was really serious about acting, especially in film and TV, that I should move down to L.A. I kind of know that. The San Francisco area is known more for theater. But in talking to other people who have tried to go down to L.A. there are so many—not that I'm afraid of the competition—talented people, so many good-looking people, so many Asian actors and actresses. Maybe I'll do it eventually. But I haven't had the guts yet to pick up and move down there and let L.A. do to me what they've done to other people that I've seen, who have gone down there before me.

When they first go down there, they're full of hope, they're energetic, the whole gung-ho thing, and because of the superficiality of L.A. they come back a little more broken down. They seem emotionally sort of chewed up and spit out. I don't think I'm emotionally strong enough to handle that right now. I don't know if I would like to go down there and have that happen to me. To the extent that I can still find enough work, whether it be paying or nonpaying, I still have a lot of personal growing to do before I want to give that a shot in L.A.

I feel that if I do go to L.A. I better be ready: mentally, emotionally, and in my acting ability. I feel like I have a little more ways to go, but I'm getting there. I'm continuing my classes as well as auditioning more now for more mainstream things. As for *Sayonara*, I wanted to see if I could even get in this musical at first. But now that I've got in, now that I know I can do it, I want to be more well-rounded and do more than theater, commercials or comedy.

In *Sayonara* I got a principal role. We had good reviews, although the material—in terms of some of the writing—still had to be worked on because it's back in the fifties and there were still some racial slurs that the playwright could have updated, but they didn't. So there are still some problems with that.

But in terms of the performing I had a great experience. It was wonderful. I think I might have found my second love in terms of doing musicals. It's really different from dramatic acting, or comedic acting. It's a tremendously positive experience for me, to act with white people for a long period of time.

In a way, I think Asian American actors tend to let ourselves be limited unreasonably, because of what we perceive as how we're being restricted. We don't tend to cross that line. But once I did try to cross it and auditioned for that musical, I got in. Luckily the experience I gained was really eye-opening, because we have our own stereotypes of how white people would treat us—especially with my background in Arkansas and Texas. I really didn't have a good experience out there. But this experience, it was great. I discovered things about myself and it's a personal growing experience.

How far would I like to go in the industry? I would like to be able to make a decent living doing what I love to do. I'd rather reach the satisfaction or the understanding for myself that I'm not doing this to be rich, I'm not doing this to be famous. It would be a huge blessing if I can just do it to sustain my own standard of living right now.

Instead of saying I want to be the Asian Sharon Stone, I want somebody else to say, "Oh, I want to be the white Linda Chuan" or the next Linda Chuan. I don't want to be patterned after somebody else. I want to be me, I want to do my own thing.

Do I feel that being Asian locks me out of the potential for super stardom? Here in the United States, it does, because in the United States, the majority of the population is white. I've had opportunities to go to Hong Kong and Taiwan, and I'm trying to get in there. However, from what I hear—and I don't have any proof, I just have friends involved in the entertainment industry—it's a little bit more underground than I would like it to be. It's not about talent, it's about who you know and how much you're willing to give up personally.

Here, I think talent has a lot to do with it. That's why I also feel strongly that if I break into Hollywood or I break into mainstream in the U.S., it'd lend me more credibility than if I did it over in Hong Kong. Because most of the time, people there would say, "Well, who did you sleep with?" And I don't want to have anything to do with that.

Breaking into mainstream here would mean that across America, in white families, they would know who I am when you say the name "Linda Chuan." When you turn on the TV, all you see are white shows. Now there are more African American shows. I wanted so badly to be the first Asian American woman to have my own sitcom. The only thing is Margaret Cho beat me to that.

After Margaret Cho's TV show—unfortunately it failed—I came to the revelation, "Okay, somebody did it." She's an Asian, wasn't me. I was pretty disappointed. But the fact that somebody else was able to do it gave me more hope of really being able to break in, as long as you have what it takes. It's still a commodity. You still have to look at yourself and ask, "Will I sell with what I have to offer in terms of talent, and looks? It's a whole package deal. Can I be a good enough commodity that movie producers or Hollywood producers, TV producers, would be willing to invest money in me and get a return?" Bottom line, that's what it comes down to. If you have that realization, it's a little easier to deal with as to whether you succeed, or whether you can break in.

I think I'd have a much easier chance as a white actor, because it's just a matter of mathematics and equations. There are more roles out there for a white person than for Asians, or ethnic minorities, even for African Americans.

But, I read something in a statistics thing today through email, that if you condensed the entire world's population into 100 people, over 67 of them would be Asian. So you would think from a world big-picture perspective, that there's a market for us. But because we're here in the United States we're minority. We don't have the buying power yet.

If somehow Hispanics and Asians and African Americans really bond together to support and promote each other's culture and performers, we would get that chance in the U.S.

Unfortunately, as talented as someone might be—it's still about bottom line. If they're going to invest hundreds of millions of dollars in doing a project with you, you better be able to pull that back. It's just like working in corporate America now. You have to know why you're there. The money that they're paying you is your salary. You have to be able to justify what you're doing to support that.

I guess that's from my accounting business background, but if you think about it in that way, take away all the intangibles of wishes and hopes and whatever, the bottom line is still being able to generate money. You have to be a box office draw.

Do I think there's a chance for an Asian to become a superstar in this country?

Yes, but maybe not in my lifetime. Somebody like Nancy Kwan. Back in the fifties, she was a megastar. But she was not pure Asian. She's Eurasian. She's half. Russell Wong—he's half. There's not a full blooded Asian American superstar in the United States. That tends to make you think you have to look somewhat like the majority. You'd almost need to be Eurasian in order for investors, producers and directors to believe that you have some kind of pull, some kind of draw at the box office. Unfortunately, that's sort of the reality. As much as I don't like it. I'd like to think people would give you a shot because they think you have the personality, or they think you have the talent, or what it takes, but it doesn't happen that way.

I think I've come to an acceptance that that's how it is here, and if I want it easier, if I wanted an easier chance at it, then I should go where I would resemble the population—namely Taiwan or Hong Kong. However, what comes with that is another factor, another price that I don't want to have to pay.

So in a way, I've come to an acceptance. I want to stay here and be true to the art, be true to myself, and I don't want to have to go through all this other stuff. I've had chances to go over there, but there was a line I didn't want to cross. I didn't want to give up my own values and my own morality for that. To me, it wasn't worth it, but at the same time, because of my love for acting and my love for performing, that doesn't mean I have to stop doing it here.

It might mean that I will perform and pursue those opportunities— gigs, jobs—that are maybe not in the mainstream, that maybe won't pay as much or not at all. But I would still do it. If you really love the art of performing and acting, you will always be able to find opportunities to do it. It's just whether you get paid for it or not.

Right now it's not a major concern only because I have this full-time job. If someone gave me a chance to go on Broadway, or on tour, even with this role that I got on *Sayonara*, I'd go. I would quit my current job. I would give up this career that I have.

Granted, it would be a huge step down financially, but it would be a chance of a lifetime. I can always come back after the tour and get a job as an accountant. I can always be an accounting manager somewhere. I can always be a purchasing manager somewhere. But to me, this opportunity won't come twice.

Joanne Takahashi

Joanne Takahashi appears to be in her early 30s. She is third generation Japanese American, born in San Francisco. She has been an actor for ten years, and has played leading roles in theater productions sponsored by the Sundance Institute, East-West Players, and the American Conservatory Theater. She has also done work with the London Shakespeare Studio, affiliated with the Royal Academy of Dramatic Arts. She started out in theater, but then moved to Los Angeles from the Bay area four years ago to break into film. She has appeared in several national commercials, including ones for Tylenol, AT&T, Puffs Tissue, and Radio Shack.

AUDITIONING AND ROLES

When I first got to Los Angeles I started out auditioning for difficult roles which I found a little offensive. An example was for a Korean café owner on a TV show. The café owner was presented as a stereotypical, offensive person who, if you were seeing it from the perspective of the protagonist's eyes, you would say yeah, that's a really obnoxious Asian café owner.

I walked into the audition and said to the casting director because I was really offended by it, "So should I do this accented or unaccented?" I spoke very clearly and they kind of looked a little embarrassed and said, no just do it without an accent. I knew then that I didn't have a shot at the role because of what I did, but there are just some things that after a while one can't play anymore. I mean if they have an accent and they're still a person and the accent is just a condition of the situation that's one thing, but if it's meant to reinforce a negative stereotype, why do it. Everybody wants to work but sometimes that's not even worth it because it makes you crazy.

Some of the other roles I auditioned for include waitresses and lots of reporters—in fact that was my first movie. I was a reporter and newscaster. Very rarely is it for psychologists or scientists. Mostly it's as a scientist's assistant where you're usually not the main scientist, but more like the student. So it's those types lately. As for commercials it's usually as a young mother or student.

When I go on a call very rarely is it generic. For TV and film, most of the time it is very ethnic specific and then they have a listing where they say submit all ethnicities.

Actually the largest project I ever did was shot like a film but ended up being a video. The level of experience that I got working on that was immense.

Joanne Takahashi

I saw during that process that I had a lot of adjustments to make in my acting style since I came from stage, and camera work is so intimate and so specific—it's like putting a thread to the needle sometimes.

I've been getting medium to small roles up to this point but I've been able to try out this year for much larger parts. I think there's much more opportunity. I could be wrong but I think it's mostly because of *The Joy Luck Club* that people started to see Asians as Asian Americans as well. Things have changed a lot more now than when I first got here. Things used to be much more specific and stereotypical. Not everybody was like this of course, but a lot of people assumed that if you had an Asian face that you were from Asia and you speak an Asian language fluently, as your first language.

Lately I have found it very, very rare that I've had to walk in and think okay, this is obviously a dialect role. They call for an Asian face, but in the script, they don't call for an accent. I just tried out for a role today where the character was first generation Japanese American and they even said don't bother with an accent—an assimilated, American accent. This is pretty new.

Sometimes there are cattle calls when they see everybody but at other times you're saying is there anything for Asians today? Anything, anything, for all ethnicities, anything.

It gets frustrating, especially if you've worked hard at training, going to school, learning your stuff, putting your time in. You get your classical training, and any other training in order to expand your range. After-wards you feel like you've tapped all that and you're ready to use it, yet they're handing you a square in that sphere and they're saying well, you know, fit in.

Let me tell you about my very first theater show I ever tried out for here. I had no idea what 99 seat theater meant in L.A. I thought it was the same thing as the quota theater they had in San Francisco, where half was equity and everybody got paid. That wasn't the way it was down here. Ninety-nine seat theater can mean anything from a good, solid company to very, very bad working conditions. I went to this one audition in Hollywood, waited for three hours. We were all sweating there in the hallway. It was a fire hazard and they put a sign-up sheet and we all signed up for it. Then three hours later people were starting to fight in the halls, and I was going, what is this? I mean, this was crazy to me. This girl stood up to this other girl and said, "Get out of my way you blank, blank, blank—I've lived in Hollywood for ten years." I thought these people were crazy. At the very end of the three or four hour wait, I don't know what was in the minds of those who were running the auditions, but they took the list off and said okay, just come in the order that you came. They didn't even care about the list or anything.

I'll tell you something even more embarrassing. I walked in there, I was the only Asian in the whole place. They gave me the man's role to read with this one actress. I mean, maybe it wasn't racial, maybe they were doing this to everybody after me but I just felt like that was really stupid.

One of my first agents (I really needed a theatrical agent at the time so I took a lot of bologna from him) he said the weirdest things to me. He said, "I know how all you Orientals are. You Orientals walk out of a contract." It was really weird. Those were bad work conditions.

When I first came here I was come on to by agents which is a really horrible experience. One agent (actually he was sort of an Asian associate) called me down in the office and played with my hair and asked me to marry him. Another time when I told him I had a boyfriend he told me to fuck off. Meanwhile I think he knew what kind of position I was in. I didn't have a lot of film credits at the time. I had a lot of theater and so he knew that I was at his mercy and so he took complete advantage of it. Of course I left him but that was after months of anguish. He messed up a deal with me in this theater project. He didn't tell them that I had to drop out of it, which I did, and when the director was calling me and screaming at me on the phone, he called her and said it was all my fault even though it was his fault he hadn't told her. Those were really horrible experiences.

Another time I walked into this play (I was just understudying) it was a prose play, with a lot of poetry in it. They told me a couple of weeks before it went that I would have to take all my clothes off. They're supposed to tell you way ahead of time so that you can make a choice. So I told the producer I don't think I can. But I felt like I couldn't leave the production because I was honoring the person who led me to this director. Now I don't feel like I have to do that anymore. But I think that's another detriment of being Asian—they tend to believe in the honor system and sometimes allow themselves to be walked all over.

Definitely not all Asians are like this, but if referred by someone you feel that you have to do it. Now I feel of course I could make the choice, but when I first got here I was very traditional in that way. Always felt like I had to honor everything, keep my word, my promises. If I promised an agent that I would come down here, and then I would come down and he would flirt with me—I couldn't say anything. This was sexual harassment. Not that I had to be passive but I felt like I just had to ignore it and sort of watch my P's and Q's. Didn't want to rock the boat kind of thing. Nobody ever said you have to sleep with me to get this role. If they did, I'd say ha, are you kidding! But it was never put that way.

I can't play anything that's too subservient. It just goes against my natural grain, and I'm sure that a lot of actresses feel this way. You read something and you think, I can't believe stuff like this is still being written. I mean I've actually turned down roles in plays because of that.

There was this one, character, just kind of like doe-doe type in a post–L.A. riots play. She was an Asian character, but the person who wrote her didn't even know there were differences in Japanese, Chinese, and Thai culture. So this character walked around just saying, "If we all just concentrated on Buddha then everything will be fine," and I was like, you don't want me to say that. I thought this was stupid. But being where I was at the time I was very, very polite about it. She had a Chinese last name but her line was, "You keep blaming us for Pearl Harbor." I was like excuse me, but I don't know if she'd say that.

Another was a play where I was cast as a Korean woman. I hated it so much it was the first play that I was ever in that was already in production that I actually walked out of. It was L.A. theater. We were doing it for free anyway so it was okay but it was another postriot play. There was so much Asian bashing in it that just sitting there in the wings listening to it just made me sick to my stomach.

It was written by an African American woman and there was a lot of African American voice in it which was fine. But they took this Korean man—this poor actor, he was a very good looking actor—and made him look so goofy with this makeup. He looked like a clown or something. They did the makeup so his eyes slanted.

First of all, he's a man, why would he be wearing all this makeup? Then they gave him these really weird looking lips, they put lipliner all over his lips. I don't even know what they were trying to get him to look like. He looked scary. I thought poor guy. He was a handsome Asian American actor. I don't know what was in their minds but that's how they saw the Korean. It was really weird. Really strange. Maybe it wasn't just Korean but that's the way they saw it. And I couldn't believe it. I was so offended.

What roles would I like to play? In theater it would be Lady Macbeth. In film and TV the best way to describe the roles I'd like would be to pick out actresses whose work I just love and whose roles I love, like Sigourney Weaver, and Michelle Pfeiffer. They are very strong actresses with very strong characters, nonapologetic, and they have to tiptoe around in the story in order to seem softer. Because I see that a lot—a sort of girlie attitude.

Do I think an Asian woman could reach the same acceptance level as Sigourney Weaver? I hope that it will be that way and soon. But at this stage we're not there yet. I think it's improving. I think all the people who worked in *Joy Luck Club* are all doing something which is really, really good but I think there's still a lot of room for improvement and it's going to take time.

Being an Asian actress in Hollywood means—and I'm not sure this is the same for every actor—that you really have to want it and you really have to like acting, and you really have to like the business. It means being patient. It does make you face yourself, your dreams, and your ambitions. You have to really know whether you want to do it. You have to want it so much that you're willing to put up with so much. When I first got here it was much easier to get harassed. People came on to you all the time and that type of thing. That's changed for me.

As far as roles—I don't want to sound negative about it because it's a positive change—but they are shifting from one figure holder to another. It used to be the prostitute, you know the opium smuggler or the sort of kimono, sunglasses type of thing. Now it's moving more towards the reporter, towards the science-lab person and the student, which I think is better.

If I had my choice, I would work in film. Number one, it's very glamorous even though it's a lot of work. I love theater, theater is in me but you can't really make very much money all the time. The whole idea of cinema is so spectacular. If I could make a solid living from film, and be recognized and respected for my work, I'd be very happy. That would be making it.

As for my work environment, it's definitely gotten much more comfortable. I'm no longer struggling so hard. I used to subsidize myself by doing temp work. I temped like a crazy person, all the time, all over the place. Just barely making enough to survive or switching to a waitress job during the day, and counting the rent money on the table and then doing a five dollar show at night. That was my life when I first came here. And now because of the commercials—I can make a living on those—I can just concentrate on the acting. And that's been very good.

It took awhile—a lot of it is timing and falling into the right places, just happening to meet the right people and the right agent because he knows a lot of people. Everyday is very different. You never know what's going to happen.

On Being an Asian American Actress in Hollywood

Hollywood is a funny place because it's one of those places where the upfront attitude is physical. Do I think I have a harder time of it than a white actress? Yes. I didn't know this, but when I did have a lead part I admittedly felt (maybe this was in my own mind) a little bit of hostility from a couple of actresses who thought that they should be the lead. I felt that the director was being nicer to them too, and saw them as more beautiful than me, and that kind of hurt my feelings. But at the same time that's the way I was feeling on the set. I started thinking that way to myself, like god, maybe I am like this.

Not all directors are like this of course but in that particular instant I felt so inadequate, I started asking myself god, am I even a good enough actress? I felt that a couple of times at auditions where everyone is blind and you just feel like god, don't look at me that way.

Is it competition or a sense of them feeling superior? I think it's both. Some do feel more superior and they feel they were born with that kind of beauty; it's something they feel is embraced today. I'm thinking about your question of what does it feel like to be in Hollywood as an Asian actress and that's part of it. You start feeling just a little inadequate and kind of ugly even though you know that you're a regular human being.

You start feeling lower. You start feeling no matter how much you studied, how much training you've done, how focused you are, or how serious you are about your work, there will be somebody who's going to look at you and say, "Well maybe you have a ton of theater training but hey, they're blond, and that makes them better," and that really hurts your feelings.

I mean it's real interesting how when I was a kid and watching TV or movies, I always looked for that Asian face just to have someone to identify with. It's really true how the media controls how you think about yourself because if you start not seeing enough Asian faces out there (who are people who look like you) you start to feel kind of invisible. Because TV does that. Television kind of hypnotizes society, you get hypnotized as well and you try to find your niche and try to keep your identity and luckily there are groups like the Asian American Theater Company all over the country that help Asian American actors. But it takes a lot of work to keep doing that when in the mainstream things are so different.

You constantly do stuff to yourself. You do a commercial with a Caucasian actress and she's getting all the lines and so you kind of rationalize with yourself and say, okay at least I'm making money off of this. Then you start thinking, are they going to need that token—where's the token?

You start doing that because you want to work. You keep telling yourself that eventually there will be a lot of Asian American shows on TV like there are Caucasian shows and, now, a lot of African American shows. There will be that equality there someday, and I hope to be a part of that. I'm going to be even more honest in saying that you kind of save yourself from thinking, oh god I'm going to hit this brick wall forever by believing that, well if that trend happens, it won't be so bad that my time passed and now those shows are on. I feel good that I was a part of that trail. Truth is, I won't feel good. I want to be a part of that trail when things change.

As for a shelf life on looks, yes, absolutely there is one. But I think Asians have an advantage compared to other actors because Asians just look young. They really do, and they're so beautiful. You can really have a wide range in age for Asian women. I think it's harder for Caucasians.

I played more glamorous roles when I was playing theaters in San

Francisco. I didn't think about it then. I trained to play every kind of role. But when I first came down here I was told some really unkind and really hurtful things. I was told that I wasn't pretty enough or that I was just too Asian. A couple of agents said that, and some Asian actors who were just being real mean to me.

When I started doing commercials they said, "Oh, you're perfect for now" and I said, "Really," and they said, "Yeah, because now we're starting to look for real people." I'm like, okay, whatever. You start thinking there is a hierarchy of looks. I think it's slowly changing because more casting directors are coming from outside of L.A. and there are a lot more women casting directors. They see women as women. They see that you're an actress and they'll give you the opportunity.

Other people are stuck in that Hollywood way—like the real model way. I can't tell you since I moved down here how many times I've said to myself, I wish I were 5' 10" and had curly hair. You just do all this to yourself—I wish I had legs that just went on forever because you know that's what a lot of these women look like here. Whoever the biggest movie star is at the time, that's who the people cast; if an actress looks like Julia Roberts, or Alicia Silverstone, for instance. I'm sure one day there will be the new Winona Ryder or the new Jane Seymour. I just saw this lady on a commercial the other day. She looked just like Jane Seymour. So they have it fixed in their heads what the standard of beauty is, and for other roles they pick real people, which is odd. It's hard to live with.

I've talked to people who were in acting and then dropped out and moved on to other things because they said they couldn't take the rejection. If you are not making a living and you are constantly being rejected it does take its toll on you after awhile. My first year here I didn't know if I could stay. I mean not only because of the cruel way people put things but just the environment; it was so vicious.

I sure hope it will get better for me. I mean, I always feel a freedom in theater, but film and TV—I don't know. I sure hope that there's much more accessibility for everyone. I am crossing my fingers and hoping that with much more liberal direction and writing there will be greater opportunities not only in the major studios but in the independent market. It's just going to take the cooperation and vision of the writers and the producers.

When I think of the independent market I think of lower budgets but also a little more freedom of vision and choices made not so much on market value but on views based on beliefs of characters as human beings in their equality—realism.

I believe that it's only going to change when more Asians come into power in the industry. And I'm not sure how that's going to happen. There's a lot of Asians in producing now but I think that there needs to be more Asians in directing and writing and I think they need to nurture their own. Some Asians want to break into the mainstream and have nothing to do with Asians or Asian work. So once they get there they don't hire any other Asians.

But there are others and I think some Asian Americans are becoming part of the independent market and casting all Asians. With the growth of that I think it'll really help. I think that's the way it's going to work. It feels a lot more open than it used to be.

What is the power of media over who we are? I think about commercials and of how a lot of music videos get put together. There are a lot of subliminal images. It's a flashing thing. People get used to seeing the flash of an image and that's what they are. I think it applies to the Asian image too. Even if people know other people who are Asian, it's the flash image that sticks. This is clearly not limited to Asians, but that's the power that it has. The way things are edited and put together, the suggestions out there.

My hope is that all this work is going to be worth it, that it's going to pay off in a big way. It's true that at this point in time I ask myself questions like will I ever get to a stance that Kevin Costner, Jane Seymour or even Whoopi Goldberg has. I have to tell you I see the chances of it happening as a little less than four years ago when I first came here.

I was so idealistic then. Hollywood! Palm trees! Hollywood was the best thing that ever happened to me, that's what I thought. It was so big. They had so many restaurants everywhere; everything was so accessible. But looking at the big picture now what I hope to be is different. I didn't know what to expect when I came here but now I look at things more realistically. What I see happening in ten years, or who I want to end up being is very different. I guess after a while you just feel a little raw.

Sharon Iwai

Sharon Iwai was born in Honolulu, and moved to California at age 11. She has been acting for 15 years, and has been in such films as the Village of the Damned, A Great Wall, *and* The Kiss. *She has also appeared in close to two dozen Asian American Theater Company productions.*

On Performing

When I performed on-stage in the past, there's a certain feeling I have just before going on. I own that role, that night. And there's nothing like that feeling of power.

It's so unlike anything I grew up with, as far as being Asian American. Every time I perform and go out there knowing that I have the power to command this group just with my energy, I feel anything is possible.

That's why I can't leave it. It keeps feeding me with this awareness of who I am and what I can do.

Sharon Iwai

Taking the Plunge

When I was about 13 I got this flash about acting. I love to watch the movies, and I would dream about what it would be like to be that person doing a role. I kept it a secret, because I knew it was a "silly" thing to want to do in a Japanese family. So I kind of kept that to myself, but I kept dreaming.

I took up speech in high school. The teacher used to be a radio announcer. The speech class used to put on these performances twice a year, and I was really anxious to be part of it, but usually only the advanced students got to do any kind of solo work or extensive performing. And so I kind of waited a little bit and watched everyone, and I finally got a chance to do a solo. It was more like an oral interpretation. It was really exciting. The speech shows were pretty elaborate. The instructor was also the director, and so he treated it as if we were actually going into performance. Not just standing up there doing a speech but actually performing. We had all of our costumes, and we had minimal sets and props, and we had a really great time. Just before I graduated, I did *Medea*, a monologue where she is talking to herself about killing her children.

I loved a lot of the classical plays: I loved Shakespeare. So when I got to college, I was studying Shakespeare, but this reality of being an actor, well, it's still a dream because it just seemed so impractical and my parents were looking at me like, Oh, it'll pass.

I was always into creative arts and I was always drawing from the time I was very little. I always planned to study art in college. And I did. Just to make my parents happy, I pretended that I wanted to be an art teacher.

But I kept going around the drama department, looking into classes to take. I did a lot of Shakespeare. I took about two or three acting classes—not very many. I rarely found any Asians in the drama department, so I was really intimidated by that. You could just count them on one hand. So I just took the classes and stayed on the periphery. I think the biggest encouragement I got was when my acting instructor made us all do a scene from *Romeo and Juliet* just before she takes the poison. He had every woman there do the scene. I did my scene and he told me that was one of the finest Juliets he's ever seen.

So that really boosted me a lot, and I sort of held that appraisal with me. I continued to audition for these small studio productions they would have. There was a rehearsal process and then you would actually have a performance, usually just for the students and the teachers. I auditioned for this one role in *No Exit*, a sad play. She's the lesbian in the trio of characters. It was the first time that I really, really wanted this role. I just kind of went aggressively at it, and so I just pushed all my fears aside and went for it.

It turned out that the acting teacher who I had before, who knew my work, was also the directing teacher. This was all done with student directors. He suggested me to the students who were directing, so I got cast in it. And oh, that was a real high, because the scene lasted for about 45 minutes—it was an incredibly long scene—I got to be angry, and I got to be insulting and a bitch and seductive. The character just goes through all ranges of emotions and it was just packed with all kinds of goodies for an actor.

So I did that, and I was getting a lot of good comments, and all this meant a lot to me because students are telling me they like it. It just gave me a good feeling about my ability.

But then I went ahead and I just got my art degree, and I never got a theater degree. The desire to act stayed with me, even though I got married and I didn't do any acting for that period. It was quite a while before I actually thought, "Well, am I going to do it or not?" All of this desire and ambition—I just kind of put it aside because it seemed impractical. How many Asians do you see up there playing roles? And you very rarely see them in movies.

It's just such a stupid thing to want to do this, but I really wanted it, so I watched a lot of Masterpiece Theater, a lot of the British television, and I really admired the actors there. They were so precise, and so full in their roles. So I studied them constantly—TV, movies. Glenda Jackson was one of my real heroines. I loved everything she did. She was so good— she wasn't beautiful, but she was so interesting to watch all the time.

Then I moved to South City [California] and had a regular job in graphics. I thought, I'm really close to San Francisco and I know that Asian American theater is there.

This was in the late seventies. I was really curious about Asians who wanted to do theater because I never heard of it before. So I stopped for some brochures and I was just kind of looking around, poking around— I was really interested in what they were doing.

They were having their classes at AATC, so it was a nice environment. It got me, and I had to keep pursuing it, because it had been so long since I actually performed. I thought, I can't let this die, because it's not going to die. It's going to keep burning up in me.

So when I took these classes at the Asian American Theater Company I thought, this was really a different kind of situation because these were all Asians, and they were all interested in the things that I was interested in. It made me really think about myself in a different way because I always thought of my ambition for acting in terms of a white audience, a white industry; being judged by white standards.

This was just a real eye-opener for me. I kind of discovered who I was and where I fit in. I didn't have to choose not to do it just because I was Asian in a white culture. Meeting all these other people at the theater—and they were all different Asians: Chinese, Japanese, Filipino—they were all so committed. I met some great people there. And I always think very, very fondly of that theater.

Before AATC I had to follow white role models and I had to follow their style. I had to present myself thinking in terms of what they would accept. Everything that I did had to be dependent on how they were going to view me as a performer.

IMAGE AND SELF IMAGE

The acting field is an image-making field. If you go into the business of the movies and put yourself out there as an image, you have to feel really confident that you're sure about what you are.

I'm not saying that all actors are, or that all the people in the business are. I think that they probably aren't, but they sure appear to be, often enough. And I just felt like I was at a disadvantage often, because I didn't have the white mindset. I grew up in a different way, and there's always that difference that I felt I had to have; that difference to the white image-making value system. When I got to AATC, I started to see we could create our own image in America. It's an American Asian image. Once I saw that in just the people I met and the goals they had, it just opened a lot of blocks. It just took them away, actually. You could dream bigger, and you could dream that anything is possible, which is how I like to think it is.

It's a struggle. I mean, the reality is that you still have to struggle with this image-making society, where the images are predominantly white and young. But it's possible now. And seeing so many Asians working in all aspects of the industry, it just made me think, the sky's the limit. It made me think of myself in a different way, not just in acting, but in art, in anything that I tried to do. It is very significant to me.

Before that the possibilities looked very limited. The only roles for me were on a meek, subservient level, because those were the only images of Asians I saw in movies. That's what the big difference was. And it wasn't my image of myself. It's like I had to keep 75 percent of myself hidden, and only present the 25 percent that, you know, has to get along with the good American society as a whole; predominantly white-owned.

By the time I left college, I felt pretty good about who I was—artistically. I felt like I had something to say, but I was still intimidated enough, graduating and going into the larger world, because I knew this industry was really harsh. It's the one industry where they can tell you, "What you are doing here? We're not even looking for Asians!" And you'd just have to eat it if they said that to you, so I was kind of afraid of trying it outside of college.

Just before I graduated, the two really significant characters I played were not really Asian roles. I did another production where I played Stella from *Streetcar*. It was just great doing people. Just having a people role instead of an Asian one.

Today, the difference for me is that if I go after a role that's not specifically Asian, I will give it the full weight of being Asian in it, as well as the character itself—the particular person involved. That's how much working with other Asians and seeing so many Asians in the industry has changed my attitudes.

There's also a lot of support. For example, say if a major film comes to town in a casting, and they have maybe a couple of roles that are for Asians in there—supporting cast. Generally the Asian performers will be bonded when it's working with a producer who's white.

It's a different thing though, when it's an Asian film. When it's Asian-directed, Asian-produced, then we get real competitive with each other.

So then, you have all of this, "Well, I have to keep certain secrets to myself because I can't give too much away or I won't get cast." Then the usual human emotions start coming into play; you start bitching about other people, just like you would anybody else.

Why is there a difference? Sometimes it's their take on the role and sometimes, you think, "Is this person really going to know—especially if they're casting for an Asian part—enough about nuances to even know whether they're casting the right person?" It's those kinds of things. I suppose every kind of ethnic group has the sort of feeling, "How could you possibly understand what it's like to be Asian when you're not one?"

In varying degrees, when Asian performers go for these auditions, and they see the band of white people [directors, etc.] sitting on the other side they feel, "We're on this side, we're in this group, and we are kind of together here." Even though we are competing for the role, that's a different issue. It's like family stuff. As opposed to outside the family.

So in this community of Asians that I do a lot of stage work with, you run the gamut of relationships and emotions; everything that a family will go through, except it's geared for performance. The thing about theater that always is so satisfying is that it's like a joint effort, everything is so focused, everybody puts out so much energy just to make it work.

And even if you have only five people in the audience, you still go out there, thinking, "Tonight's going to be a good show." And you go out there and you just perform … and when you have so many people in the cast all believing the same thing, there's really a different energy at work there that's hard to repeat anywhere else.

I think this is why so many actors like working on shows and films. There's something happening over here in front of the camera, but there's a lot of bonding going on behind.

When you have all Asians working on the same show, you get along pretty well, even though you have spats here and there. Ultimately it all comes together right on opening night. That's a fantastic feeling. I got a lot of that when I was working at Asian American. Real special.

Every show is different, because you work with different people. You get close to some people, and you never want to work with others again. And you get to know where people's flaws are, and if you really want to take advantage of them, you can move in on them too. There's some of that going on, and it's very competitive.

As for roles I've had: By the time I got enough experience, got my union cards, and was able to go out for commercials I was sort of in an age range. This was an aspect I didn't think about when I wanted to be an actor, but it hits a woman really quick.

At 35, you can be placed in a certain age range and stereotyped real fast. Whenever I was called for an audition, it was because they wanted an older woman or mother or grandmother. Sometimes, I got called for being a news anchor—in fact, I did a little industrial for that—that was kind of fun.

I get a lot of calls for mothers, not too much for grandmothers, especially on films, because generally they want you to be older. It puts me in sort of a weird place now, which is another reason I haven't been acting that much. I'm in an age range now where you don't see too many roles for women 40–50. There are roles for women in their thirties, but not so much 40, 45, to 50 or 55.

FUTURE PLANS

In this period where I haven't been acting so much, I've been trying to think of what I can do to get more control. The only way I can think of doing that is by writing, acting, and making a film myself. Or at least writing and performing, and trying to get people who are interested in making something.

I'm not thinking on a feature film or anything like that. I'm just trying to work everything out. I'm thinking of maybe along the line of a short film.

As for being an Asian American actress and opportunities, I still think it's fewer than what a white actor could do. But it's become less significant in that if your attitudes change and you don't think that you have to be molded by what they think you should be, then you can create your own opportunities.

I think there are a lot of opportunities for young Asian Americans—men and women. Especially the ways things are now, I've seen more and more young people, Asian people, in different roles, small roles, big roles. At least they're out there. But because I'm running into that age thing now, there's still not enough roles for women who are in that age range from 35–55. And the filmmakers have had a lot to do with putting the Asian image up there, so people can see it and get used to it, so that you can get more Asian images out there.

So I think there's more opportunity out there now, but I think it's namely if you're younger. The problem's across the board for white women as well—but it's even worse if you're ethnic. African American women seem to be creeping in there a lot more, but then, they've been in the business longer too.

So I think that Asians being in the business is sort of new—it's still seems to be sort of a new idea. I think there's a lot of people in the industry that just sort of have to get used to it because I don't think we're going to leave.

A LACK OF ROLES FOR ASIANS

I haven't done too much theater lately, because the roles that I have been offered over the last four years have pretty much been the roles I've played before. They're generally mothers, varying in ages of mothers. As I get older, mothers get older. Then it goes to grandmothers. I've played grandmothers. I don't really like playing them over and over again, and theater takes a lot of energy. If you don't love the role, love the character you're playing, it's really hard to keep that energy up.

As for Asian American actresses, I don't know too many who are in my age range, I don't know too many. There's just a lack of roles. And I think that in order to get cast again, you have to wait until you're older-looking actually—character actors. Sixty-five to seventy, maybe, you might get cast more often in that age range than you would from 40–55 or 60. And I think it's because no one is writing for women at that middle age range. I guess that's the age range I would hit, because it's really a shame. Women at that age are so much fuller. They've seen a lot more, they've experienced a lot more. They have a lot of ideas about who they are, and in fact, they're more sure about who they are, and they have a lot of power.

But they never get to exercise that power, and this is what I would to see. I would want to see more examples of that, beyond having more Asian American faces out there. That's great, but I would love to see women in that age range out there being very strong women, because I think there are a lot of strong women.

I would measure success at this point if I could write and act in a short film. That would be a really great success for me, because I've kind of learned, from when I came back to theater, and I was doing theater at Asian American, that I look for the goals that are reachable and it usually leads to something bigger.

If I just keep focusing on what I really feel confident I can handle, then it usually opens doors. This would make me very happy if I could do this. And if it opens up any doors beyond that, then that would be great. But this is what I'm thinking of doing right now.

As for the possibility of an Asian American superstar—I think it's there. How about the issue of race? I could see a superstar being half–Asian and half-white. That maybe is more plausible, I think than a full-blooded Asian. Why? Physical appearance, mostly. It's a very image-conscious industry. I think the Asian person who makes it as a superstar would have to have extraordinary looks. I'm not sure if you could just do it on pure energy. I think it has to do something with your physical looks, because it's a business of image making, and the person has to have something extraordinary.

Why do I stay in the business? I think it's the excitement, the sense of power. The energy that you can exchange with other kinds of actors is really special too because whenever you get on-stage, it's like you're naked. Your emotions are bare and you're going to have to trust that other person on stage to make it work. When that happens it's pretty fantastic. When you really link with another actor and you know there's this energy going back and forth and you know the audience is with you, that's really an amazing feeling. There's all this energy and this power, and it's just— nothing like it. Actually I've never supported myself fully by acting. I've always had a job. Now I work as a graphic designer, and do acting on the side. That's my passion. Last year I didn't have roles. The year before, I had a movie. I played an optometrist. Great little role, I got to scream, get my eyes burned up. It's a horror film. That was a real competitive one, too. I was really surprised when I got it. A lot of people I knew wanted it too. It wasn't an Asian-specific role. Latinos, Filipinos and some Caucasians tried for it too. It was mixed. It was open, just wide open. It one of those nice roles, like, "Wow, it's open!"

Is success in a mainstream way important? I don't think so, because I think I measure success by how I feel about myself. And if I feel real good about what I'm doing, and I feel like I've accomplished a lot, then that's success. I don't think there's anything that can beat that.

I've always been interested in movies, and that's the direction I've wanted to go. The stage, while it had some exciting moments, is kind of limited in a sense. You can't do some of the creations that I have in my mind. Film is really subtle. You can do a different kind of acting with film, and I've always considered myself more of a subtle actor. When you're on-stage, you have to be a lot larger. And there's a lot of thinking that's going on when you're playing a character. All of that can be read through a camera, and that is what really interests me more in acting.

A lot of the auditions I've attended have been frustrating in that they hardly have any meat in them. When you look over the lines before your audition, you think, "Wow, what can I create out of this?" I mean, you're just asking for a glass of water or something like that. It's pretty minimal and there's not much you can invest in it.

I think the only reason actors keep going into that is because it keeps you active in the business itself. It gets your name known to agents and casting directors. I did it a lot, thinking that's the way to get into the business and to be seen and all this. But I guess this is why I haven't been going out for much because I've done it. After a while I just got tired of getting all my energy up for this little spot thing that I probably wouldn't get anyway. It's kind of demeaning, you know. You have to get in there to get all pumped up for one line and that's all that you can shoot for. You go to countless auditions and after awhile, you're just tired of it, so I guess I just stopped going to them. I'd rather put my energy somewhere else. I was just kind of picking and choosing. My agent wouldn't call me for that, and I guess as a result, he doesn't call me much at all because that's all that seems to be out there.

Success and Future Goals

Success to me does not mean making a lot of money, being in some mainstream film—you know that'd be nice—but I still want to do it my own way. I don't want to have to compromise even more on these stupid little one-line auditions just to be in the same place—so that when the role comes up, maybe you might get. I'd rather spend my time creating something myself.

I love San Francisco, so it would be very hard for me to move. But I had thought about L.A. at one point, and I just couldn't deal with that lifestyle out there. It's so superficial and I just don't think of myself that way. I'm just going to have to create myself if I'm going to have to do it at all.

Am I a character type? I can be. Actually, some of the roles that I've enjoyed more than any have been comic roles, and it's a great feeling when the audience laughs. It's really wonderful, and I really have a lot of fun.

I can see myself playing roles as I get older and as I get more into the kind of character look that's out there, but I don't know. I really think that the future is more in terms of what I want to do with my acting right now, how I want to mold it, how I want to create it.

When I think of the future, I don't think of it as the mainstream control. I'd like to think in terms of what I'm going to do, so I try to think pretty much in the present. As far as short term goals, this is what I want to work on right now, this is what I want to create, this is where my energy is going to be focused. And I'll just go with that, and if takes me somewhere, great. But if it doesn't—I've done it and I'll just move from that point on.

I think I get bored too easily, that's why, I have to keep being stimulated. Even with the visual arts, I have to keep moving into different areas and thinking of different ideas.

Were there roles I wouldn't have played as an Asian woman? I think one movie called *Taipan*. Joan Chen played that role and I was cringing when I saw her because it was so stereotyped. I thought that that is really not the direction I'd like to see an Asian actress go because it's just going to reinforce that image of the Asian woman as the exotic, kittenish woman who would do whatever her man wants her to do. That's one role that really kind of sticks in my head.

But then some of the roles have changed. When I saw *The Wash*, I thought that was a beautiful piece. I love the fact that these were people, and they had a life that was just filled with a lot of conflict. It was just wonderful to be able to see actors do more than be the race, basically, just a face. So that's—I think that's moving ahead.

I see a lot of young Asian roles where it's just beautiful people type of roles, but I'm not sure if that's particularly just Asian, because I've seen that with just about every race.

Often I see a lot of roles where the action goes to like a Chinatown or something, and you see a stereotypical shopkeeper—a woman and a man. That's pretty stereotyped too. It would be nice if that could change, but then they don't ever give them enough lines or scripts to show anything else. So, I don't know, I keep seeing that.

I get disappointed, but, disappointed to a degree. It's just that it's not different and we've made advances in a lot of different aspects. But there's still a lot of the old stuff that's hanging on there. It seems that I see a lot of the older people in the stereotyped kind of roles more than I do younger people.

Looking back at my life, I'm glad I went into acting. I think if I hadn't gone back into acting after that long period (after college), I would've been a very disappointed person. I dropped it for ten years.

As for race, I think it will always be there. But I don't think it has to be a negative thing because if I meet someone, or if someone sees me onstage, I want them to know that I'm Asian, but I don't want that to be the major thing. I want them to see the full person, and being Asian is a good part of me. It's a certain attitude that I really had reinforced when I was working with other Asian actors.

Would art ever transcend race to a point that no one is racially distinguishable and everyone would look at the pure art form? Well, looking at the way things are now, I think it would be very difficult. There's a lot of things that have to be in place before people could be that free in our attitudes. I think it'd be great if you kept trying, but I don't know how it would come off. I'd like to see that happen, but the way things are now, I can't see that happening.

I'm happy that I'm looking to a new direction, because I think we need to have Asians out there thinking on that line too, especially women, because there are just not enough out there.

Karen Lee

Karen Lee has been an actor for about ten years. She majored in theater arts at San Francisco State University, and attended classes at the American Conservatory Theater. Most of her work has been in nonprofit theater and corporate video. (She is not related to Karen Tsen Lee of New York.)

ACTING EXPERIENCES

I think being an Asian American actor makes you fluctuate between having the same kinds of dreams as any other actor does in the types of roles you want to play and in the success that you see yourself having. Then the flip side of it is just sort of being really disillusioned either when you watch movies or when you go through the audition process and then seeing what kinds of roles you are even offered or allowed to read for. So at least for me personally I kind of go through the highs and lows of feeling very limited or not.

The bulk of the work I've done is in smaller, nonprofit or even fringed type of theater and then some commercial work. Certainly people would like to have a lot more commercial work than there is in this area but it's quite limited, and especially more limited for actors of color.

In terms of tiers, the American Conservatory Theater and Berkeley Repertory Theater are the highest theaters in the Bay area. I haven't worked in those theaters but I have been working in some of the lower, midsized theaters. The Asian American Theater Company in San Francisco is one of four in the country and that's where I've done probably half of my work.

I think for a lot of actors, especially actors of color, including Asian Americans, you are doing midsized theater; you are doing a lot of new stuff because there are a lot of new Asian American playwrights.

I'm not a full-time actor in the sense that I can pay all my bills with it. I don't do it forty hours a week. Right now I'm taking a break. I'm going to school; I'm taking some classes. It's pretty tough in this area to make a living in acting. I've done like office work, secretarial work, things like that.

The last theater piece I did was a show that was with the Asian American Theater Company. Last summer I did my first, sort of, independent, full length film which was shot in the East bay which I don't even know if it's been edited yet or so, that was a bigger project that I did.

The filmmaker was this young guy and it was his first film. It was a really passionate project for him because he had been working on getting the money to make it and the script for a long time. I think it was semi-autobiographical about his college experiences. The lead character was this young man in college who was torn between his sexual identity and all these other types of things. The character I played was supposed to be this woman that he becomes involved with on campus and the character was actually supposed to be Eurasian. It was the first time that I've actually played a character with that kind of background so it was a unique experience in that way.

My father is Chinese and my mother is Swiss. I spoke Swiss-German for some time when I was younger. My father is second generation from Hawaii. My grandparents spoke Chinese but none of the next generation picked it up.

I have an agent for commercial work which is what people have agents for—anything that's on camera: national commercials, or movie parts, or the corporate films that I was talking about.

The commercial work that I've done has not been extensive. Most of what I have played has been designated as Asian American roles. A lot of the commercial roles are standard where you are playing very public roles or a business person or something like that. I've played a businesswoman maybe a handful of times. In commercial work the stuff that you're going to get called in for as an Asian American female actor is not going to be a lead role. It's going to be something that's sort of like a side type role. Like in a corporate film you might play somebody's boss but you're not going to be the center of what the product is about.

Do I like what I do? For the most part. I have my ups and downs and I never know when I'm going to slump, which I haven't done recently. I've been taking other classes, I've been doing other things, I never know whether I'm tired of being an actor or whether I'm going through one of those actor/artist type of phases, where either you're not doing anything or you're not doing anything that you're satisfied with so you don't like being an actor at that point in your life.

I think my idea of success as an actress is being able to do projects that I feel are high quality that I feel satisfied with the work. You know, I think that you're definition of success probably changes over the years, like with anybody in any profession.

I think when you first start acting you just want to do it and whatever else you can. I think when you're young too, you think of success as making a bunch of money and getting well known for anything that you're doing. But having been an actor and having gotten work and having been in projects where I feel unsatisfied by it—even though it might be something where it might be looked at as having been successful—you know, I think my definition of success has changed.

Being Asian defines a lot of what you do. You're limited to the types of roles that you can get being an Asian American person trying to be an actor and in Hollywood, especially. But I think even in theater which is thought of being a little more alternative or progressive there are a lot of limitations if you're not a Caucasian actor.

The things that you are getting an opportunity to read for the things that people are going to see you as, define what you do much more so than people in any other profession. Whether it's racism or whatever kind of racial awareness—in hiring practices—you're never really sure how much that has to do with getting a job in a lot of professions. But when you're an actor it's one of those professions where you get called in to read a part because you are Asian or you're not allowed to read for a part because you are Asian, so it's clear cut.

I can't imagine anybody who would say they are okay with that. In general you're not going to get a shot at the lead roles in most projects unless it's an Asian American piece. Try to name some movies where you've seen Asian American actors or actresses in lead roles that are not Asian specific.

I don't think I've developed an exact theory for why that's the case. It's probably a lot combination of things. Part of it is that Asian Americans as a culture have not embraced the arts. So part of it can fall back on Asian American culture itself because we are still a small part of the population that's not that big of an influence on society in general.

I don't think it's overt racism like they're thinking oh, we don't want an Asian American, or an African American. That doesn't even enter their mind. But if somebody were to suggest how about Joan Chen for that role, then they'd take that step back—and think that's not really the type that we were looking for.

Nontraditional Casting

The Bay area theater circuit from what I know of it is really known for casting a good percentage of nontraditional roles, nontraditional acting—having an actor of color play the role of Hamlet. The minority of times that I have done that, I've probably done that a few, I don't even know if it's been a handful of times, I think from what I could remember, they usually bring fairly large casts and they're usually a lot of Caucasians and they add some people of color. And they have definitely been small roles for Asians, roles in which it might not bother somebody too much to see a nonwhite actor in.

Do I feel a lot of these good roles are shut out to me because I'm Asian American? Yes. Not necessarily Shakespearean roles. I guess it sort of comes back to whatever the lead roles are; lead roles are basically reserved for white actors in film, in television, in stage.

The majority of Asian roles, I mean I can't give you a number like ninety percent or whatever, but the majority of roles that Asian American actors end up playing is I'd say are the '90s version of the house boy or whatever other stereotype that existed fifty years ago. I haven't seen that change much in the last ten years.

How do actors deal with it? Acknowledging it as a condition is one thing, and accepting it as something that's never going to change is something else. I don't think I have the belief that things are going to change so drastically in the next ten or fifteen years that doors are going to open for me if I just hang in there and keep acting. I think the shelf life of an actor that's an Asian American woman is something like that similar to a model's career. I would like to think that that will change somehow someday, but I don't see it changing in the near future. I think part of my dilemma with it is that I've never felt very much, personality wise with the characters that I've seen myself doing. The kind of parts that Asian American women are asked to read for I've never identified heavily with so that in itself feels like a little restriction there. And how much that has to do with the fact that I go up and down in acting I don't know; I'm sure it's a big part of it. Still, I'd like to keep acting for as long as I can.

So how do I survive in an industry where there really aren't any role models? Well that makes it even more difficult. Having a role model or having someone you can follow at least provides a path or map to imitate. But when there's nothing that you can achieve or imitate or something to resemble in any way then you're just searching.

I've sort of had to keep myself going. I'm not making a ton of money, I'm not doing any projects all the time that I like being called for. I think I've just developed this attitude for myself that it's just this journey I'm going through, and if I get really tired of it, I stop and I'll stop for good one day. I think you sort of adjust to what it is you want out of it.

What I want out of it would be to make a living at it. Although I know this may sound pessimistic—to make a living out of it and at the same time to do work that you're very satisfied with as an Asian American actor is probably a pretty tall order—but as close as I could get to that as possible.

That's why I take acting classes occasionally, or I'll take audition workshops just to keep myself going, and I take breaks too. I've been taking a break for awhile and I concentrate on just one kind of work. I think mostly what keeps me going is just other stuff that I like to do in my non–acting related life.

How do I think my experience differs from a white actress? I don't know how the odds are against every white woman just based on how many roles there are and the number of people going up for them. At least for me, I feel that as an Asian American actor, no matter what the numbers are, I am limited to a certain extent. A Caucasian actress who is twenty-six years old and blond is not going to be allowed to read for a character who is a red head and forty-five. Every actor has limitations based on physical appearance. But I think when you add race into the mix, that's a real limitation that's placed on you from outside. That's a real struggle that a white actor doesn't face.

Why do I stay on? I've thought about that a lot over the last few years and I think part of the reason is I do see myself as an artist. I just think I have that kind of personality for whatever reason. Someday I'll find another way or form to express that, which will be more gratifying, or maybe I won't. For the last ten years this is the form that I have chosen so I think that in part is a very independent, somewhat spiritual journey that doesn't encompass all the race stuff. It's the independent part of it that really keeps me going. When it comes to race in general I think there's what you identify yourself as—a human being—and then there's what you define yourself as in the context of the environment in which you live. Living in the United States in 1997, especially as an actor, race is a really important part of that. In any profession I think it is big, no matter what you do. So part of waking up every day as someone living in this country—there's who you are, and then there's dealing with the race issue. Some people don't deal with it at all.

It's hard not to dwell on it in the sense that it affects the work that you are able to do and the kind of abilities you have as an individual. As an actor of color you can be aware of the kinds of limitations that have been placed on you, but you can't let those limitations from the outside affect the ability that you know you have, and I think that's one of the dangers.

Things just have to be more color blind and people just have to be judged by their craft but it's not going to happen any time soon, just like it's not going to happen within the American culture. I think racism is a really, really big issue right now that a lot of people are turning a blind eye to in general.

I don't talk to any other family members about this. I think it's hard to express to a lot of people who are outside the business what the acting profession means to you because there are so many misconceptions about what it is to be an actor and so many preconceived ideas. To most people, your average man on the street, being an actor is like Hollywood. On top of that, being an actor of color, there are so many subtleties and difficulties you go through that it's almost not worth talking about with someone from the outside.

What I would say to young people about the acting profession if they were going into it as Asian Americans? I'd tell them that it was a very hard thing they were going to undertake. I wouldn't say don't do it because I think we're led by a lot of other forces too. But I would just say to really identify what it is you really want out of it and try not to be affected by the limitations imposed on you. Develop your craft as much as you can and be confident in that—to own that—and to be confident in that. It takes a certain personality. You have to be able to let that stuff roll off your back, which I think actors struggle with all the time too.

Do I think there really are shades of changes happening for Asian American actors? That's the thing, they're shades. It's very small, small steps that we're taking. I was reading, and I don't remember who was it that wrote this—I think it was a white writer—it was something about race relations and he referred to Asian Americans at one point as probationary whites. Asian Americans seem very marginalized on the outside. Yet they seem to have assimilated to a point where I think of them either as first generation immigrants, or third or fourth generation Asian Americans who have blended into white society and have become a part of it without really having their own separate voice, identity and power.

How long will I stay in this business? It could be for the rest of my life and it could be for just months—six months. I'd say for at least a few years more. I guess it will depend on how much I want to do it. I mean if I find myself really enjoying my life, doing something else, with this incredible passion for something else then there would be no point in doing something that doesn't completely satisfy me.

What drives me is probably a combination of things. The fact that I have been doing it for a long time builds on itself, where I think, I can't stop now. It's almost like a race where you've run eight miles in a ten mile race and you want to make it to the finish line. Also it's my artistic expression. Probably a combination of those two things.

The finish line might be if I turned around one day and feel I have no desire to do this anymore and something else is calling me. I'm still chasing something, definitely. I don't know, maybe it's just a feeling that I get sometimes. I remember somebody coming up to me after a show that I had done and it was a character that I didn't really enjoy playing that much. I remember not identifying with all that much, but somebody said, that was like my life. I can't believe that, you sort of seemed to know everything I was thinking. I remember not feeling particularly moved or anything but it's a comment that I've remembered for years and years. So maybe it's just that feeling you get every once in awhile, that you realize you've made an impact on somebody. I think that's why artists crave what it is they do. They feel that that's their way of making contact with other human beings in some way.

Would it be any easier if I were a white actor? I can't say for sure that it would be. I certainly wouldn't have the same kind of limitations, but I don't know. I could be a white actor who's been out of work. As hard as it is to be an Asian American actor, you can bond with other Asian Americans in a way that other white actors can't with others. You feel you do have a certain, stronger link to a certain culture from which you want to express things, so that's hard to say. I don't know if I'd be any happier— I'd probably just have different problems.

6

Veteran Actors in California

Lane Nishikawa

Lane Nishikawa appears to be in his early 40s. He is an actor, writer, director, and served as the artistic director of the Asian American Theater Company in San Francisco for eight years. For the past 18 years he has been involved as actor, writer, director, and dramaturg in over 55 productions at AATC. He has written various plays, among them: Mifune and Me, *a one-man show about Asian American images in the media;* I'm on a Mission from Buddha; *and* The Gate of Heaven. *He has various film and television credits, with the bulk of his work in theater.*

Lane is third generation Japanese American, born in Hawaii and raised in San Francisco. He started out in the 1970s writing and performing his own street poetry for audiences at street fairs and even San Quentin prison. After his first dramatic role in theater, he said everything fell into place and he knew acting was what he wanted to pursue.

WORKING IN THEATER

Why did I choose to concentrate on theater? Well, it's not that I choose it; I have done the ten years of going back and forth to Los Angeles and all of that. I don't want to be just a martial arts actor in film. All the plays that I have done are truthful. They're meaningful. We communicate to an audience our experience as Asian Americans in this country. They need a different opinion of who we are. I play supporting and lead roles on stage.

When you go on an audition for Hollywood, there are no plays that even have any kind of substance. Every once in a while, a film will come by; I've auditioned for many of them, and I've been in the running for many of them. I was even very close to one. It was a television miniseries that I really wanted to be in. The director said, "You have a lot of things going against you as an Asian man when your voice is too low. You have a voice that any theater actor would kill for, but for these guys, the producers I'm bringing you in

Lane Nishikawa

front of, they're gonna tell you you're voice is too low for them. They don't picture this guy, this Asian guy, as having such a low voice. You're also a little bit tall. You also have to shave that mustache of yours and get your hair cut. Think about the time. It takes place in 1940. Get some wire-rimmed glasses." He says, "You gotta look weak. You're too strong. You enter a room, you take it over. You can't do that." I said "okay." So, I did all those things. Cut my hair, got some glasses, shaved my mustache, walked in there, tried to make my voice higher—but it didn't work. I didn't get cast. The director called me and said, "I was pushing for you, but the producers went with another guy." I knew then that I wasn't what Hollywood wanted. I'm not half white like Russell Wong. I'm cut from a different cloth, I guess. I know martial arts, but it's not on the same level as Jason Scott Lee.

They got those guys, which is fine, and, to me, to do any one of my shows that are good in front of 500 students at the University of Chicago is worth more than my being a day player and getting paid for maybe one line.

Americans don't look for a strong, Asian American man, not really. I bet Hollywood wouldn't know what to do with Asian actors, they really don't.

Why do I think it's so? It's a racist country. It's a racist business.

Is the racism driven by racism, or is it tied more to box office receipts and money? I think it's a combination. If you look at other minorities, they have been able to rise, that's for certain. But it's been a lot of hard work, and it's also been a lot of exploitation on the part of Hollywood.

Black Americans have a very strong political voice, so that combination with strong images, like Michael Jordan, Tiger Woods, along with political clout and box office drawings have helped. They haven't figured this out with Asians yet.

With women, it's a different story. With men, it's I think, the combination of all the wars we've had with Asia that have made Asians look like the enemy. That's an image that is very hard to get over. Also, we as Asian Americans in this country don't have the political voice. Additionally, the numbers aren't there yet for the mega box office support. So it's a combination of factors.

But then I think this is all theory, it's Hollywood's theory. Take for example, *The Gate of Heaven* [written by Nishikawa]. It's about a Japanese American soldier who saves a Jewish survivor during the war. It played in the Old Globe of San Diego, one of the biggest theaters, if not the biggest theater of San Diego, to packed houses. It wasn't a Jewish or Japanese audience, but a mainstream America which came to see the play. We also staged it at Ford Theater in Washington, D.C., where Lincoln got shot. I mean, it's just theatergoers coming to see the play. If there's a story with substance and meaning and affects people, then they will come.

But Hollywood wouldn't give it a chance. If you say, "I have this play that could be made into a film, I have this other book that we could do something with..." they're gonna say, "Well, is it a bestseller?" They're gonna put up everything they can before they're going to truly give you their time.

ASIAN IMAGES IN MEDIA

Over the years we've taken a lot of shots as Asian Americans in the terms of media, which perpetuate a very negative, weak, dangerous stereotype of who Asian Americans are. And every time I'm out there doing a show, I'm up against it.

We've grown up with certain images: a woman wants a blond, blue-eyed Ken, and a man wants a busty, blonde Barbie. We, even in our own communities, have to deal with it. So you can imagine what your average person on the street thinks of that; what the ultimate partner should be. Asian women are a little bit higher than Asian men, when it comes to perception. But it is because of positive images of women.

When I'm talking about images I'm not just talking about acting images, but what also supports those images. I mean, the fact is you can turn on almost any station in the country and see a woman broadcaster, which is a strong, positive, legitimate image. Whereas that is not the case with Asian men. At most they might be in a Macy's ad; that might be a positive image, I guess, I don't know.

On the negative side look at the fact that one of the most prevalent images of the Vietnam War involved Asians as enemies who tortured you, killed you, killed your sons, your fathers; these films were huge hits. And it's still going on today. I mean the fact that a guy like Sylvester Stallone can kill 500 of us in two hours, that's pretty amazing.

Look at the film *Year of the Dragon*. San Francisco has a pretty good Chinatown and I know a lot of the Chinatown guys. It's a laugh, you know how the men came off as gangsters and thugs. That was Hollywood's image rather than the reality of who we were. Asian women had a pretty bad image in the film too—there's an Asian news reporter who ends up with Mickey Rourke! At least she survived and wasn't killed off in the end.

But it's not to say that all the roles for Asian women are great either; there are terrible Asian women's roles. Look at *Miss Saigon*. I never hear complaints about the fact that Jonathan Pryce was cast as this Asian guy— the lead role—in the first Broadway production. It's about an Asian woman who falls in love with this American soldier, gets pregnant, he goes away, so she kills herself. Nobody talks about it in that way. I mean, as an Asian woman, how do you feel about that, how would you want your daughter to think about that?

It's about the lack of self-worth of Asians. The images out there are constantly reinforcing this.

If you tracked film or television during prime time for a couple of months looking at the number of Hollywood releases which cast Asians as cops—you won't see very many. Maybe you'll have an Asian cop some-where but he probably won't have any lines. Perhaps you might find a coroner, because we're "supposed to be" very scientific and very good with, you know, analyzing. But definitely there will be a female Asian reporter. What I'm saying is the roles are going to be pretty small—way down the line in the terms of supporting roles. You don't even get to supporting roles.

Although I have to admit B.D. Wong's appearance as a marine in the film *Executive Decision* was a nice, contemporary breakthrough. But then I can't think of any other Asian male doing that in the last year. Actually, I think that's about it for the whole year. When you think that Hollywood puts out over 400 major films a year, and maybe there was one Asian cast in a role like B.D.'s in *Executive Decision*, it kind of shows you the reality of the business.

Asian men and women actors have to deal with all the various issues of race on a daily basis. Their masculinity, their exoticism, are questioned every day, every audition they go out on. They have to deal with characters that have no character whatsoever. It's almost like this mindless, heartless, senseless face. And that's what you audition for because those are the characters that are relegated to Asians.

It makes me realize that I have to work harder, you know? Because, I know what our history is about, what is important to me as an Asian American. I grew up partly in Hawaii. And that feeling, I try to convey it—a sense of strength about myself, and who I am as an Asian person. I try to do whatever I can in all of my plays to work against the image that's out there. To say that I am a real human being and I'm gonna connect with this audience, I'm gonna make them laugh, I'm gonna make them cry, I'm gonna make them think. That's what I try to do with every one of my shows. I think each one of my plays probably has something like 10–12,000 lines. Now, I don't think everybody could do that.

Can I ever be an artist outside of my Asian American experience? I think I can. But I don't know if I want to. I've toured 75 cities around the U.S., Canada, Europe. I remember this show, actually it was in Chicago, and this Asian guy, in the audience, after the show ... because a lot of places I go, they don't really see an Asian American guy or get much theater. We're very fortunate in San Francisco, Seattle, L.A., N.Y., to have a theater company in a city that does plays regularly. But I remember this was years ago, 10–12 years ago in Chicago, and this guy says, "Well, I'm a writer, and I don't write anything about being an Asian. And I don't think you have to write about being an Asian American person." Okay, that's fine. So then, the audience started to react to him, about what they just saw and what he just said. They just started to have their own discussion about it.

I thought about that, about what he said. I'll never forget it. But as one of my writing instructors very early on said, "Your best writing is going to be what you know. What you truly know. It's going to be your best writing." That's what I've always stuck with.

To me what is important is the sad fact that an Asian can walk down the street and get his head beaten in because some idiots think he's Chinese, when he's really Japanese. Or he's Japanese, and they think he's Chinese; kids getting shot in the playground. It's important to speak out about race-related crimes.

There are things which are not in the history books ... I'm talking about those groups who also fought during World War II: black soldiers, Asian soldiers, the Native American soldiers. We're just kind of pushed to the side.

This country boasts that it is a melting pot. "Give me your poor, your needy." It boasts that, and yet it does so much to keep us separate because it is run by this small group of corporate, powerful people. I don't buy it, you know? When I see a film about black American fighter pilots, it strikes a chord in me, as much as seeing *Air Force One* with Harrison Ford. Watching our president kick ass. That's my feeling as far as being an American.

I'm not panning on Hollywood. I've given up on Hollywood a long, long time ago. I truly think that independent filmmakers are basically the ones that give roles—supporting and leading—to Asian Americans. We're going to have to create our own.

My own material gives me freedom. The more I work, the more it allows me to work. In terms of the more I can tour, the more time it gives me to write, develop. I'm working on three more plays right now. I'm touring four. I worked about ten months last year, mostly in theater.

The Future

Film looks a lot like real life. I think independents are going to make a big move in the next five years, in their projects, that will include Asian Americans. I see young filmmakers that have their little short films who in five years are going to be somebody to be reckoned with. Their stories are all about being fourth generation, fifth generation in this country as Asian Americans. And they've got blond hair, they've got rings in there noses, they've got tattoos up the wazoo, and they're just like any American teenager. They are reckoning with their identity, their way of life. So it's going to be interesting. I'm always excited about what's coming. I just think that what I see for the future is going to be slow, it's going to take a long time.

If I retired now and just became a carpenter or chef, I'd be very happy because I've toured so much and with so many people. I'm very happy. What I'd like to see is more of my work documented for the future. That's just something that I would like to achieve now, now that I don't have to run a theater company anymore.

You know, in 18 years, we've staged about 100 plays at AATC. I'm very proud of that. So, for the next 18 years, I would just like to do a film. It doesn't have to be a big feature film. Some kind of a film project, a small piece, or a television piece. What I'd also like to do is embrace artists, develop them. That's my interest now. Going more towards video, and keep creating more work for the future. That's a goal, so I have something that I can now reach for. I'm very happy about what I've achieved so far, but every show makes me think of the next one.

With every audience, it's a new day.

Cherylene Lee

Cherylene Lee started acting at the age of 3. She is fourth generation Chinese American, raised in Los Angeles. As a child star she was dubbed the Chinese Shirley Temple. She was in numerous television shows, among them M*A*S*H, Dennis the Menace, Bachelor Father, Ben Casey, *and* My Three Sons. *She appeared in TV specials with stars such as Gene Kelly, Dinah Shore, and Frank Sinatra.*

Today she is a playwright, poet, and fiction writer. Her plays have toured the country as staged readings, as well as productions. They include Carry the Tiger to the Mountain, Arthur and Leila, Wong Bow Rides Again, Knock Off Balance, *and* The Ballad of Doc Hay. *She talks about the transition from child actor.*

THE BEGINNING

My sister, Virginia, tried out for the CBS Playhouse 90 television show *The Family Nobody Wanted*. But the producer said she was a little too tall for one of the parts. Remembering our mother's training to always be positive at auditions, she said, "I have

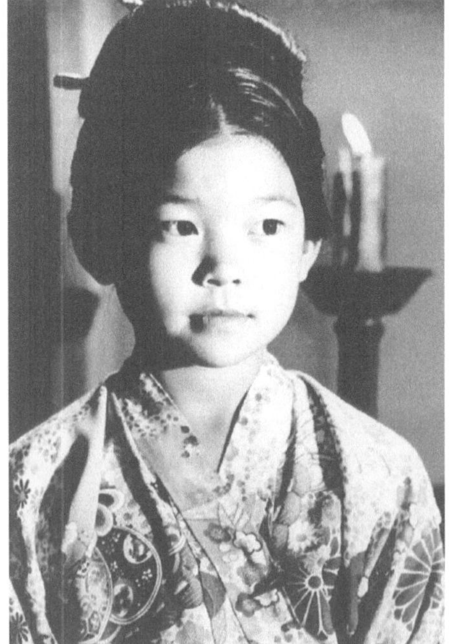

Cherylene Lee

a younger sister who's three." So that's how I started my first professional job. I played a Korean orphan. This was 1956. My first speaking part was the word "Hi." That was what started me off.

My family had actually been in a lot of television and film before that. My grandmother was often called upon to play Indian roles in the old western shows. My sisters and brother were in the movie *The King and I*. At the time the Chinese community was not that big in Los Angeles. Everybody knew everybody else and whenever they needed Chinese Americans, Asian Americans in any of the movies, people called each other. In fact Bessie Loo—the first Chinese-American agent in Hollywood (she started her agency in the 1930s, and handled all the Asian performers)—told me she had this phone tree for getting actors or extras for movies or television. That's how people got parts. My family all spoke English and my grandmother spoke English very well, so whenever studios needed an older woman, they always called her because she was somebody whom they could communicate with. So my family was already very much in the loop.

My sister, Virginia, took class at the American School of Ballet, where she met Dinah Shore's daughter, Melissa, and became very good friends with her. Melissa invited Virginia over for dinner one day. As I was there, we went together. We ended up showing Dinah Shore one of our dance routines after dinner and she asked us to be on her show. That was our start as an act—the Lee Sisters. After that things just kind of snowballed. I auditioned for the *Gene Kelly Spectacular*, at age five. That was a TV special, and it was wonderful. Liza Minnelli performed and Carl Sandburg read some poetry that Gene Kelly danced to. It was really amazing. When I think of Gene Kelly dancing to poetry, I still remember watching him rehearse with Carl Sandburg, and Liza practicing with Gene Kelly when she was 14 or so.

Then my sister and I were asked to do a night club act in Las Vegas at the New Frontier Hotel. The first show we did was in 1960. It was an all Asian review. The storyline was a Hollywood agent who would go to the Far East to look at talent and bring it back for the Ed Sullivan show. It had production numbers and also this one nude scene with Miss Tokyo. It was a conglomeration of variety acts. There were singers, a comic, traditional Japanese dancers, traditional Chinese instrumentalists—a hodgepodge. But the owner of the hotel just thought that my sister and I were so wonderful that even after that show ended he kept inviting us back as a special added attraction, the Lee Sisters.

We were in Las Vegas for four summers. That started when I was seven. After the Gene Kelly special I also began doing a lot of the sitcoms.

I was a semi-regular on *Bachelor Father*. I played Sammy Tong's niece, Blossom, who comes to visit. I played the girlfriend of *Dennis the Menace* in three episodes. I was bossier than Margaret and I would teach Dennis to eat with chop sticks. Of course Margaret would get very jealous. It was an interesting episode. Dennis took me to a place to eat ice cream and I remember eating ice cream for hours. I was almost sick because we had to reshoot this scene so many times.

This was the fifties and sixties. I often played a Korean orphan, brought in for adoption as in an episode of *Mr. Smith Goes to Washington*. That was a television series which didn't run very long, but I was a Korean orphan that was brought in so that a family would adopt me. The same thing happened in *My Three Sons* where they found me and I would be sort of adopted for one episode. My sister and I also did the movie *Flower Drum Song* together. We sang the song "The Other Generation." I was 7 and my sister was 14.

I was very outgoing as a child and very precocious and I had a memory as a child where I could read something once and remember it. Directors only had to tell me to do something once and I would remember to do it. I wanted to please people. I think that had to do with hearing that applause. If I was told to do something, I did it. I was extremely malleable.

I really enjoyed that time in my life. I mean I was definitely the center of a lot of attention as a child.

I was working almost all the time up until I was about 13, 14, 15 and then roles started getting fewer and far between.

Virginia kept on dancing. She did a lot of television shows as a dancer, *The Smothers Brothers Show*, and *The Jim Nabors Show*. Our sister act eventually ended when I grew to be the same height she was. When I was younger, we were not the same height, the act was cute—the thing that worked for us was no longer working when I grew up, so she continued to perform on her own. Then she got married.

I began to spend a lot of my time at the La Brea tar pits in Los Angeles, which to me was really interesting. From 14 to 17, my interest was focusing on reconstructing bones and doing all this scientific stuff. That's what I went into in college to study. I didn't go into drama, I didn't go into writing, I went to UC–Berkeley majoring in paleontology, so I really took this 180 degree turn. I continued taking dance class for exercise, but my interest started going much more into the scientific realm. I was just sort of fascinated by this reconstruction of the past, which I think ended up affecting my writing later on.

It was a gradual shift out of acting. I didn't realize this was happening. I knew that I was interested in something else, yet I would still go out for parts even though I was too old. I couldn't go out for the young parts that were being written. Up until I was 11, I was really short for my age. I could play 6 year olds, even when I was 9, 10, 11. Of course I was a very good reader and I was more mature. I worked a lot playing younger roles, but when I grew up there weren't that many roles for me to play.

I think also there was a shift during the period I was growing up. There was less interest in the Korean War and less interest in having Asian roles in the situations that I had been in, in the sitcoms; those roles just weren't there. I was going out on fewer auditions. I was getting fewer jobs. It happened gradually; I didn't realize it was happening. I think my conscious choice when I was ready to go to college was that I would pursue something scientific and not something in the business. Acting was something that I had done so much of on a practical basis that I didn't feel really drawn to learning about theater in college. I was really drawn much more to learning about science.

What were my thoughts about the industry? To me it was just fun. I grew up doing it and I started at such a young age that it was just part of my life. It didn't feel like it was something very special; oh, today I'm going to school, today I'm going out on an audition, today I'm going to the dentist. My mother wanted to make sure that my sister and I grew up normally. She kept us in public school, except for the times when we were working when we would have someone on the set to teach us. When we were in Las Vegas we had a private tutor too. We always had to keep up with our assignments; everybody had to keep up with family chores. So it didn't feel like it was something that was all that different.

I didn't even think about whether this would be for the rest of my life. I just noticed when I stopped working that things were not happening the way they had been. Showbusiness came sort of given to me; it was something that I fell into. It was never something that was sought out, I mean, I certainly did my best when I was performing, and I wanted to do well and remember the steps and the lines and not screw up, but I never thought about it in the long term as a child.

Did I have aspirations about being a star as a child? I think I did for a while. Everything came very quickly to me as a child, and I think that by the time I was 12, 13, 14 those aspirations came down. It was like, I know I have the talent to do this, I was working before, but the roles weren't there. Gradually there was a realization that I wasn't going to continue in this, that the demand for me as a child performer was just not happening anymore, and that coming of age was a difficult time. I had these aspirations and yet was not having the outlet that I used to have as a child, and wondering why that was so. Part of it was knowing that the roles weren't there as they had been and then realizing I did have other resources too. The science research that I was doing was so introverted compared to being so extroverted. It was a 180 degree turn. Drawing these bones or trying to identify this sabertooth tiger part, that was private as opposed to being public. It was a very difficult shift but I was very grateful that I had the intelligence and the awareness that there was a world beyond showbusiness. It was a very interesting time for me to find another way of expressing myself.

I don't find acting as challenging now as the writing. As an artist, as a writer, my contribution is unique. It is something that no one else will do. Even as an actor the roles will come and go, another person will get cast in a play that I have done; I might have originated a role but it's not mine, perhaps someone else will perform the role later. But as a writer my contribution is truly unique and to me that was such a revelation. In science, a scientist's work must be repeatable, that is the basis of the scientific method, repeatability is the test of a hypothesis, but in writing, no one else will write the way I write. That is where I have been concentrating, that has been my main calling for the past 15 or 16 years. I write for the theater because when I started writing, it was dialogue almost immediately and I think that came from having to learn dialogue as a really young child. I like the sound and rhythm of words, I have always been an avid reader, and to me, words have power.

Beyond Acting

I started writing 15 years ago. At the time, I was living in Seattle and I wasn't able to get work as a performer or as a scientist and it was really out of desperation that I started to write because I wasn't able to get any work.

One of the first poems that I wrote was about the Vincent Chin case and it was published in the *International Examiner*, the Asian American newspaper in Seattle. That helped convince me that I did have a voice. My first play was accepted in the Bay Area Playwrights Festival and later was produced in Hawaii. It was on interracial marriage. That acted as reinforcement to help me say yes, I can do this.

Most of my writing now is about Asian Americans. I want my writing now to show the character complexity that wasn't in plays or shows when I was growing up. It was hard for me to understand, growing up, that certain things in my childhood were exceptions. It was a pretty unusual life. Reflecting back, that's influenced my writing today.

Did I ever go through a period where I was either angry or bitter about understanding the rules of the game when it came to how Asian actors actually fit into the hierarchy of the film industry? Not when I was growing up and was in it. I was just too young to really recognize anything. I think as a writer I understand the hierarchy more, with trying to get my work produced.

Because I write mostly for theater, mainstream producers look at my work and think that perhaps it is not exotic enough, because it has a very American rhythm. The characters are generally second or third generation Americans. The stories are American. Perhaps my work lacks that exoticized perception of what non–Asians think Asian American plays are. Perhaps that has held my work back from getting produced by more mainstream theaters. Most of my work is produced by Asian American theaters. This is my interpretation of why some of my plays have not been done in non–Asian theaters. I did a play about the Hong Kong turnover to China, but it's from the perspective of a Chinese American, rather than from the point of view of someone born in China. I believe American audiences identify much more with a Chinese American point of view, but are unaware of what that view is; people think in terms of American or Chinese, not that there is a blend of both.

When I first started writing I just wanted to be a writer and express myself as I needed to, not to be categorized as an Asian American writer or as an Asian American woman writer. But now having been writing for a long time, having gone through pitfalls, ups and downs, having seen material that's produced, I feel that if I don't write the stories of Asian Americans in the way that I see them, I don't think they will be expressed by other people. I feel that I do have a very unique viewpoint and perception because I have four generations of being in this country behind me and I have a sort of evolutionary perspective and I want to be able to express that; I mean I do see differences in immigration and immigrants now from families which have been here a long time.

I've written 15 plays and had eight produced, mostly in Asian American theaters. I want my plays to get bigger and go to bigger theaters and regional theaters. They should be seen as widely as possible because these plays are part of the American landscape. They're very American stories, these are issues that I think everyone encounters: finding your place, finding your identity and where you fit in society's class structure. These are issues told from an Asian American perspective but are issues every American goes through.

If I had a choice would I do acting or write? Definitely write. I feel much more in control and powerful as a writer. The challenges are much greater to me as a writer than they were as a performer. Also I'm older now, and I haven't the energy to pursue those things one has to do as a performer. To me as a writer, my voice is much more unique. I create an entire world as a writer, whereas as a performer I am a part of someone else's world. So for me I have no desire to go back and perform again, although I have, on occasion, performed my own work and I think I still have the dramatic/comedic timing to do it.

Being an Asian American are there any barriers to my work? Yes. There are barriers in that there's just a smaller percentage of people who are willing to go see Asian American works. So that's something that's part of the demographics.

I also think it is more difficult as an Asian American woman playwright, just to be visible and to be heard. Women novelists can do very well, because it's more private writing. They write on the page, they don't have to put their work in a collaborative situation.

When will I feel that I've made it? When my plays are on Broadway. I don't know that they'll get there in my lifetime. But I have hopes. I suspect my plays have a point of view more geared towards those who are second or third generation. It may take a few more generations where there's a larger population which share the same perspective. Right now there are many people who are first generation, who my experience doesn't really speak to. I think down the line that will change.

I plan to continue writing for a long time. Most of my living has been as a writer for the past few years but it's getting harder and harder to be able to earn a living at it, just because arts funding is drying up, we live in a society which doesn't value art, but the ability to make money. But regardless of how I make my money, the writing will definitely continue.

Nancy Kwan

Nancy Kwan is most well known for her leading roles in The World of Suzie Wong *and* Flower Drum Song. *Additionally she starred in such films as* The Main Attraction *and* Honeymoon Hotel *opposite Robert Goulet,* Fate is the Hunter *opposite Glenn Ford,* Lt. Robinson Crusoe USA *opposite Dick Van Dyke,* The Wrecking Crew *opposite Dean Martin,* Arrivederci Baby *opposite Tony Curtis,* Nobody's Perfect *with Doug McClure, and the* McMasters *with David Carradine and Jack Palance. During the 1970s Kwan moved back to Hong Kong with her son where she entered film production as managing director of Nancy Kwan Films.*

Nancy Kwan

She returned to the United States in 1980, and appeared in such television series as Fantasy Island, Knots Landing *and* Trapper John. *She recently produced the* Biker Poet, *a feature film.*

She is the spokesperson for Oriental Pearl Cream.

The Beginning

I used to go home for the summer holidays to Hong Kong where my parents were living. I was attending the Royal Ballet School in England, studying ballet, which was my first love.

My father, an architect, had designed this studio that was owned by my uncle in Hong Kong (it's all kind of connected) and I went up there to see some of my favorite Chinese actresses testing out for the role of *The World of Suzie Wong.* I was standing around, looking, finding it very fascinating when suddenly someone said to me, "Young lady, young lady." I said "What," and he said, "Would you like to do a screen test?" So I went, "Screen test. What's that?" He said, "Well all you have to do is stand in front of the camera and we'll ask you a few questions." So I said, "Sure why not."

They sat me on the stool and there was this camera and they asked me how old I was, and what I was doing there and you know, very simple questions and that was that. A couple of months later I was ready to go back to school in England and we got a letter asking whether I would like to come to Hollywood on contract and do another screen test for *The World of Suzie Wong.* I had never been to America at this point so I said, "Yeah! I'll go." My father said well, okay, as long as she can stay somewhere in like a safe place and be looked after because I was still relatively young—eighteen years old. They said that they would pay me a certain amount of money for a week, I'd go to acting school, and then when the time came, do another screen test.

I stayed at the Hollywood Studio Club, which at that time was for women only, and a very nice lady ran this place, called Ms. Williams. Kim Novak and all these other actresses stayed there. I've never seen so many beautiful women in one place in my life. Subsequently a lot of these women became actresses—quite well known.

I studied for three months then did another screen test for Paramount. At that time the play *The World of Suzie Wong* was going on in New York and they asked me whether I would I like to do the play on tour. They said, "Look, we'll put you under contract and you go on tour and learn some more about acting and everything, and then later on we'll find a movie for you." So I went to New York and the Broadway production was going to go on tour for I think about six months, all around the United States. About a month or two later, I think, we were in Canada on tour, and I get a phone call. Apparently there had been problems and the director and the actress were both dismissed—fired. They said we would like you to come to London and do a screen test this time, with Bill Holden.

At that time they already shot the exteriors, the locations in Hong Kong and they were coming back to London to do the interiors. And I said, "Well what happens if it doesn't work out, what do I do then?" They said, "You could make up your own mind. You could re-join the show or whatever." So I said okay. So being very adventurous, I packed my bags and I went to London. I did a screen test and they said, "Fine, you got the role."

So you know, that's what's strange in life. What is meant to be, will be. I mean, they had already been filming and everything else. So then we started, we did all the interiors in London which was like three or four months shooting and I thought, my goodness, making a movie takes forever. I had never made a film so I didn't know the length of time it took. Today you can do a movie in four weeks and eight weeks; in those days it took months. After a while I asked, "Well, are we finished?" and they said, "Oh, no, because we're going back to Hong Kong and redo the exteriors." Which was another two or three months and so all together it was about five, six months making this film. And then, so that was, *The World of Suzie Wong*. That was my first film, how I got into films.

It was very well received. They had premieres all over the place. It opened in London for the Queen and the Duke with a royal premiere and there were premieres in New York and Los Angeles. That was fun and then I went back to Hong Kong for a rest, I went home.

The first time I realized the change in my life was: I remember walking in the street doing shopping with my stepmother in this material store and I saw all these people standing around staring. So I said, "What are they looking at?" and then I realized they were looking at me! I thought, oh this is really nerve-wracking, and then before we knew it the whole shop was full of people, gaping at us. It was a very strange experience I must say. Life slowly changed. I mean, people gaping in the streets—and in Hong Kong they kind of say what they feel, they're not quite as polite as over here, you know, whatever comes into mind. They say whether they liked the movie or they didn't like the movie, whether they liked you or they didn't like you, when you're a public figure. But then I kind of realized my life had changed because of the privacy. In the beginning it was quite a shock. I wasn't even quite twenty yet.

When I returned, both *Flower Drum Song* and *Suzie Wong* were on Broadway, it was very strange. This was the early sixties, there were two very big Asian productions on Broadway pretty much at the same time.

I came back to Hollywood and was under contract. In those days you were under contract in the studio system. I'm glad I didn't miss that era. It was very exciting because you met a lot of young actors, actors coming up during that time. The studio took care of everyone, and they nurtured the young, up and coming actors.

I signed a seven year contract. You get paid every week, and they would loan you out. Let's say, for example, *Flower Drum Song*. I was at a party with my producer, and Ross Hunter the producer of *Flower Drum Song* was there too. It was the opening of some film. Ross saw me, and he came up to me, and said, "Linda Lo!" I didn't know what he was talking about so I said, "I beg your pardon." He said, "I'm making a film called *Flower Drum Song*. You've heard about it?" and I said, "Sure, you know, Broadway." He said, "Have you seen it?" At that time I hadn't seen it. He said, "You should go and see it. You're perfect for the role of Linda Lo." And I said, "Oh really." So then I get a call a few days later from my producer who said, "Would you like to do a musical (*Flower Drum Song*)?" and I said, "Would I?" I said, it'd be great. You know I could dance—basically I'm still a dancer from ballet. That's how I got *Flower Drum Song*, which is I guess, kind of by fluke. So within six to eight months I was onto my next movie.

I was on a loan-out to Universal. It was great because we had six or eight weeks' dance rehearsals. We got to know all the dancers, and actors got to know each other. We had rehearsal time which today you don't get as much unless you're doing a play, so I really enjoyed doing *Flower Drum Song*. That was my first movie also in Hollywood. It was called big studio, first all–Asian American cast; that was the first time ever. At that time there were a lot of Asian American actors just coming up from *Suzie Wong* and *Flower Drum Song* and other productions because there were a lot of tours and things. There are friends whom I have kept in touch with to this day. Some of them are still in the business and some of them are married and have children, and god knows what else.

Then they wanted me to do a film which I didn't want to do. What happens when you're under contract is they loan you out and if you feel you don't want to do this film or you feel that it's not right for you, they can suspend you. That means they won't pay you until you decide that you want to work again or they find a new project for you. I didn't want to work in the film, I didn't feel I was right for it, so I got suspended.

I used to take off and they used to search for me all over the place. Sometimes you do films for various reasons. In those days, I could play quite a few roles

I bummed around Europe and saw all my friends and had a good time and then they said, Nancy, how would you like to play a non–Asian role. They said that would be very good for you. It would open up the market more than only playing Asian roles because there aren't that many Asian roles. So I said, sure, why not, great. So I made a movie as a circus performer. It was an Italian background and I had Italian parents. Then I played the French girl. In those days I guess because I had a name and I was a so-called "hot actress" they would cast you just for your name sake. I also played a Mexican; it was kind of wide open still, there wasn't quite that awareness yet.

I thought well, it's a smart move to have opportunities to play other roles. They even one time sent Francis Ford Coppola to Hong Kong to write a screenplay for me. It never got made, I think Francis told me he had a great time in Hong Kong, writing the screenplay but it never got made.

Things like that. So I did the Italian film *Main Attraction*, which didn't do well. Then I got married and lived in Europe. They said you better come back to Los Angeles and I said no, I'm going to live in Europe, and had a son. I also played an English girl—believe it or not—with English parents. It was a film called "The Last Days of Sandra Lee" I think. A very good English actor-comedian played my boss and I played a secretary or something with English parents. It wasn't a big time budget film and it was a first-time director who had done documentaries previously. Well, the film died, he didn't do anything. Then there was a movie in Tahiti. I thought I could do that one. I mean I look like everyone else; I seem to fit in there quite well. My father's Chinese and my mother's English. I'm Eurasian.

So I got to play quite a variation of different nationalities which was nice. It was a good learning process. I was very lucky I was in my position because of *Flower Drum Song* and *Suzie Wong*. Those two films gave me the opportunity to play other roles.

As for expectations, in *The World of Suzie Wong* I had none because I had no real idea of what I was doing. I mean I happen to have a very good actor who was very giving. I had a terrific role that I could do something with and he enhanced the role for me—I mean my performance. Then my director really took care of me. But I had no idea. I thought you do a film and that's it. It opened a lot of doors; it was really successful.

Flower Drum Song was the first time we were an all–Asian cast and we were very excited about that. I thought wow, this is great. After *Flower Drum Song* I had a lot of letters about being a role model. A lot came from young Asians who wanted to be in the film business. Then there were those who said we made an image for Asian Americans; at the time there were far fewer Asian Americans compared to today. It was the first time they said they could identify with someone on the screen in a mainstream film which made a lot of money and had all Asians. I think the Asian Americans said "I Enjoy Being a Girl" was one of the favorite songs.

It was kind of nice if I helped in any way; or that I was a pioneer to give them some sort of pride in seeing an Asian American fit in a country that is their country.

AFTER *THE WORLD OF SUZIE WONG* AND *FLOWER DRUM SONG*

In the early '70s, I wanted to go to Asia. It was a personal thing. My father was sick and I wanted to live in Asia to spend at least a year there. My son was very young and I thought well, if I don't do it now, I'll never do it. I remember my agent saying to me, "Don't do that. You stay here because you have to be around, you have to be seen. I thought no, no. I had gotten divorced and I was back here and I said, no, I felt there was something missing. All my life I had been traveling and I had never really spent time as an adult in Asia. I said I wanted to take a year and do that. My agent said, "Don't," and I said, "Well, I have to. If I don't do it now, I won't do it."

So I took off. I took my son. My parents were still living in Hong Kong at that time and my father was quite sick so I went back and I stayed there a year. A man from Australia wanted to open up a film company in Hong Kong and he asked whether I would be interested in doing some directing and producing commercials. At that time I was looking to the other side of the camera and I felt it would be nice that I would have an overall knowledge of the film business. So when I was in Hong Kong

I did a lot of films in Southeast Asia. I worked in the Philippines, I worked in Thailand, I worked in Hong Kong, I did well, I only did one Chinese-speaking film, but the rest was shot on location and I would come back here once in a while and do a TV show or a movie of the week.

I stayed in Hong Kong for almost eight years instead of that one year. American films would shoot there and English films would shoot there and they would use me in Southeast Asia and my base was Hong Kong.

When my son got to be high school age I thought I better bring him back here, because in Hong Kong there's only Hong Kong U and it's pretty limited. He wanted to come back too. So I brought him back here and by then it was difficult. I was in my mid-thirties-going into my late thirties and it was difficult re-establishing myself, because the momentum is gone, and the whole batch of new people come up and the whole film business had changed substantially. Now there was a lot of independent filmmakers. I had to go meet them, and I had to read, and just kind of like re-establish myself. When you get to a certain age, that's another issue that you have to deal with, especially for Asians. There weren't that many roles for the young, and now your middle age and it's even more limited.

I wanted to do everything when I came back, especially act. I wanted to keep on acting because it's something that I do well; I know I'm good at it. I still worked once in awhile and so it wasn't as though completely I didn't have any work and I might have said well, I should concentrate more on producing. I was also producing and writing. When you write you develop things that you would like to do. I found I liked it. In the beginning I worked with another writer or friends, but after a while I found that I could do it myself so now I write by myself.

At this point I consider myself a filmmaker and I'm glad that I started out acting because it makes it much easier for me to work with other actors. I see when they need help and that's a great help. Even about lighting and stuff—as a producer I learned more. So I think the more knowledge you have the better you become—the more secure you become. In television where they don't take time with the young actors, I see them getting lost; the directors don't have time—they have to cover so many pages a day. Today especially in television, they've got to move and they don't have time. So you pick up bad habits or you're just at a loss so you become insecure. I'm glad for the background I have. But I consider myself a filmmaker and I think that I will always act too. I love the business.

ASIAN AMERICAN IMAGES ON SCREEN

When I first came back from Hong Kong in the late '70s—I did this tape for Tai Chi Chuan and was in San Francisco promoting it. An Asian lady was talking to me about the tape and all of a sudden she said to me, "Do you know that because of Suzie Wong you made a bad impression for a lot of Asian American women." I said, "What are you trying to say?" So she said, "You know, because Suzie Wong was a prostitute a lot of Americans got the wrong idea and they thought that all Asian woman were prostitutes." I said, "I don't have any problems with the movie and I don't know why you bring this up because I think it's up to you and how you feel about yourself. It's only a role and it happened to be a very successful film and I'm sure that you feel that way."

Then she went on about *Flower Drum Song* and said, "Do you know that *Flower Drum Song* was very stereotypical of Asian Americans in Chinatown in San Francisco?" I said, "I've been out of the country for quite a while but I hadn't heard of that." She said, "Oh, yeah, and people think that they behave that way." I said, "I just happen to know that *Flower Drum Song* was the first Asian cast mainstream movie that made a lot of money in this country, and I think it actually helped enhanced the Asian Americans in this country." Then I was told that in the '70s this whole Asian awareness, politically incorrect or correct, was going on; I don't know, that I apparently had missed from being in Hong Kong all that time and not being in this country. Now all that has changed around. Just recently in San Francisco someone said you're being honored for *Flower Drum Song* in October from the Asian community. So how things change. When you ask about Asian American awareness in this country—how has it evolved—I guess what goes around comes around.

I guess they blamed me for that image, yes of being a prostitute. The first time I heard it I thought well, if she had been a nun it would have been a whole different thing, but because she was a prostitute they thought that every Asian woman was a Suzie Wong.

I've never seen myself as an icon for Asian American women. I'm an actor and I play these roles; one happens to be a prostitute, next it's another role. But I never even thought of myself as a role model.

I still do not feel there are enough roles coming out of Hollywood for Asian Americans; especially males. Females have more than males. I mean how many male Asian Americans do you see here that are working in the film business? None, really, none.

Why do I think there are so few roles? I think it comes in waves. In the '60s there were *Flower Drum Song* and *Suzie Wong*. Then there was

The Last Emperor. It's numbers. Bottom line it's dollars. More and more Asians settle in this country, building demand for Asian film, Asian whatever, anything. And so, and the bottom line is where the demands are. Still predominantly this is white, Caucasian, this country. The Asians are two percent. So, it's money. The bottom line is it's commerce.

Do I think it's dollars and box office draw or do I think there's something more there tied to race? Oh I think definitely. I think there will always be that, unfortunately. It's like human nature. People judge people by color. It happens all the time and we know it. It's not only Asians. But I think the bottom line is still dollars. Believe me if we came up today with a fantastic film with Asians in it, this Asian actor or actress would keep on working for a while if the demand is there. They are always judged by the last movie they did or the last work and that's the way it goes.

As for my being not confined to certain roles when I was younger—today let's say somebody comes up and makes a fantastic film and it was a great success and everything. I don't know if this Asian actor could—let's say in the next film—play a Latino or someone non–Asian. Let's say that this Asian is going to be in this big movie and let's say the lead is going to be this big Latino role. What do you think the Latinos would say to that? They'd say, oh, wait a minute, we've got very good Latino actors. Why are you not using us, why are you using an Asian? A few years ago I remember going on an interview. It was for a Latino role. This Latino actress said to me, what are you doing here? You know, so, because they say well, we're minorities, we don't have enough roles for ourselves too, why are you taking our roles. I mean in the old days I played an Italian. I had English parents. I mean, I didn't think twice about it. You're an actor, you can play anything you want. Asians played Shakespeare, and Shakespeare's roles were always written, at that time, for Caucasians because there were no Asians around to cast.

Today I think in the theater you could do that. But I don't know about film. They wouldn't cast you, I don't think, unless you were so much in demand and such a hot commodity that they'd say oh, it doesn't matter what you play, you can play anything. If an Asian actor says, I want to play Juliet in *Romeo and Juliet* why not? If you were in that position and willing to invest—especially mainstream movies today cost 30 or 40 million dollars—then you could do it. But I don't think anybody would risk it. The bottom line is dollars. They'd say are you crazy.

Do I think casting is more race driven now ? No. I still think the bottom line still is money. If it was an Asian and very hot commodity and they wanted to do that, someone might say well, okay, he or she is so hot, let's give it a shot and they might do it once.

Do I think there can be an Asian superstar? Of course. I think it's luck. Being in the film business I always say, I was in the right place at the right time and it was meant to be. Sure, I think definitely so, and I think it will happen—I mean it will happen again.

You might get lucky and you'll get in a very successful film and then you become very well known, but you have to sustain it. That's why I always said in order to sustain it you need material. As long as there are not enough Asian writers, Asian directors, Asian producers, Asian executive producers working on projects for Asians, how are you going to sustain that career? You need the roles to sustain it. How many good Asian scripts do you get? Very few. So I really encourage Asians not only to become actors but writers. We need directors, we need producers and executive producers in order to develop projects for Asians.

Look at Jackie Chan. Now Jackie has had two careers. Twenty years ago he tried to break into the American market; didn't make it. Now he's trying again and I think his pictures are getting better, more Asians are settling here so they go see the film because he's well known in Asia and internationally. So now he's trying to break into the American market. I hope he makes it. It's opened up the market for Asian male actors, who have a worse time than Asian women.

Until you get Asians really developing roles for their own people, things won't happen. The Caucasian is not going to do it—why should they do it? The Westerners, they're successful with their own race, their own people and maybe they like to see their own people on screen. I'm sure that has a lot to do with it.

I just finished a screenplay about an Asian American family in Los Angeles. Culturally there's the grandmother too. I wanted to introduce the American people to some of our customs and culture. We are all human beings, we might be different colors, but we share the same emotions and I hope to touch them on that level. We all get married, we all love, we all have children; the basic things that we go through emotionally. I would like to touch them on that level.

I don't know if you know about my thing with *The Joy Luck Club* but I turned it down because they had this very insulting scene about Suzie Wong in the script. In one scene something derogatory was said about Suzie Wong. I asked whether they would mind taking that line out because that's not even in the book and I don't know why it was even put in. Why promote animosity between Asians. But they wouldn't do that, so then I said well I won't be in the film; I'll come to see it and that's it. I can't do it. I'm very proud of *The World of Suzie Wong*; the film set my career off.

In *The Joy Luck Club* I think also it made the men look wimpy. So the balance was off, I think. I'm happy that it got good reviews and that it did so well, because people became more aware of Asians. It went mainstream and it did well. There was a lot of interest and talk about it. But I think it depicted the men in not a very good light in. I heard that Asian males were quite angry and disappointed about it and I don't blame them for that. I think the women did great, but not the men.

ROLES AND THE FUTURE

Success for me at this point? I guess I'm on a quest, but it's an inward journey. I feel that as I get older I seem to search more inwardly than outwardly and the things that were important to me, especially the material things and everything else, is not so important anymore. I hope it will continue to be so with the drive, with the ambition. I would like to keep on making films that come from the heart, that have something that I can be proud of to say. The fact is I'm in a position where I don't have to work in order to survive and I think a lot of people out there have to work because they have to survive, they have to make the next meal.

You say a lot of people look at me and see me as the success story to the Asian American actor. I don't know about that. I'm not aware of it. I see myself as an actor and I know most of the actors, every age; it's a small circle and I have some good friends in that circle, but I just don't see it that way.

I feel that I've been in the business a long time and maybe we're survivors—the older group—because we've hung in there and we're still doing it. I do get a lot of letters, and I do have the respect of a lot of young actors. They come up to me and say, Nancy what do you think. I try to help them as much as I can in my way, but I don't feel I am this role model. I have letters from people about how much they've enjoyed the film and how proud they are for Asians but it's not something I carry on me.

I'm very proud of my heritage. I was brought up as an Asian. You see, when I came to this country people said to me you know Nancy, Asian Americans are quite different, they have many complexes. I said, what do you mean. They said, when they're born here they have to deal with white people all the time and even though they're Asians they think American; which is true because a lot of my friends' kids are second or third generation. You look Asian, but you think Caucasian and that's the difference between the Asians from Asia that come over here. So with Asian Americans I think it's quite a delicate balance and it's really difficult for them. They're competing very hard and in America it's always about competition.

Over here you always have to be number one. That's one of the reasons why the children are messed up today—this whole emphasis where the parents warn their kids they have to be the best, that they have to be number one. The only thing my father said to me when I wanted to be an actor was get your education, and do what you want. After that you'll always have something to fall back on. With Asians I think education is always number one; that's why I think Asians excel so much. Parents instill in the children those values and that's something that I really admire from the Asian families.

In the Bruce Lee story I played the Asian woman who instilled into Bruce Lee the importance of going to college—he was a dishwasher in my restaurant. Last year for personal reasons I didn't work. As for roles, the last role I tried out for was an Asian doctor.

There isn't that much out there and the roles I was going up for were Asian roles. I keep telling my agent, put me up for roles that are non-nationality; just a good role that's the right age. The last week I went up for something but it's also an Asian role.

Even when they are Asian roles, they tend to be intelligent, professional roles. Otherwise I wouldn't go for them. My agent knows that.

Oh, I just thought of one now, they asked me to go in. They were looking for an East Indian doctor for a TV series. So first I said I don't look East Indian, I don't think I'm right. Then they said, oh, no, maybe Asian too. So I said to my agent, you're sure now, Asian? So he said, yes. So I went in and I met the producer and the casting director. I even read and used an East Indian accent. They asked me if I would mind darkening my skin. I said wait a second—if I'm Asian I don't have to darken it. So I came home and told my agent, East Indian, okay, I could do the accent but the darkening of the skin, why don't they just look for an East Indian? In the end it turned out that way—they went for East Indian because they felt that I would stick out too much. So you get things like that, which I think are quite interesting.

Are there characters I wouldn't play at all or would consider demeaning to an Asian? Yes. If it was demeaning I certainly wouldn't do it, or I would say, hey, this is demeaning. I mean I have a big mouth too. And I think maybe they would want to know. Sometimes you read a screenplay and it's demeaning from an Asian point of view and they might not be aware of it. I would point it out through my agent or say directly to them, Asians would not like that. If they were doing it on purpose, maybe they wouldn't change it. But if they weren't, then they might say oh, you're right, we shouldn't do that. It's insulting or whatever. I think it's very important that I set standards because I have to live with them.

Summary of Interviews with California Actors

All the actors interviewed on the West Coast clearly had very strong feelings about the issue of race as related to their acting experiences. As a group they were far more direct in pointing out the role of race in affecting their attempts to enter into and navigate the world of film, theater and television. Despite the barriers and limitations, all reflected a strong determination to continue acting. Much of it comes from a fundamental love of acting. It is this desire that has apparently kept them going. Just about all said theater was the key channel that enabled them to enter into acting. To this end, the Asian American Theater Company in San Francisco, and the East-West Players in Los Angeles are important support structures for aspiring Asian American actors.

A second major point for why Asian American actors go into acting derives from their experiences as a minority. Acting afforded them opportunities of self-expression, a chance to confront issues of Asian American identity head-on—through acting them out on stage.

As for roles, the recurring response from males was again the paucity of meaningful roles. For men, the type of roles have changed little over the past decade. They continue to be called for minor roles primarily as kung-fu types, gangsters, gamblers, and villains in films or television. Things are changing in commercials and industrials, but very slowly. Occasionally there are roles such as a businessman or professional worker.

For women the opportunity to play meaningful roles seems somewhat greater. Some say they have been asked to audition as reporters, students, and professional women. Looks play a significant role, as Joanne Takahashi said. The Hollywood image of beauty—and therefore race—remains a major factor of success. There is also a keen awareness of the relationship of box office draw to the chances of superstardom.

As for the image of Asian Americans as depicted in film, theater and television, many of the actors felt what they saw on screen ultimately does have an impact on the societal perceptions of Asian Americans in general. Correspondingly, the roles Asians get to play contributes to a general sense of how Asians are perceived.

Epilogue

One of the key aims of this research was to examine the perspectives of Asian American actors in the context of being a minority in an industry where physical appearance, in particular racial features, plays a key role to success. The materials provided by the aspiring actors outline a broad picture of their personal views relative to their individual experiences. Media ecologists however also strive to see everything as interrelated. So the stories of Asian American actors are not just individual narratives, they are also discourse from a particular community which is a subset of a much larger system, a system within the mass media universe of television, film and theater.

The work done here is best understood by reference to three important concepts that grow out of media studies: systems theory, economic determinism, and development of self. Chief influences in pursuing these realms of study are works by Laszlo (1972), Schiller (1989), and Mead (1934).

Laszlo asserts that systems theory is a mode of organizing existing findings in reference to the concept of systems and systemic properties and relationships. He asserts, if we want to know more about the behavior of complex phenomena we must approach them as systems, as wholes with properties of their own ... some knowledge of connected complexity is preferable even to a more detailed knowledge of atomized simplicity ... to have an adequate grasp of reality we must look at things as systems, with properties and structures of their own (1972, p. 12, 13, 14).

He describes open systems as natural systems that maintain their own states by exchanging energy and information with their environment, and subsystems. Natural systems also evolve new structures and new functions. A natural system as defined by Laszlo is "any system which does not owe its existence to conscious human planning and execution" (p. 23).

Furthermore Laszlo states that systems have complex hiearchies. They are goal oriented, self-maintaining, and create their own expressions of order and adjustments.

Systems theory looks at various parts in terms of the whole; it discovers repeating patterns in the organization, and evaluates these as so many variations on a common theme. Because of the interdependence of elements in an open system, change is not additive. Change in one part will affect another.

Through the lens of systems theory, it is possible to understand various dichotomies in the experiences of some of the participants. First, mass media can be seen as a suprasystem in which the systems of film, television and theater function. Environmental changes affect all parts of the system as the elements are interdependent. The marketing of films in a global arena for instance, will have an effect on the domestic market environment. Therefore Peter Kwong's view that opportunities are opening up for Asian American actors—using the Jackie Chan phenomenon as an example—can be explained in terms of changes within the mass media suprasystem affecting the subsystem environment—namely the community of actors. Jackie Chan is a Hong Kong star who has achieved recognition in the United States for his kung fu films. Even though he is a foreign actor, the fact that he can make it as a "star" in this country is seen by Peter Kwong as an indicator that things are changing for the Asian American actor.

In contrast, but not contradition, Ray Moy's views that race remains the imbreachable barrier to superstardom, can be explained in terms of the tendency of open systems toward segregation and systemization.

Along the same vein Karen Tsen Lee's experience as an Asian American woman who is getting more opportunities to do television commercials could be a reflection of an environmental adjustment to market driven realities occurring in the mass media suprasystem. Television commercials are designed to sell products. With an increased Asian American population comes the potential for more Asian American consumers. Including Asian American actors in the stable to peddle goods on television is a logical development in this regard. This supports Laszlo's view that open systems are self-regulating, and that the "highly developed organism regulates its own internal environment, much as a thermostat regulates the temperature of a house" (p. 41).

How can the proliferation of Asian American acting companies over the past decade be explained if the ultimate opportunities for stardom are still elusive to the Asian American actor? Laszlo's explanation of an open system's tendency toward equilibrium could be applied here. He offers that natural systems evolve new structures and new functions; they create themselves in time (p. 47). The pool of Asian Americans interested in pursuing acting has increased with the population, and with opportunities still limited, Asian American actors are turning to acting companies such as the Pan Asian Repertory. It is analogous to the subsystem of Asian American actors undertaking to create a new structure within the system of film, theater and television. In open systems progressive segregation and progressive systematization may occur simultaneously or sequentially. Off Broadway and off-off-Broadway sprang up in part to accommodate Asian American actors and others who may have been shut out of the existing system structure (Broadway). There continues to be a Balkanization at various levels of achievement in film, television, and theater, so that for Asian American actors such as Mel Gionson, performing at regional theater levels and off-off-Broadway do not translate into greater acting roles and opportunities.

Applying Laszlo's systems view of the world to explain the range of complexity surrounding the Asian American acting community has provided an analytical frame through which to understand and generalize about some of the responses which Asian American actors interviewed for this study have provided. But is it possible to use Laszlo's philosophical viewpoint as a critical tool from which to identify ways Asian American actors can break the barrier of race in film, theater and television?

If the film, theater and television industries are systems within a suprasystem, then altering the environments may be one possible approach to tackling the issue. For instance, find a way to make it more profitable to produce films using Asian American actors. Attracting a mainstream audience is consistent with the system's fundamental needs. What would have to change therefore is the environment in which Asian American actors navigate the system. Pumping more mainstream-style works from Asian American writers into the system would increase the pool of material and provide greater opportunities for Asian American actors. Analogous to this are Spike Lee's films on African American experiences. His films drew large audiences, paving the way for additional African American films; films that would not have been possible without a black audience and the potential for profitability.

More films with wide audience appeal, such as Amy Tan's *The Joy Luck Club* (1993), as well as movies from Asia like *Eat, Drink, Man, Woman* (1993) and *The Wedding Banquet* (1992), will add to the growing interest and opportunities for Asian works.

But mass media as a system is also driven by profits. Schiller (1989) asserts that cultural industries—of which film, theater and television are a part—are segments of a rapidly emerging transnational information system driven by commercial profitability. The domination of culture through media by information conglomerates is condemned by Schiller as a form of economic determinism whereby decisions for what audiences see are driven solely by profitability factors. Ultimately the cultural message is determined by what will sell in the marketplace. In this environment audience choice is limited by what the cultural imagemakers deem is commercially viable.

The corporate voice now constitutes the national symbolic environment. "If a creative project, no matter what its inherent quality, cannot be viewed as a potential money-maker, salable in a large enough market, its production is problematic at best.... To the extent then that the creative process has been absorbed by industries producing for the market, the commercial imperative prevails. General awareness that profitability is the ultimate determinant of cultural production becomes internalized in the creative mindset. Scriptwriters, authors, videomakers and film directors shape their efforts, consciously or not, with rare exceptions to the deep-structured demands of salability and prospective returns" (Schiller, 1989, p. 43).

Case in point: The world of acting is seen as biased by actors such as Raymond Moy, Fay Ann Lee, and just about all the actors interviewed from the West Coast. Yet Donna DeSeta's perspective as a casting director is that discrimination against Asian American actors does not exist. Instead she explains limited opportunities for Asians in terms of certain realities within the industry. This also contradicts directly with Michael Amato's opinions. As a talent agent who represents various minorities he sees opportunities for Asians as basically stagnant. Michael blames a certain mindset among those in power when it comes to picking actors—that is, to go for those who are big box office draws.

Her struggles over a lifetime as an Asian American performer not withstanding, Jadin Wong—as manager and agent—has accepted commercial viability as a paradigm for success. Much of the same was acknowledged by Linda Chuan and Nancy Kwan. The nature of the beast is to make money by catering to the largest audiences possible. In the United States that means producing films and shows geared to predominantly white audiences. Thus Asian actors who long for the opportunities of becoming major movie stars must be able to generate huge profits as well. Unless there is a fundamental change in what drives the system (profitability), the rules dictating opportunities for Asian American—and other actors—will remain chained to the draw of audiences to the box office.

But changes in the media environment for Asian American actors are underway, linked in large part to global marketing of cultural products as well as heightened economic-based interests. As Asian nations are seen more and more as market economies, cultural products tailored to audience tastes will continue to proliferate. Schiller would see this not as a democratizing of media, however. Asian faces appearing more and more on screens result as a recognition of market demand. Genres within film, television and theater tend to be mimetic, and roles as enacted for audiences require a reflection of reality.

Huston (1992) asserts that programming depicting all white or all black shows on television leave the viewer with a constructed view of the world as a segregated place. Audiences may turn on the television for entertainment, but there is a socialization process which occurs simultaneously. For Asians in American media, their presence in films, theater, and television remain, for the most part, negligible. From the vantage point of development of self-image, this is problematic.

Mead (1934) has written that the image of self is constructed through a social process. "The self, as that which can be an object to itself, is essentially a social structure, and it arises in social experience ... it is impossible to conceive of a self arising outside of social experience" (p.140). In order to be aware of oneself, one has to have another stance from which to gaze at oneself as object.

According to Mead: "There are two general stages in the full development of the self. At the first of these stages, the individual's self is constituted simply by an organization of the particular attitudes of other individuals.... But at the second stage in the full development of the individual's self that self is constituted not only by an organization of these particular individual attitudes, but also by an organization of social attitudes of the generalized other or the social group as a whole to which he belongs" (p. 158).

Choices of self derive from a construction of generalized others, such as parents, teachers, and friends. Interaction with these sorts of groups, according to Mead, constitute primary socialization processes because contact evokes response. Media messages—such as from film and television—constitute secondary socialization processes as they are not interactive.

"The vast importance of media communication such as those involved in journalism is seen at once, since they report situations through which one can enter into the attitude and experience of other persons" (Mead, p. 257).

Though this statement refers to journalism, it does not preclude inclusion of other forms of media communication such as film, television and theater. Their images are also part of the generalized other derived from secondary socialization processes.

It is as he takes the attitude of the other that the individual is able to realize himself as a self, asserts Mead. But the paucity of Asian American images in film, theater, and television provides little opportunity for the development of self beyond a white context, as most of what is seen in media are non–Asian images.

Billy Chang said his first moment of personal pride as an Asian in the United States came at the age of 12, when he saw Bruce Lee on screen in a kung fu movie; what he was also implying was that up to that point there were no other Asian images on screen that "looked like him" and through which he could validate himself culturally and socially.

Mel Gionson said what attracted him to the theater and New York was seeing Shakespeare on public television. "I saw people who looked like me participating in the classics. People like Raul Julia and James Earl Jones mixed in Shakespeare. I thought it was neat. It was something I was striving for.

"Everything is based on looks in the business, and race is part of looks. Everything is based on imagery. The problem of stereotypes is the imagery—the perception of certain groups and how they fit into that imagery. Say there are good guys and bad guys—how society sees what is a good guy versus a bad guy. Good is clear skin, blond hair, blue eyes, a certain look. Openness will denote goodness. Pockmarked face and bad hair will be bad. A lot of times the bad, or the other, is perceived in terms of race," said Gionson.

Essentially we are a subset of interpersonal communications, imported inward, a generalized other. "We cannot realize ourselves except in so far as we can recognize the other in his relationship to us. It is as he takes the attitude of the other that the individual is able to realize himself as a self" (Mead p.194).

So when Asian American male actors appearing on screen—as pointed out by Raymond Moy and Billy Chang—repeatedly play roles as gangsters and grocers, rather than as the guy next door on films and television, this imagery of Asian Americans males eventually affects the social construction of the way Asian American males are seen.

Similarly when Fay Ann Lee touched on the reasons she left *Miss Saigon,* she talked about the "horrible stereotype of Asian women" being portrayed as prostitutes on stage. One might argue that an actor is only playing a role, but media images contribute in constructions of the generalized other and ultimately influence how Asian Americans are socially perceived; the attitude of the generalized other, according to Mead, is also the attitude of the whole community.

The application of Laszlo's systems view of the world from which to examine the various issues raised by Asian American actors regarding the film, movie and theater industries is an attempt to better understand through a theoretical frame issues related to the realm of the Asian American acting experience. Laszlo's assumptions do not address every aspect or concern raised, but could serve as a prism through which changes and shifts in the Asian American acting experience can be viewed and studied. This raises the need to further study mass media as a suprasystem impacting other systems, such as cultures. In essence when one system collides with another how do systems respond?

The experiences of the actors in this study is a minuscule part of a much larger picture. Billy Chang said audiences today want to see more of the average guy succeed on screen. He believes he has it in himself to appeal to that and therefore becoming a superstar and box office draw in those terms is not impossible. He believes in the system as it is. But Raymond Moy does not. His answer to it is to essentially drop out of it. As actors, both belong to an open system. Yet their views on how they can navigate that system are very different. Lane Nishikawa has determined his course in acting is to focus on theater (both in acting and writing), where the opportunity to play meaningful roles as an Asian American are within reach.

The question of how and whether an Asian American actor can attain superstar status in the United States is tied into the way the systems of film, television and theater are structured. To overcome the barriers within the system one needs to change the existing environment.

Stardom in mass media is difficult for not only Asian Americans but for other minority groups, as well as the general population. How does the experience of Asian American actors compare with that of whites and other ethnic groups? That is one question that was not addressed in the overall context of this book, and leaves open possibilities for further study.

Veteran actor Peter Kwong, and Greg Watanabe of San Francisco, believe that art reflects culture and society. They suggested that if news and other forms of mass media portray Asians in certain ways then films will echo that. In his own way he is saying that by altering the environment, the system will be impacted. Comparison of Asian images in the news against Asian characterizations in film, television and theater merits attention. This would be part of a larger area of study for media ecologists looking at the impact of mass media on culture and images.

The belief among the actors is that those in control such as film and television producers will not chance the casting of Asians in leading roles because of the financial risk. Superstardom as tied to revenues is inextricably linked to the belief that in general Caucasians prefer to see other Caucasians in leading roles. Audiences expect genre to be mimetic of some level of reality. Jadin Wong clearly believes this. But is it the audience that defines the cultural product, or is it, as Schiller asserts, that American mass media content is controlled by multinational corporations with generating profit as their primary objective? Both audience and multinational corporations are part of the mass media suprasystem and both affect the system environment.

This study was undertaken as a piece of a larger inquiry within the general area of prejudice and cultural domination in mass media. Little has been written about the problem of exclusion in film, television and theater as related to the Asian American acting experience and its impact on concepts of development of self. Market forces and expectations within the genre may foster certain exclusionary conditions pertaining to minorities, but these should not preclude discourse and research of issues pertaining to media fairness and cultural domination. This study will, it is hoped, serve as a starting point from which to conduct further exploration. From a media ecology perspective the experiences of Asian American actors are but a subset of concerns within a much larger system, a system within the mass media universe of television, film and theater.

Bibliography

Armes, R. (1987). *Third world film making and the West*. Berkeley: University of California Press.

Bagdikian, B. (1992). *Media monopoly* 4th ed. Boston: Beacon Press.

Blockbuster Video Guide to Movies and Videos. (1995). [CD Rom]. Blockbuster Entertainment.

Bogdan, R. C., & Biklen, S. K. (1992). *Qualitative research for education: An introduction to theory and methods*. Boston: Allyn & Bacon.

Brown, S. A. (1972). *Negro poetry and drama* 2d. ed. New York: Atheneum.

Chan, K., & Hune, S. (1995). "Racialization and panethnicity: From Asians in America to Asian Americans" W. Hawley, & A. Jackson (eds.), in *Toward a common destiny: Improving race and ethnic relations in America*. San Francisco: Jossey-Bass.

Corrigan, T. (1991). *Cinema without walls: Movies and culture after Vietnam*. New Brunswick, NJ: Rutgers University Press.

Cowen, P. (1991). "A social-cognitive approach to ethnicity in films." L. D. Friedman (ed.), *Unspeakable images: Ethnicity and the American cinema* (pp. 353–378). Urbana: University of Illinois Press.

Creswell, J. W. (1994). *Research design: Qualitative and quantitative approaches*. Thousand Oakes, CA: Sage.

Cripps, T. (1990). "Making movies Black." J. L. Dates, & W. Barlow (Eds.), *Split image: African Americans in the mass media*. Washington, DC: Howard University Press.

Daniels, R., & Kitano, H. (1970). *American racism: Exploration of the nature of prejudice*. Englewood Cliffs, NJ: Prentice-Hall.

J. L. Dates, & W. Barlow (ed.), *Split image: African Americans in the mass media*. Washington DC: Howard University Press.

Dissanayake, W. (1994). "Asian cultural texts and western theory." N. Masavisut, G. Simson, & L. Smith (eds.), *Gender and culture in literature and film East and West: Issues of perception and interpretation* (pp. 280–291). Honolulu: University of Hawaii and the East-West Center.

Donahue, S. M. (1987). *American film distribution: The changing marketplace.* Ann Arbor, MI: UMI Research Press.

Ely, M., with Anzul, M., Friedman, T., Garner, D., & Steinmetz, A. (1991). *Doing qualitative research: Circles within circles.* Bristol, PA: Falmer Press.

Ewen, S. (1976). *Captains of consciousness: Advertising and the social roots of the consumer culture.* New York: McGraw-Hill.

Fredrickson, G. M. (1971). *The Black image in the White mind.* Middletown, CT: Wesleyan University Press.

Friedman, L. D., (ed.) (1991). *Unspeakable images: Ethnicity and the American cinema.* Chicago: University of Illinois Press.

Gitlin, T. (1983). *Inside prime time.* New York: Pantheon Books.

Gitlin, T. (1989). "Postmodernism: Roots and politics." *Dissent,* (Winter), pp. 100–108.

Gomery, D. (1992). *Shared pleasures: A History of movie presentation in the United States.* Madison: University of Wisconsin Press.

Higashi, S. (1991). "Ethnicity, class and gender in film: DeMille's *The Cheat.*" L. D. Friedman (ed.), *Unspeakable images: Ethnicity and the American cinema* (pp. 112–139). Urbana: University of Illinois Press.

Hilton, M. (1982). *The constructed message in the motion picture medium.* Unpublished doctoral dissertation, New York University.

Huston, A. (1992). *Big world, small screen.* Lincoln: University of Nebraska Press.

Izod, J. (1988). *Hollywood and the box office, 1895–1986.* New York: Columbia University Press.

Jowett, G., & Linton, J. M. (1980). *Movies as mass communication.* Beverly Hills, CA: Sage.

Kaplan, E. A. (ed.) (1988). *Postmodernism and its discontents: Theories, practices.* London: Verso.

Kellner, D. (1987). "Television, ideology and emancipatory popular culture." H. Newcomb (ed.), *Television: The critical view* (4th ed.). New York: Oxford University Press.

Landy, R. J. (1993). *Persona and performance: The meaning of role in drama, therapy, and everyday life.* New York: The Guilford Press.

Laszlo, E. (1972). *Systems view of the world.* New York: George Braziller.

Leong, R. (ed.) (1991). *Moving the image: Independent Asian Pacific American media arts.* Los Angeles: UCLA Asian American Studies Center.

Lincoln, Y. S., & Guba, E. G. (1985). *Naturalistic inquiry.* Beverly Hills, CA: Sage.

Marchetti, G. (1993). *Romance and the "Yellow Peril": Race, sex, and discursive strategies in Hollywood fiction.* Berkeley and Los Angeles: University of California Press.

Masavisut, N., Simson, G., & Smith, L. (ed.) (1994). *Gender and culture in literature and film East and West: issues of perception and interpretation.* Honolulu: University of Hawaii Press.

Mead, G. H. (1934). *Mind, self, and society: From the standpoint of a Social Behaviorist.* Chicago: University of Chicago Press.

Moy, J. S. (1993). *Marginal sights.* Iowa City: University of Iowa Press.

Oehling, R. A. (1980). "The yellow menace: Asian images in American film." R. M. Miller (ed.), *The kaleidoscopic lens: How Hollywood views ethnic groups* (pp. 182–206). Englewood, NJ: Jerome S. Ozer.

Palmer, E., Smith, K., & Strawser, K. (1993). "Rubik's tube: Developing a child's television worldview." G. Berry, & J. K. Asamen *Children & television: Images in a changing sociocultural world*. Newberry, CA: Sage.

Postman, N. (1985). *Amusing ourselves to death: Public discourse in the age of show business*. New York: Penguin.

Prindle, D. F. (1993). *Risky business: The political economy of Hollywood*. Boulder, CO: Westview Press.

Schiller, H. I. (1984). *Communication and cultural domination*. Armonk, New York: M.E. Sharpe, Inc.

______. (1989). *Culture, Inc.* Oxford, NY: Oxford University Press.

Silk, C., & John Silk. (1990). *Racism and anti racism in American popular culture*. Manchester, NH: Manchester University Press.

Summerfield, E. (1993). *Crossing cultures through film*. Yarmouth, ME: Intercultural Press.

Tesch, R. (1990). *Qualitative research: Analysis types and software tools*. New York: Falmer.

Toplin, R. B., ed. (1993). *Hollywood as mirror: Changing views of "outsiders and enemies" in American movies*. Westport, Conn.: Greenwood Press.

Wong, E. F. (1978). *On visual media racism: Asians in the American motion pictures*. New York: Arno Press.

Index